RHETORIC
AND
ON POETICS

ARISTOTLE

RHETORIC
AND
ON POETICS

THE FRANKLIN LIBRARY
Franklin Center, Pennsylvania

A NOTE ON THE ILLUSTRATIONS

With the writing of *Rhetoric* and *On Poetics*, Aristotle turned from the abstractions of logic and science to the more pragmatic task of illuminating ideas by means of allusion. *Rhetoric* includes the earliest known theory on the proper use of metaphor; *On Poetics* treats the role of symbolism in drama and poetry. In both works Aristotle assumes that myth and history provide the best frame of reference for metaphorical language. This was the central assumption of *iconography*, the tradition by which the writer, artist, or sculptor relied on universally acknowledged symbols to convey his message.

By the sixteenth century, this tradition had become the dominant trend in the arts. It had also spawned *iconology*, the investigation of symbols themselves. The illustrations selected for this edition are derived from Cesare Ripa's *Iconologia*, generally considered the greatest of these investigations. With its publication in 1593, Ripa rose from the obscurity of a Cardinal's kitchen to the highest ranks of knighthood. Drawing heavily from the great classical writers, including Aristotle, his *Iconologia* provided Baroque writers and artists with a symbolic codification of such abstract concepts as Age, Wisdom, and Victory. It also provides an interesting counterpoint to the definitions of these concepts in *Rhetoric* and *On Poetics*.

The sixteen engravings in this Franklin Library edition are taken from the 1759 edition of Ripa's work, published by Johann Hertel in Augsburg, Germany. Of the more than twenty versions in which the *Iconologia* appeared during the seventeenth and eighteenth centuries, Hertel's was the most elaborate. For it, the artist Gottfried Eichler the Younger was commissioned to express Ripa's allegories in visual terms; from his designs the finest engravers in Europe created the plates. The vision and effort that produced these illustrations make them a worthy complement to the writings of Aristotle.

CONTENTS

RHETORIC
AND
ON POETICS

RHETORIC

ρητορικη

THE TRANSLATION OF
W. RHYS ROBERTS

BOOK I

1 • Rhetoric, the counterpart of Dialectic

Rhetoric is the counterpart of Dialectic. Both alike are concerned with such things as come, more or less, within the general ken of all men and belong to no definite science. Accordingly all men make use, more or less, of both; for to a certain extent all men attempt to discuss statements and to maintain them, to defend themselves and to attack others. Ordinary people do this either at random or through practice and from acquired habit. Both ways being possible, the subject can plainly be handled systematically, for it is possible to inquire the reason why some speakers succeed through practice and others spontaneously; and every one will at once agree that such an inquiry is the function of an art.

Now, the framers of the current treatises on rhetoric have constructed but a small portion of that art. The modes of persuasion are the only true constituents of the art: everything else is merely accessory. These writers, however, say nothing about enthymemes, which are the substance of rhetorical persuasion, but deal mainly with non-essentials. The arousing of prejudice, pity, anger, and similar emotions has nothing to do with the essential facts, but is merely a personal appeal to the man who is judging the case. Consequently if the rules for trials which are now laid down in some states—especially in well-governed states—were applied everywhere, such people would have nothing to say. All men, no doubt, *think* that the laws should prescribe such rules, but some, as in the court of Areopagus, give practical effect to their thoughts and forbid talk about non-essentials. This is sound law and custom. It is not right to pervert the judge by moving him to anger or envy or pity—one might as well warp a carpenter's rule before using it. Again, a litigant has clearly nothing to do but to show that the alleged fact is so or is not so, that it has or has not happened. As to whether a thing is important or unimportant, just or unjust, the judge must surely refuse to take his instructions from the litigants: he must decide for himself all such points as the law-giver has not already defined for him.

Now, it is of great moment that well-drawn laws should themselves define all the points they possibly can and leave as few as may be to the decision of the judges; and this for several reasons. First, to find one man, or a few men, who are sensible persons and capable of legislating and administering justice is easier than to find a large number. Next, laws are made after long consideration, whereas decisions in the courts are given at short notice, which makes it hard for those who try the case to satisfy the claims of justice and expediency. The weightiest reason of all is that the decision of the law-giver is not particular but prospective and general, whereas members of the assembly and the jury find it *their* duty to decide on definite cases brought before them. They will often have allowed themselves to be so much influenced by feelings of friendship or hatred or self-interest that they lose any clear vision of the truth and have their judgement obscured by considerations of personal pleasure or pain. In general, then, the judge should, we say, be allowed to decide as few things as possible. But questions as to whether something has happened or has not happened, will be or will not be, is or is not, must of necessity be left to the judge, since the law-giver cannot foresee them. If this is so, it is evident that any one who lays down rules about other matters, such as what must be the contents of the 'introduction' or the 'narration' or any of the other divisions of a speech, is theorizing about non-essentials as if they belonged to the art. The only question with which these writers here deal is how to put the judge into a given frame of mind. About the orator's proper modes of persuasion they have nothing to tell us; nothing, that is, about how to gain skill in enthymemes.

Hence it comes that, although the same systematic principles apply to political as to forensic oratory, and although the former is a nobler business, and fitter for a citizen, than that which concerns the relations of private individuals, these authors say nothing about political oratory, but try, one and all, to write treatises on the way to plead in court. The reason for this is that in political oratory there is less inducement to talk about non-essentials. Political oratory is less given to unscrupulous practices than forensic, because it treats of wider issues. In a political debate the man who is forming a judgement is making a decision about his own vital interests. There is no need, therefore, to prove anything except that the facts are what the supporter of a measure maintains they are. In forensic oratory this is not enough; to conciliate the listener is what pays here. It is other people's affairs that are to be decided, so that the judges, intent on their own satisfaction and listening with partiality, surrender themselves to the disputants instead of judging between them. Hence in many places, as we have said already, irrelevant speaking is forbidden in the law-courts: in the public assembly those who have to form a judgement are themselves well able to guard against that.

It is clear, then, that rhetorical study, in its strict sense, is concerned with the modes of persuasion. Persuasion is clearly a sort of demonstration, since we are most fully persuaded when we consider a thing to have been demonstrated. The orator's demonstration is an enthymeme, and this is, in general, the most effective of the modes of persuasion. The enthymeme is a sort of syllogism, and the consideration of syllogisms of all kinds, without distinction, is the business of dialectic, either of dialectic as a whole or of one of its branches. It follows plainly, therefore, that he who is best able to see how and from what elements a syllogism is produced will also be best skilled in the enthymeme, when he has further learnt what its subject-matter is and in what respects it differs from the syllogism of strict logic. The true and the approximately true are apprehended by the same faculty; it may also be noted that men have a sufficient natural instinct for what is true, and usually do arrive at the truth. Hence the man who makes a good guess at truth is likely to make a good guess at probabilities.

It has now been shown that the ordinary writers on rhetoric treat of non-essentials; it has also been shown why they have inclined more towards the forensic branch of oratory.

Rhetoric is useful (1) because things that are true and things that are just have a natural tendency to prevail over their opposites, so that if the decisions of judges are not what they ought to be, the defeat must be due to the speakers themselves, and they must be blamed accordingly. Moreover, (2) before some audiences not even the possession of the exactest knowledge will make it easy for what we say to produce conviction. For argument based on knowledge implies instruction, and there are people whom one cannot instruct. Here, then, we must use, as our modes of persuasion and argument, notions possessed by everybody, as we observed in the *Topics*[1] when dealing with the way to handle a popular audience. Further, (3) we must be able to employ persuasion, just as strict reasoning can be employed, on opposite sides of a question, not in order that we may in practice employ it in both ways (for we must not make people believe what is wrong), but in order that we may see clearly what the facts are, and that, if another man argues unfairly, we on our part may be able to confute him. No other of the arts draws opposite conclusions: dialectic and rhetoric alone do this. Both these arts draw opposite conclusions impartially. Nevertheless, the underlying facts do not lend themselves equally well to the contrary views. No; things that are true and things that are better are, by their nature, practically always easier to prove and easier to believe in. Again, (4) it is absurd to hold that a man ought to be ashamed of being unable to defend himself with his limbs, but not of being unable to defend himself with speech and reason, when the use of rational speech is more distinctive of a human being than the use of his limbs. And if it be objected that one who uses such power of speech unjustly might do great harm, *that* is a charge which may be made in common against all good things except virtue, and above all against the things that are most useful, as strength, health, wealth, generalship. A man can confer the greatest of benefits by a right use of these, and inflict the greatest of injuries by using them wrongly.

It is clear, then, that rhetoric is not bound up with a single definite class of subjects, but is as universal as dialectic; it is clear, also, that it is useful. It is clear, further, that its function is not simply to succeed in persuading, but rather to discover the means of

[1] *Topics*, I.

coming as near such success as the circumstances of each particular case allow. In this it resembles all other arts. For example, it is not the function of medicine simply to make a man quite healthy, but to put him as far as may be on the road to health; it is possible to give excellent treatment even to those who can never enjoy sound health. Furthermore, it is plain that it is the function of one and the same art to discern the real and the apparent means of persuasion, just as it is the function of dialectic to discern the real and the apparent syllogism. What makes a man a 'sophist' is not his faculty, but his moral purpose. In rhetoric, however, the term 'rhetorician' may describe either the speaker's knowledge of the art, or his moral purpose. In dialectic it is different: a man is a 'sophist' because he has a certain kind of moral purpose, a 'dialectician' in respect, not of his moral purpose, but of his faculty.

Let us now try to give some account of the systematic principles of Rhetoric itself—of the right method and means of succeeding in the object we set before us. We must make as it were a fresh start, and before going further define what rhetoric is.

2 · A definition of rhetoric, and a discussion of persuasive arguments

Rhetoric may be defined as the faculty of observing in any given case the available means of persuasion. This is not a function of any other art. Every other art can instruct or persuade about its own particular subject-matter; for instance, medicine about what is healthy and unhealthy, geometry about the properties of magnitudes, arithmetic about numbers, and the same is true of the other arts and sciences. But rhetoric we look upon as the power of observing the means of persuasion on almost any subject presented to us; and that is why we say that, in its technical character, it is not concerned with any special or definite class of subjects.

Of the modes of persuasion some belong strictly to the art of rhetoric and some do not. By the latter I mean such things as are not supplied by the speaker but are there at the outset—witnesses, evidence given under torture, written contracts, and so on. By the former I mean such as we can ourselves construct by means of the principles of rhetoric. The one kind has merely to be used, the other has to be invented.

Of the modes of persuasion furnished by the unspoken word there are three kinds. The first kind depends on the personal character of the speaker; the second on putting the audience into a certain frame of mind; the third on the proof, or apparent proof, provided by the words of the speech itself. Persuasion is achieved by the speaker's personal character when the speech is so spoken as to make us think him credible. We believe good men more fully and more readily than others: this is true generally whatever the question is, and absolutely true where exact certainty is impossible and opinions are divided. This kind of persuasion, like the others, should be achieved by what the speaker says, not by what people think of his character before he begins to speak. It is not true, as some writers assume in their treatises on rhetoric, that the personal goodness revealed by the speaker contributes nothing to his power of persuasion; on the contrary, his character may almost be called the most effective means of persuasion he possesses. Secondly, persuasion may come through the hearers, when the speech stirs their emotions. Our judgements when we are pleased and friendly are not the same as when we are pained and hostile. It is towards producing these effects, as we maintain, that present-day writers on rhetoric direct the whole of their efforts. This subject shall be treated in detail when we come to speak of the emotions.[2] Thirdly, persuasion is effected through the speech itself when we have proved a truth or an apparent truth by means of the persuasive arguments suitable to the case in question.

There are, then, these three means of effecting persuasion. The man who is to be in command of them must, it is clear, be able (1) to reason logically, (2) to understand human character and goodness in their various forms, and (3) to understand the emotions—that is, to name them and describe them, to know their causes and the way in which they are excited. It thus appears that rhetoric is an offshoot of dialectic and also of ethical studies.

[2] II. 2–11.

Ethical studies may fairly be called political; and for this reason rhetoric masquerades as political science, and the professors of it as political experts—sometimes from want of education, sometimes from ostentation, sometimes owing to other human failings. As a matter of fact, it is a branch of dialectic and similar to it, as we said at the outset. Neither rhetoric nor dialectic is the scientific study of any one separate subject: both are faculties for providing arguments. This is perhaps a sufficient account of their scope and of how they are related to each other.

With regard to the persuasion achieved by proof or apparent proof: just as in dialectic there is induction on the one hand and syllogism or apparent syllogism on the other, so it is in rhetoric. The example is an induction, the enthymeme is a syllogism, and the apparent enthymeme is an apparent syllogism. I call the enthymeme a rhetorical syllogism, and the example a rhetorical induction. Every one who effects persuasion through proof does in fact use either enthymemes or examples: there is no other way. And since every one who proves anything at all is bound to use either syllogisms or inductions (and this is clear to us from the *Analytics*[3]), it must follow that enthymemes are syllogisms and examples are inductions. The difference between example and enthymeme is made plain by the passages in the *Topics*[4] where induction and syllogism have already been discussed. When we base the proof of a proposition on a number of similar cases, this is induction in dialectic, example in rhetoric; when it is shown that, certain propositions being true, a further and quite distinct proposition must also be true in consequence, whether invariably or usually, this is called syllogism in dialectic, enthymeme in rhetoric. It is plain also that each of these types of oratory has its advantages. Types of oratory, I say: for what has been said in the *Methodics* applies equally well here; in some oratorical styles examples prevail, in others enthymemes; and in like manner, some orators are better at the former and some at the latter. Speeches that rely on examples are as persuasive as the other kind, but those which rely on enthy-

[3] *Prior Analytics*, II. 23, 24; *Posterior Analytics*, I. 1.
[4] *Topics*, I. 1, 12.

memes excite the louder applause. The sources of examples and enthymemes, and their proper uses, we will discuss later.[5] Our next step is to define the processes themselves more clearly.

A statement is persuasive and credible either because it is directly self-evident or because it appears to be proved from other statements that are so. In either case it is persuasive because there is somebody whom it persuades. But none of the arts theorize about individual cases. Medicine, for instance, does not theorize about what will help to cure Socrates or Callias, but only about what will help to cure any or all of a given class of patients: this alone is its business: individual cases are so infinitely various that no systematic knowledge of them is possible. In the same way the theory of rhetoric is concerned not with what seems probable to a given individual like Socrates or Hippias, but with what seems probable to men of a given type; and this is true of dialectic also. Dialectic does not construct its syllogisms out of any haphazard materials, such as the fancies of crazy people, but out of materials that call for discussion; and rhetoric, too, draws upon the regular subjects of debate. The duty of rhetoric is to deal with such matters as we deliberate upon without arts or systems to guide us, in the hearing of persons who cannot take in at a glance a complicated argument, or follow a long chain of reasoning. The subjects of our deliberation are such as seem to present us with alternative possibilities: about things that could not have been, and cannot now or in the future be, other than they are, nobody who takes them to be of this nature wastes his time in deliberation.

It is possible to form syllogisms and draw conclusions from the results of previous syllogisms; or, on the other hand, from premisses which have not been thus proved, and at the same time are so little accepted that they call for proof. Reasonings of the former kind will necessarily be hard to follow owing to their length, for we assume an audience of untrained thinkers; those of the latter kind will fail to win assent, because they are based on premisses that are not generally admitted or believed.

The enthymeme and the example must, then, deal with what is in the main contingent, the example being an induction, and the

[5] II. 20–24.

enthymeme a syllogism, about such matters. The enthymeme must consist of few propositions, fewer often than those which make up the normal syllogism. For if any of these propositions is a familiar fact, there is no need even to mention it; the hearer adds it himself. Thus, to show that Dorieus has been victor in a contest for which the prize is a crown, it is enough to say 'For he has been victor in the Olympic games', without adding 'And in the Olympic games the prize is a crown', a fact which everybody knows. There are few facts of the 'necessary' type that can form the basis of rhetorical syllogisms. Most of the things about which we make decisions, and into which therefore we inquire, present us with alternative possibilities. For it is about our actions that we deliberate and inquire, and all our actions have a contingent character; hardly any of them are determined by necessity. Again, conclusions that state what is merely usual or possible must be drawn from premises that do the same, just as 'necessary' conclusions must be drawn from 'necessary' premises; this too is clear to us from the *Analytics*.[6] It is evident, therefore, that the propositions forming the basis of enthymemes, though some of them may be 'necessary', will most of them be only usually true. Now the materials of enthymemes are Probabilities and Signs, which we can see must correspond respectively with the propositions that are generally and those that are necessarily true. A Probability is a thing that usually happens; not, however, as some definitions would suggest, anything whatever that usually happens, but only if it belongs to the class of the 'contingent' or 'variable'. It bears the same relation to that in respect of which it is probable as the universal bears to the particular. Of Signs, one kind bears the same relation to the statement it supports as the particular bears to the universal, the other the same as the universal bears to the particular. The infallible kind is a 'complete proof' (τεκμήριον); the fallible kind has no specific name. By infallible signs I mean those on which syllogisms proper may be based: and this shows us why this kind of Sign is called 'complete proof': when people think that what they have said cannot be refuted, they then think that they are bringing forward a 'complete proof', meaning that

[6] *Prior Analytics*, I. 8, 12–14, 27.

the matter has now been demonstrated and completed (πε-
περασμένον); for the word πέρας has the same meaning (of 'end'
or 'boundary') as the word τέκμαρ in the ancient tongue. Now
the one kind of Sign (that which bears to the proposition it supports the relation of particular to universal) may be illustrated
thus. Suppose it were said, 'The fact that Socrates was wise and
just is a sign that the wise are just'. Here we certainly have a Sign;
but even though the proposition be true, the argument is refutable, since it does not form a syllogism. Suppose, on the other
hand, it were said, 'The fact that he has a fever is a sign that he is
ill', or, 'The fact that she is giving milk is a sign that she has lately
borne a child'. Here we have the infallible kind of Sign, the only
kind that constitutes a complete proof, since it is the only kind
that, if the particular statement is true, is irrefutable. The other
kind of Sign, that which bears to the proposition it supports the
relation of universal to particular, might be illustrated by saying,
'The fact that he breathes fast is a sign that he has a fever'. This
argument also is refutable, even if the statement about the fast
breathing be true, since a man may breathe hard without having a
fever.

It has, then, been stated above what is the nature of a Probability, of a Sign, and of a complete proof, and what are the differences between them. In the *Analytics*[7] a more explicit description
has been given of these points; it is there shown why some of these
reasonings can be put into syllogisms and some cannot.

The 'example' has already been described as one kind of induction; and the special nature of the subject-matter that distinguishes it from the other kinds has also been stated above. Its
relation to the proposition it supports is not that of part to whole,
nor whole to part, nor whole to whole, but of part to part, or like
to like. When two statements are of the same order, but one is
more familiar than the other, the former is an 'example'. The argument may, for instance, be that Dionysius, in asking as he does
for a bodyguard, is scheming to make himself a despot. For in the
past Peisistratus kept asking for a bodyguard in order to carry out
such a scheme, and did make himself a despot as soon as he got it;

[7] *Prior Analytics*, II. 27.

and so did Theagenes at Megara; and in the same way all other instances known to the speaker are made into examples, in order to show what is not yet known, that Dionysius has the same purpose in making the same request: all these being instances of the one general principle, that a man who asks for a bodyguard is scheming to make himself a despot. We have now described the sources of those means of persuasion which are popularly supposed to be demonstrative.

There is an important distinction between two sorts of enthymemes that has been wholly overlooked by almost everybody — one that also subsists between the syllogisms treated of in dialectic. One sort of enthymeme really belongs to rhetoric, as one sort of syllogism really belongs to dialectic; but the other sort really belongs to other arts and faculties, whether to those we already exercise or to those we have not yet acquired. Missing this distinction, people fail to notice that the more correctly they handle their particular subject the further they are getting away from pure rhetoric or dialectic. This statement will be clearer if expressed more fully. I mean that the proper subjects of dialectical and rhetorical syllogisms are the things with which we say the regular or universal Lines of Argument are concerned, that is to say those lines of argument that apply equally to questions of right conduct, natural science, politics, and many other things that have nothing to do with one another. Take, for instance, the line of argument concerned with 'the more or less'. On this line of argument it is equally easy to base a syllogism or enthymeme about any of what nevertheless are essentially disconnected subjects — right conduct, natural science, or anything else whatever. But there are also those special Lines of Argument which are based on such propositions as apply only to particular groups or classes of things. Thus there are propositions about natural science on which it is impossible to base any enthymeme or syllogism about ethics, and other propositions about ethics on which nothing can be based about natural science. The same principle applies throughout. The general Lines of Argument have no special subject-matter, and therefore will not increase our understanding of any particular class of things. On the other hand, the better the selection one makes of propositions suitable for special Lines of Argument, the nearer one comes, unconsciously, to setting up a science that is distinct from dialectic and rhetoric. One may succeed in stating the required principles, but one's science will be no longer dialectic or rhetoric, but the science to which the principles thus discovered belong. Most enthymemes are in fact based upon these particular or special Lines of Argument; comparatively few on the common or general kind. As in the *Topics*,[8] therefore, so in this work, we must distinguish, in dealing with enthymemes, the special and the general Lines of Argument on which they are to be founded. By special Lines of Argument I mean the propositions peculiar to each several class of things, by general those common to all classes alike. We may begin with the special Lines of Argument. But, first of all, let us classify rhetoric into its varieties. Having distinguished these we may deal with them one by one, and try to discover the elements of which each is composed, and the propositions each must employ.

3 · The three kinds of rhetoric: political, or deliberative; forensic, or legal; and epideictic, or ceremonial oratory of display

Rhetoric falls into three divisions, determined by the three classes of listeners to speeches. For of the three elements in speech-making—speaker, subject, and person addressed—it is the last one, the hearer, that determines the speech's end and object. The hearer must be either a judge, with a decision to make about things past or future, or an observer. A member of the assembly decides about future events, a juryman about past events: while those who merely decide on the orator's skill are observers. From this it follows that there are three divisions of oratory—(1) political, (2) forensic, and (3) the ceremonial oratory of display.

Political speaking urges us either to do or not to do something: one of these two courses is always taken by private counsellors, as well as by men who address public assemblies. Forensic speaking either attacks or defends somebody: one or other of

---

[8] Cf. *Topics*, I. 10, 14; III. 5.

these two things must always be done by the parties in a case. The ceremonial oratory of display either praises or censures somebody. These three kinds of rhetoric refer to three different kinds of time. The political orator is concerned with the future: it is about things to be done hereafter that he advises, for or against. The party in a case at law is concerned with the past; one man accuses the other, and the other defends himself, with reference to things already done. The ceremonial orator is, properly speaking, concerned with the present, since all men praise or blame in view of the state of things existing at the time, though they often find it useful also to recall the past and to make guesses at the future.

Rhetoric has three distinct ends in view, one for each of its three kinds. The political orator aims at establishing the expediency or the harmfulness of a proposed course of action; if he urges its acceptance, he does so on the ground that it will do good; if he urges its rejection, he does so on the ground that it will do harm; and all other points, such as whether the proposal is just or unjust, honourable or dishonourable, he brings in as subsidiary and relative to this main consideration. Parties in a law-case aim at establishing the justice or injustice of some action, and they too bring in all other points as subsidiary and relative to this one. Those who praise or attack a man aim at proving him worthy of honour or the reverse, and they too treat all other considerations with reference to this one.

That the three kinds of rhetoric do aim respectively at the three ends we have mentioned is shown by the fact that speakers will sometimes not try to establish anything else. Thus, the litigant will sometimes not deny that a thing has happened or that he has done harm. But that he is guilty of injustice he will never admit; otherwise there would be no need of a trial. So too, political orators often make any concession short of admitting that they are recommending their hearers to take an inexpedient course or not to take an expedient one. The question whether it is not *unjust* for a city to enslave its innocent neighbours often does not trouble them at all. In like manner those who praise or censure a man do not consider whether his acts have been expedient or not, but often make it a ground of actual praise that he has neglected his own interest to do what was honourable. Thus, they praise

Achilles because he championed his fallen friend Patroclus, though he knew that this meant death, and that otherwise he need not die: yet while to die thus was the nobler thing for him to do, the expedient thing was to live on.

It is evident from what has been said that it is these three subjects, more than any others, about which the orator must be able to have propositions at his command. Now the propositions of Rhetoric are Complete Proofs, Probabilities, and Signs. Every kind of syllogism is composed of propositions, and the enthymeme is a particular kind of syllogism composed of the aforesaid propositions.

Since only possible actions, and not impossible ones, can ever have been done in the past or the present, and since things which have not occurred, or will not occur, also cannot have been done or be going to be done, it is necessary for the political, the forensic, and the ceremonial speaker alike to be able to have at their command propositions about the possible and the impossible, and about whether a thing has or has not occurred, will or will not occur. Further, all men, in giving praise or blame, in urging us to accept or reject proposals for action, in accusing others or defending themselves, attempt not only to prove the points mentioned but also to show that the good or the harm, the honour or disgrace, the justice or injustice, is great or small, either absolutely or relatively; and therefore it is plain that we must also have at our command propositions about greatness or smallness and the greater or the lesser—propositions both universal and particular. Thus, we must be able to say which is the greater or lesser good, the greater or lesser act of justice or injustice; and so on.

Such, then, are the subjects regarding which we are inevitably bound to master the propositions relevant to them. We must now discuss each particular class of these subjects in turn, namely those dealt with in political, in ceremonial, and lastly in legal, oratory.

RHETORIC

4 · The subjects of political oratory: ways and means; peace and war; national defence; food supply; and legislation

First, then, we must ascertain what are the kinds of things, good or bad, about which the political orator offers counsel. For he does not deal with all things, but only with such as may or may not take place. Concerning things which exist or will exist inevitably, or which cannot possibly exist or take place, no counsel can be given. Nor, again, can counsel be given about the whole class of things which may or may not take place; for this class includes some good things that occur naturally, and some that occur by accident; and about these it is useless to offer counsel. Clearly counsel can only be given on matters about which people deliberate; matters, namely, that ultimately depend on ourselves, and which we have it in our power to set going. For we turn a thing over in our mind until we have reached the point of seeing whether we can do it or not.

Now to enumerate and classify accurately the usual subjects of public business, and further to frame, as far as possible, true definitions of them, is a task which we must not attempt on the present occasion. For it does not belong to the art of rhetoric, but to a more instructive art and a more real branch of knowledge; and as it is, rhetoric has been given a far wider subject-matter than strictly belongs to it. The truth is, as indeed we have said already, that rhetoric is a combination of the science of logic and of the ethical branch of politics; and it is partly like dialectic, partly like sophistical reasoning. But the more we try to make either dialectic or rhetoric not, what they really are, practical faculties, but sciences, the more we shall inadvertently be destroying their true nature; for we shall be re-fashioning them and shall be passing into the region of sciences dealing with definite subjects rather than simply with words and forms of reasoning. Even here, however, we will mention those points which it is of practical importance to distinguish, their fuller treatment falling naturally to political science.

The main matters on which all men deliberate and on which political speakers make speeches are some five in number: ways and means, war and peace, national defence, imports and exports, and legislation.

As to Ways and Means, then, the intending speaker will need to know the number and extent of the country's sources of revenue, so that, if any is being overlooked, it may be added, and, if any is defective, it may be increased. Further, he should know all the expenditure of the country, in order that, if any part of it is superfluous, it may be abolished, or, if any is too large, it may be reduced. For men become richer not only by increasing their existing wealth but also by reducing their expenditure. A comprehensive view of these questions cannot be gained solely from experience in home affairs; in order to advise on such matters a man must be keenly interested in the methods worked out in other lands.

As to Peace and War, he must know the extent of the military strength of his country, both actual and potential, and also the nature of that actual and potential strength; and further, what wars his country has waged, and how it has waged them. He must know these facts not only about his own country, but also about neighbouring countries; and also about countries with which war is likely, in order that peace may be maintained with those stronger than his own, and that his own may have power to make war or not against those that are weaker. He should know, too, whether the military power of another country is like or unlike that of his own; for this is a matter that may affect their relative strength. With the same end in view he must, besides, have studied the wars of other countries as well as those of his own, and the way they ended; similar causes are likely to have similar results.

With regard to National Defence: he ought to know all about the methods of defence in actual use, such as the strength and character of the defensive force and the positions of the forts—

The political orator aims at establishing the expediency or the harmfulness of a proposed course of action; if he urges its acceptance, he does so on the ground that it will do good; if he urges its rejection, he does so on the ground that it will do harm; and all other points, such as whether the proposal is just or unjust, honourable or dishonourable, he brings in as subsidiary and relative to this main consideration. (Page 17)

J. Wachsmuth Sc.

this last means that he must be well acquainted with the lie of the country—in order that a garrison may be increased if it is too small or removed if it is not wanted, and that the strategic points may be guarded with special care.

With regard to the Food Supply: he must know what outlay will meet the needs of his country; what kinds of food are produced at home and what imported; and what articles must be exported or imported. This last he must know in order that agreements and commercial treaties may be made with the countries concerned. There are, indeed, two sorts of state to which he must see that his countrymen give no cause for offence, states stronger than his own, and states with which it is advantageous to trade.

But while he must, for security's sake, be able to take all this into account, he must before all things understand the subject of legislation; for it is on a country's laws that its whole welfare depends. He must, therefore, know how many different forms of constitution there are; under what conditions each of these will prosper and by what internal developments or external attacks each of them tends to be destroyed. When I speak of destruction through internal developments I refer to the fact that all constitutions, except the best one of all, are destroyed both by not being pushed far enough and by being pushed too far. Thus, democracy loses its vigour, and finally passes into oligarchy, not only when it is not pushed far enough, but also when it is pushed a great deal too far; just as the aquiline and the snub nose not only turn into normal noses by not being aquiline or snub enough, but also by being too violently aquiline or snub arrive at a condition in which they no longer look like noses at all.

It is useful, in framing laws, not only to study the past history of one's own country, in order to understand which constitution is desirable for it now, but also to have a knowledge of the constitutions of other nations, and so to learn for what kinds of nation the various kinds of constitution are suited. From this we can see that books of travel are useful aids to legislation, since from these we may learn the laws and customs of different races. The political speaker will also find the researches of historians useful. But all this is the business of political science and not of rhetoric.

These, then, are the most important kinds of information which the political speaker must possess. Let us now go back and state the premisses from which he will have to argue in favour of adopting or rejecting measures regarding these and other matters.

5 · The premisses of the political speaker: happiness and its constituents

It may be said that every individual man and all men in common aim at a certain end which determines what they choose and what they avoid. This end, to sum it up briefly, is happiness and its constituents. Let us, then, by way of illustration only, ascertain what is in general the nature of happiness, and what are the elements of its constituent parts. For all advice to do things or not to do them is concerned with happiness and with the things that make for or against it; whatever creates or increases happiness or some part of happiness, we ought to do; whatever destroys or hampers happiness, or gives rise to its opposite, we ought not to do.

We may define happiness as prosperity combined with virtue; or as independence of life; or as the secure enjoyment of the maximum of pleasure; or as a good condition of property and body, together with the power of guarding one's property and body and making use of them. That happiness is one or more of these things, pretty well everybody agrees.

From this definition of happiness it follows that its constituent parts are: — good birth, plenty of friends, good friends, wealth, good children, plenty of children, a happy old age, also such bodily excellences as health, beauty, strength, large stature, athletic powers, together with fame, honour, good luck, and virtue. A man cannot fail to be completely independent if he possesses these internal and these external goods; for besides these there are no others to have. (Goods of the soul and of the body are internal. Good birth, friends, money, and honour are external.) Further, we think that he should possess resources and luck, in order to make his life really secure. As we have already ascertained what happiness in general is, so now let us try to ascertain what each of these parts of it is.

Now good birth in a race or a state means that its members are indigenous or ancient: that its earliest leaders were distinguished men, and that from them have sprung many who were distinguished for qualities that we admire.

The good birth of an individual, which may come either from the male or the female side, implies that both parents are free citizens, and that, as in the case of the state, the founders of the line have been notable for virtue or wealth or something else which is highly prized, and that many distinguished persons belong to the family, men and women, young and old.

The phrases 'possession of good children' and 'of many children' bear a quite clear meaning. Applied to a community, they mean that its young men are numerous and of good quality: good in regard to bodily excellences, such as stature, beauty, strength, athletic powers; and also in regard to the excellences of the soul, which in a young man are temperance and courage. Applied to an individual, they mean that his own children are numerous and have the good qualities we have described. Both male and female are here included; the excellences of the latter are, in body, beauty and stature; in soul, self-command and an industry that is not sordid. Communities as well as individuals should lack none of these perfections, in their women as well as in their men. Where, as among the Lacedaemonians, the state of women is bad, almost half of human life is spoilt.

The constituents of wealth are: plenty of coined money and territory; the ownership of numerous, large, and beautiful estates; also the ownership of numerous and beautiful implements, live stock, and slaves. All these kinds of property are our own, are secure, gentlemanly, and useful. The useful kinds are those that are productive, the gentlemanly kinds are those that provide enjoyment. By 'productive' I mean those from which we get our income; by 'enjoyable', those from which we get nothing worth mentioning except the use of them. The criterion of 'security' is the ownership of property in such places and under such conditions that the use of it is in our power; and it is 'our own' if it is in our own power to dispose of it or keep it. By 'disposing of it' I mean giving it away or selling it. Wealth as a whole consists in using things rather than in owning them; it is really the activity—that is, the use—of property that constitutes wealth.

Fame means being respected by everybody, or having some quality that is desired by all men, or by most, or by the good, or by the wise.

Honour is the token of a man's being famous for doing good. It is chiefly and most properly paid to those who have already done good; but also to the man who can do good in future. Doing good refers either to the preservation of life and the means of life, or to wealth, or to some other of the good things which it is hard to get either always or at that particular place or time—for many gain honour for things which seem small, but the place and the occasion account for it. The constituents of honour are: sacrifices; commemoration, in verse or prose; privileges; grants of land; front seats at civic celebrations; state burial; statues; public maintenance; among foreigners, obeisances and giving place; and such presents as are among various bodies of men regarded as marks of honour. For a present is not only the bestowal of a piece of property, but also a token of honour; which explains why honour-loving as well as money-loving persons desire it. The present brings to both what they want; it is a piece of property, which is what the lovers of money desire; and it brings honour, which is what the lovers of honour desire.

The excellence of the body is health; that is, a condition which allows us, while keeping free from disease, to have the use of our bodies; for many people are 'healthy' as we are told Herodicus was; and these no one can congratulate on their 'health', for they have to abstain from everything or nearly everything that men do.—Beauty varies with the time of life. In a young man beauty is the possession of a body fit to endure the exertion of running and of contests of strength; which means that he is pleasant to look at; and therefore all-round athletes are the most beautiful, being naturally adapted both for contests of strength and for speed also. For a man in his prime, beauty is fitness for the exertion of warfare, together with a pleasant but at the same time formidable appearance. For an old man, it is to be strong enough for such exertion as is necessary, and to be free from all those deformities of old age which cause pain to others. Strength is the power of moving some one else at will; to do this, you must either pull, push, lift, pin, or grip him; thus you must be strong in all of those ways or at least in some. Excellence in size is to surpass ordinary people in height, thickness, and breadth by just as much as will not make one's movements slower in consequence. Athletic excellence of the body consists in size, strength, and swiftness; swiftness implying strength. He who can fling forward his legs in a certain way, and move them fast and far, is good at running; he who can grip and hold down is good at wrestling; he who can drive an adversary from his ground with the right blow is a good boxer: he who can do both the last is a good pancratiast, while he who can do all is an 'all-round' athlete.

Happiness in old age is the coming of old age slowly and painlessly; for a man has not this happiness if he grows old either quickly, or tardily but painfully. It arises both from the excellences of the body and from good luck. If a man is not free from disease, or if he is not strong, he will not be free from suffering; nor can he continue to live a long and painless life unless he has good luck. There is, indeed, a capacity for long life that is quite independent of health or strength; for many people live long who lack the excellences of the body; but for our present purpose there is no use in going into the details of this.

The terms 'possession of many friends' and 'possession of good friends' need no explanation; for we define a 'friend' as one who will always try, for your sake, to do what he takes to be good for you. The man towards whom many feel thus has many friends; if these are worthy men, he has good friends.

'Good luck' means the acquisition or possession of all or most, or the most important, of those good things which are due to luck. Some of the things that are due to luck may also be due to artificial contrivance; but many are independent of art, as for example those which are due to nature—though, to be sure, things due to luck may actually be contrary to nature. Thus health may be due to artificial contrivance, but beauty and stature are due to nature. All such good things as excite envy are, as a class, the outcome of good luck. Luck is also the cause of good things that happen contrary to reasonable expectation: as when, for instance, all your brothers are ugly, but you are handsome yourself; or when you find a treasure that everybody else has overlooked; or when a missile hits the next man and misses you; or when you are the only man not to go to a place you have gone to regularly, while the others go there for the first time and are killed. All such things are reckoned pieces of good luck.

As to virtue, it is most closely connected with the subject of Eulogy, and therefore we will wait to define it until we come to discuss that subject.

6 · The aims of the political speaker: goodness and utility

It is now plain what our aims, future or actual, should be in urging, and what in depreciating, a proposal; the latter being the opposite of the former. Now the political or deliberative orator's aim is utility: deliberation seeks to determine not ends but the means to ends, i.e. what it is most useful to do. Further, utility is a good thing. We ought therefore to assure ourselves of the main facts about goodness and utility in general.

We may define a good thing as that which ought to be chosen for its own sake; or as that for the sake of which we choose something else; or as that which is sought after by all things, or by all things that have sensation or reason, or which will be sought after by any things that acquire reason; or as that which must be prescribed for a given individual by reason generally, or is prescribed for him by his individual reason, this being his individual good; or as that whose presence brings anything into a satisfactory and self-sufficing condition; or as self-sufficiency; or as what produces, maintains, or entails characteristics of this kind, while preventing and destroying their opposites. One thing may entail another in either of two ways—(1) simultaneously, (2) subsequently. Thus learning entails knowledge subsequently, health entails life simultaneously. Things are productive of other things in three senses: first as being healthy produces health; secondly, as food produces health; and thirdly, as exercise does—i.e. it does so usually. All this being settled, we now see that both the acquisition of good things and the removal of bad things must be good; the latter entails freedom from the evil things simultaneously, while the former entails possession of the good things subsequently. The acquisition of a greater in place of a lesser good, or of a lesser in place of a greater evil, is also good, for in proportion as the greater exceeds the lesser there is acquisition of good or removal of evil. The virtues, too, must be something good; for it is by possessing these that we are in a good condition, and they tend to produce good works and good actions. They must be severally named and described elsewhere.[9] Pleasure, again, must be a good thing, since it is the nature of all animals to aim at it. Consequently both pleasant and beautiful things must be good things, since the former are productive of pleasure, while of the beautiful things some are pleasant and some desirable in and for themselves.

The following is a more detailed list of things that must be good. Happiness, as being desirable in itself and sufficient by itself, and as being that for whose sake we choose many other things. Also justice, courage, temperance, magnanimity, magnificence, and all such qualities, as being excellences of the soul. Further, health, beauty, and the like, as being bodily excellences and productive of many other good things: for instance, health is productive both of pleasure and of life, and therefore is thought the greatest of goods, since these two things which it causes, pleasure and life, are two of the things most highly prized by ordinary people. Wealth, again: for it is the excellence of possession, and also productive of many other good things. Friends and friendship: for a friend is desirable in himself and also productive of many other good things. So, too, honour and reputation, as being pleasant, and productive of many other good things, and usually accompanied by the presence of the good things that cause them to be bestowed. The faculty of speech and action; since all such qualities are productive of what is good. Further—good parts, strong memory, receptiveness, quickness of intuition, and the like, for all such faculties are productive of what is good. Similarly, all the sciences and arts. And life: since, even if no other good were

[9] Chapter 9.

the result of life, it is desirable in itself. And justice, as the cause of good to the community.

The above are pretty well all the things admittedly good. In dealing with things whose goodness is disputed, we may argue in the following ways:—That is good of which the contrary is bad. That is good the contrary of which is to the advantage of our enemies; for example, if it is to the particular advantage of our enemies that we should be cowards, clearly courage is of particular value to our countrymen. And generally, the contrary of that which our enemies desire, or of that at which they rejoice, is evidently valuable. Hence the passage beginning:

> How happy Priam and Priam's sons would be . . .[10]

This principle usually holds good, but not always, since it may well be that our interest is sometimes the same as that of our enemies. Hence it is said that 'evils draw men together'; that is, when the same thing is hurtful to them both.

Further: that which is not in excess is good, and that which is greater than it should be is bad. That also is good on which much labour or money has been spent; the mere fact of this makes it seem good, and such a good is assumed to be an end—an end reached through a long chain of means; and any end is a good. Hence the lines beginning:

> . . . leave her [Helen] in Priam's hands,
> the boast for every Trojan;[11]

and

> Ah, but still it would be utter shame
> to stay so long and sail home empty-handed.[12]

and there is also the proverb about 'breaking the pitcher at the door'.

That which most people seek after, and which is obviously an

[10] *Iliad*, I. 304.
[11] *Iliad*, II. 184–85.
[12] *Iliad*, II. 345–46.

object of contention, is also a good; for, as has been shown, that is good which is sought after by everybody, and 'most people' is taken to be equivalent to 'everybody'. That which is praised is good, since no one praises what is not good. So, again, that which is praised by our enemies [or by the worthless]; for when even those who have a grievance think a thing good, it is at once felt that every one must agree with them; our enemies can admit the fact only because it is evident, just as those must be worthless whom their friends censure and their enemies do not. (For this reason the Corinthians conceived themselves to be insulted by Simonides when he wrote:

Against the Corinthians hath Ilium no complaint.)

Again, that is good which has been distinguished by the favour of a discerning or virtuous man or woman, as Odysseus was distinguished by Athena, Helen by Theseus, Paris by the goddesses, and Achilles by Homer. And, generally speaking, all things are good which men deliberately choose to do; this will include the things already mentioned, and also whatever may be bad for their enemies or good for their friends, and at the same time practicable. Things are 'practicable' in two senses: (1) it is possible to do them, (2) it is easy to do them. Things are done 'easily' when they are done either without pain or quickly: the 'difficulty' of an act lies either in its painfulness or in the long time it takes. Again, a thing is good if it is as men wish; and they wish to have either no evil at all or at least a balance of good over evil. This last will happen where the penalty is either imperceptible or slight. Good, too, are things that are a man's very own, possessed by no one else, exceptional; for this increases the credit of having them. So are things which befit the possessors, such as whatever is appropriate to their birth or capacity, and whatever they feel they ought to have but lack—such things may indeed be trifling, but nonetheless men deliberately make them the goal of their action. And things easily effected; for these are practicable (in the sense of being easy); such things are those in which every one, or most people, or one's equals, or one's inferiors have succeeded. Good also are the things by which we shall gratify our friends or annoy our enemies; and the things chosen by those whom we admire: and the things for which we are fitted by nature or experience, since we think we shall succeed more easily in these: and those in which no worthless man can succeed, for such things bring greater praise: and those which we do in fact desire, for what we desire is taken to be not only pleasant but also better. Further, a man of a given disposition makes chiefly for the corresponding things: lovers of victory make for victory, lovers of honour for honour, money-loving men for money, and so with the rest. These, then, are the sources from which we must derive our means of persuasion about Good and Utility.

7 · A comparison of 'good' things, and a consideration of degree—the lore of 'less or more'

Since, however, it often happens that people agree that two things are both useful but do not agree about which is the more so, the next step will be to treat of relative goodness and relative utility.

A thing which surpasses another may be regarded as being that other thing plus something more, and that other thing which is surpassed as being what is contained in the first thing. Now to call a thing 'greater' or 'more' always implies a comparison of it with one that is 'smaller' or 'less', while 'great' and 'small', 'much' and 'little', are terms used in comparison with normal magnitude. The 'great' is that which surpasses the normal, the 'small' is that which is surpassed by the normal; and so with 'many' and 'few'.

Now we are applying the term 'good' to what is desirable for its own sake and not for the sake of something else; to that at which all things aim; to what they would choose if they could acquire understanding and practical wisdom; and to that which tends to produce or preserve such goods, or is always accompanied by them. Moreover, that for the sake of which things are done is the end (an end being that for the sake of which all else is done), and for each individual that thing is a good which fulfils these conditions in regard to himself. It follows, then, that a greater number of goods is a greater good than one or than a smaller number, if that one or that smaller number is included in the count; for then the larger number surpasses the smaller, and the smaller quantity is surpassed as being contained in the larger.

Again, if the largest member of one class surpasses the largest member of another, then the one class surpasses the other; and if one class surpasses another, then the largest member of the one surpasses the largest member of the other. Thus, if the tallest man is taller than the tallest woman, then men in general are taller than women. Conversely, if men in general are taller than women, then the tallest man is taller than the tallest woman. For the superiority of class over class is proportionate to the superiority possessed by their largest specimens. Again, where one good is always accompanied by another, but does not always accompany it, it is greater than the other, for the use of the second thing is implied in the use of the first. A thing may be accompanied by another in three ways, either simultaneously, subsequently, or potentially. Life accompanies health simultaneously (but not health life), knowledge accompanies the act of learning subsequently, cheating accompanies sacrilege potentially, since a man who has committed sacrilege is always capable of cheating. Again, when two things each surpass a third, that which does so by the greater amount is the greater of the two; for it must surpass the greater as well as the lesser of the other two. A thing productive of a greater good than another is productive of is itself a greater good than that other. For this conception of 'productive of a greater' has been implied in our argument. Likewise, that which is produced by a greater good is itself a greater good; thus, if what is wholesome is more desirable and a greater good than what gives pleasure, health too must be a greater good than pleasure. Again, a thing which is desirable in itself is a greater good than a thing which is not desirable in itself, as for example, bodily strength than what is wholesome, since the latter is not pursued for its own sake, whereas the former is; and this was our definition of the good. Again, if one of two things is an end, and the other is not, the former is the greater good, as being chosen for its own sake and not for the sake of something else; as, for example, exercise is chosen for the sake of physical well-being. And of two things, that which stands less in need of the other, or of other things, is the greater good, since it is more self-sufficing. (That which stands 'less' in need of others is that which needs either *fewer* or *easier* things.) So when one thing does not exist or cannot come into existence without a second, while the second can exist without the first, the second is better. That which does not need something else is more self-sufficing than that which does, and presents itself as a greater good for that reason. Again, that which is a beginning of other things is a greater good than that which is not, and that which is a cause is a greater good than that which is not; the reason being the same in each case, namely that without a cause and a beginning nothing can exist or come into existence. Again, where there are two sets of consequences arising from two different beginnings or causes, the consequences of the more important beginning or cause are themselves the more important; and conversely, that beginning or cause is itself the more important which has the more important consequences. Now it is plain, from all that has been said, that one thing may be shown to be more important than another from two opposite points of view: it may appear the more important (1) because it is a beginning and the other thing is not, and also (2) because it is not a beginning and the other thing is—on the ground that the end is more important and is not a beginning. So Leodamas, when accusing Callistratus, said that the man who prompted the deed was more guilty than the doer, since it would not have been done if he had not planned it. On the other hand, when accusing Chabrias he said that the doer was worse than the prompter, since there would have been no deed without some one to do it; men, said he, plot a thing only in order to carry it out.

Further, what is rare is a greater good than what is plentiful. Thus, gold is a better thing than iron, though less useful: it is harder to get, and therefore better worth getting. Reversely, it may be argued that the plentiful is a better thing than the rare, because we can make more use of it. For what is often useful surpasses what is seldom useful, whence the saying

The best of things is water.

More generally: the hard thing is better than the easy, because it is rarer: and reversely, the easy thing is better than the hard, for it is as we wish it to be. That is the greater good whose contrary is the greater evil, and whose loss affects us more. Positive goodness and

badness are more important than the mere *absence* of goodness
and badness: for positive goodness and badness are ends, which
the mere absence of them cannot be. Further, in proportion as the
functions of things are noble or base, the things themselves are
good or bad: conversely, in proportion as the things themselves
are good or bad, their functions also are good or bad; for the nature of results corresponds with that of their causes and beginnings, and conversely the nature of causes and beginnings
corresponds with that of their results. Moreover, those things are
greater goods, superiority in which is more desirable or more honourable. Thus, keenness of sight is more desirable than keenness
of smell, sight generally being more desirable than smell generally;
and similarly, unusually great love of friends being more honourable than unusually great love of money, ordinary love of friends
is more honourable than ordinary love of money. Conversely, if
one of two normal things is better or nobler than the other, an
unusual degree of that thing is better or nobler than an unusual
degree of the other. Again, one thing is more honourable or better than another if it is more honourable or better to desire it; the
importance of the object of a given instinct corresponds to the importance of the instinct itself; and for the same reason, if one
thing is more honourable or better than another, it is more honourable and better to desire it. Again, if one science is more
honourable and valuable than another, the activity with which it
deals is also more honourable and valuable; as is the science, so is
the reality that is its object, each science being authoritative in its
own sphere. So, also, the more valuable and honourable the object
of a science, the more valuable and honourable the science itself is
in consequence. Again, that which would be judged, or which has
been judged, a good thing, or a better thing than something else,
by all or most people of understanding, or by the majority of men,
or by the ablest, must be so; either without qualification, or inso-
far as they use their understanding to form their judgement. This
is indeed a general principle, applicable to all other judgements
also; not only the goodness of things, but their essence, magnitude, and general nature are in fact just what knowledge and understanding will declare them to be. Here the principle is applied

to judgements of goodness, since one definition of 'good' was 'what beings that acquire understanding will choose in any given case': from which it clearly follows that that thing is *better* which understanding declares to be so. That, again, is a better thing which attaches to better men, either absolutely, or in virtue of their being better; as courage is better than strength. And that is a greater good which would be chosen by a better man, either absolutely, or in virtue of his being better: for instance, to suffer wrong rather than to do wrong, for that would be the choice of the juster man. Again, the pleasanter of two things is the better, since *all* things pursue pleasure, and things instinctively desire pleasurable sensation *for its own sake;* and these are two of the characteristics by which the 'good' and the 'end' have been defined. One pleasure is greater than another if it is more unmixed with pain, or more lasting. Again, the nobler thing is better than the less noble, since the noble is either what is pleasant or what is desirable in itself. And those things also are greater goods which men desire more earnestly to bring about for themselves or for their friends, whereas those things which they least desire to bring about are greater evils. And those things which are more lasting are better than those which are more fleeting, and the more secure than the less; the enjoyment of the lasting has the advantage of being longer, and that of the secure has the advantage of suiting our wishes, being there for us whenever we like. Further, in accordance with the rule of co-ordinate terms and inflexions of the same stem, what is true of one such related word is true of all. Thus if the action qualified by the term 'brave' is more noble and desirable than the action qualified by the term 'temperate', then 'bravery' is more desirable than 'temperance' and 'being brave' than 'being temperate'. That, again, which is chosen by all is a greater good than that which is not, and that chosen by the majority than that chosen by the minority. For that which *all* desire is good, as we have said; and so, the more a thing is desired, the better it is. Further, that is the better thing which is considered so by competitors or enemies, or, again, by authorized judges or those whom they select to represent them. In the first two cases the decision is virtually that of every one, in the last two that of authorities and experts. And sometimes it may be argued that what all share is the better thing, since it is a dishonour not to share in it; at other times, that what none or few share is better, since it is rarer. The more praiseworthy things are, the nobler and therefore the better they are. So with the things that earn greater honours than others —honour is, as it were, a measure of value; and the things whose absence involves comparatively heavy penalties; and the things that are better than others admitted or believed to be good. Moreover, things look better merely by being divided into their parts, since they then seem to surpass a greater number of things than before. Hence Homer says that Meleager was roused to battle by the thought of

> . . . *all the ills that come to men*
> *whose town is taken: soldiers put to the sword;*
> *the city razed by fire; alien hands*
> *carrying off the children and the women.*[13]

The same effect is produced by piling up facts in a climax after the manner of Epicharmus. The reason is partly the same as in the case of division (for combination, too, makes the impression of great superiority), and partly that the original thing appears to be the cause and origin of important results. And since a thing is better when it is harder or rarer than other things, its superiority may be due to seasons, ages, places, times, or one's natural powers. When a man accomplishes something beyond his natural power, or beyond his years, or beyond the measure of people like him, or in a special way, or at a special place or time, his deed will have a high degree of nobleness, goodness, and justice, or of their opposites. Hence the epigram on the victor at the Olympic games:

In time past, bearing a yoke on my shoulders, of wood unshaven,
I carried my loads of fish from Argos to Tegea town.

So Iphicrates used to extol himself by describing the low estate from which he had risen. Again, what is natural is better than

[13] *Iliad*, IX. 719–22.

what is acquired, since it is harder to come by. Hence the words of Homer:

> No one taught me; deep in my mind a god
> shaped all the various ways of life in song.[14]

And the best part of a good thing is particularly good; as when Pericles in his funeral oration said that the country's loss of its young men in battle was 'as if the spring were taken out of the year'. So with those things which are of service when the need is pressing; for example, in old age and times of sickness. And of two things that which leads more directly to the end in view is the better. So, too, is that which is better for people generally as well as for a particular individual. Again, what *can* be got is better than what cannot, for it is good in a given case and the other thing is not. And what is at the end of life is better than what is not, since those things are ends in a greater degree which are nearer the end. What aims at reality is better than what aims at appearance. We may define what aims at appearance as what a man will not choose if nobody is to know of his having it. This would seem to show that to receive benefits is more desirable than to confer them, since a man will choose the former even if nobody is to know of it, but it is not the general view that he will choose the latter if nobody knows of it. What a man wants to *be* is better than what a man wants to *seem,* for in aiming at that he is aiming more at reality. Hence men say that justice is of small value, since it is more desirable to seem just than to be just, whereas with health it is not so. That is better than other things which is more useful than they are for a number of different purposes; for example, that which promotes life, good life, pleasure, and noble conduct. For this reason wealth and health are commonly thought to be of the highest value, as possessing all these advantages. Again, that is better than other things which is accompanied both with less pain and with actual pleasure; for here there is more than one advantage; and so here we have the good of feeling pleasure and also the good of not feeling pain. And of two good things that is

[14] *Odyssey,* XXII. 363–64.

the better whose addition to a third thing makes a better whole than the addition of the other to the same thing will make. Again, those things which we are seen to possess are better than those which we are not seen to possess, since the former have the air of reality. Hence wealth may be regarded as a greater good if its existence is known to others. That which is dearly prized is better than what is not—the sort of thing that some people have only one of, though others have more like it. Accordingly, blinding a one-eyed man inflicts worse injury than half-blinding a man with two eyes; for the one-eyed man has been robbed of what he dearly prized.

The grounds on which we must base our arguments, when we are speaking for or against a proposal, have now been set forth more or less completely.

8 · The powers of persuasion of the political speaker enhanced by a knowledge of the four sorts of governments—democracy, oligarchy, aristocracy, and monarchy—and their characteristic customs, institutions, and interests

The most important and effective qualification for success in persuading audiences and speaking well on public affairs is to understand all the forms of government and to discriminate their respective customs, institutions, and interests. For all men are persuaded by considerations of their interest, and their interest lies in the maintenance of the established order. Further, it rests with the supreme authority to give authoritative decisions, and this varies with each form of government; there are as many different supreme authorities as there are different forms of government. The forms of government are four—democracy, oligarchy, aristocracy, monarchy. The supreme right to judge and decide always

---

It is those who have been loyal to the national institutions that hold office under an aristocracy. These are bound to be looked upon as 'the best men'. (Page 40)

rests, therefore, with either a part or the whole of one or other of these governing powers.

A Democracy is a form of government under which the citizens distribute the offices of state among themselves by lot, whereas under oligarchy there is a property qualification, under aristocracy one of education. By education I mean that education which is laid down by the law; for it is those who have been loyal to the national institutions that hold office under an aristocracy. These are bound to be looked upon as 'the best men', and it is from this fact that this form of government has derived its name ('the rule of the best'). Monarchy, as the word implies, is the constitution in which one man has authority over all. There are two forms of monarchy: kingship, which is limited by prescribed conditions, and 'tyranny', which is not limited by anything.

We must also notice the ends which the various forms of government pursue, since people choose in practice such actions as will lead to the realization of their ends. The end of democracy is freedom; of oligarchy, wealth; of aristocracy, the maintenance of education and national institutions; of tyranny, the protection of the tyrant. It is clear, then, that we must distinguish those particular customs, institutions, and interests which tend to realize the ideal of each constitution, since men choose their means with reference to their ends. But rhetorical persuasion is effected not only by demonstrative but by ethical argument; it helps a speaker to convince us, if we believe that he has certain qualities himself, namely, goodness, or goodwill towards us, or both together. Similarly, we should know the moral qualities characteristic of each form of government, for the special moral character of each is bound to provide us with our most effective means of persuasion in dealing with it. We shall learn the qualities of governments in the same way as we learn the qualities of individuals, since they are revealed in their deliberate acts of choice; and these are determined by the end that inspires them.

We have now considered the objects, immediate or distant, at which we are to aim when urging any proposal, and the grounds on which we are to base our arguments in favour of its utility. We have also briefly considered the means and methods by which we shall gain a good knowledge of the moral qualities and institutions peculiar to the various forms of government—only, however, to the extent demanded by the present occasion; a detailed account of the subject has been given in the *Politics*.[15]

9 • The concerns of the epideictic speaker—virtue and vice; epideictic rhetorical devices, especially amplification

We have now to consider Virtue and Vice, the Noble and the Base, since these are the objects of praise and blame. In doing so, we shall at the same time be finding out how to make our hearers take the required view of our own characters—our second method of persuasion. The ways in which to make them trust the goodness of other people are also the ways in which to make them trust our own. Praise, again, may be serious or frivolous; nor is it always of a human or divine being but often of inanimate things, or of the humblest of the lower animals. Here too we must know on what grounds to argue, and must, therefore, now discuss the subject, though by way of illustration only.

The Noble is that which is both desirable for its own sake and also worthy of praise; or that which is both good and also pleasant because good. If this is a true definition of the Noble, it follows that virtue must be noble, since it is both a good thing and also praiseworthy. Virtue is, according to the usual view, a faculty of providing and preserving good things; or a faculty of conferring many great benefits, and benefits of all kinds on all occasions. The forms of Virtue are justice, courage, temperance, magnificence, magnanimity, liberality, gentleness, prudence, wisdom. If virtue is a faculty of beneficence, the highest kinds of it must be those which are most useful to others, and for this reason men honour most the just and the courageous, since courage is useful to others in war, justice both in war and in peace. Next comes liberality; liberal people let their money go instead of fighting for it, whereas other people care more for money than for anything else. Justice is the virtue through which everybody enjoys his own possessions in

---

[15] *Politics*, III, IV.

41

accordance with the law; its opposite is injustice, through which men enjoy the possessions of others in defiance of the law. Courage is the virtue that disposes men to do noble deeds in situations of danger, in accordance with the law and in obedience to its commands; cowardice is the opposite. Temperance is the virtue that disposes us to obey the law where physical pleasures are concerned; incontinence is the opposite. Liberality disposes us to spend money for others' good; illiberality is the opposite. Magnanimity is the virtue that disposes us to do good to others on a large scale; [its opposite is meanness of spirit]. Magnificence is a virtue productive of greatness in matters involving the spending of money. The opposites of these two are smallness of spirit and meanness respectively. Prudence is that virtue of the understanding which enables men to come to wise decisions about the relation to happiness of the goods and evils that have been previously mentioned.

The above is a sufficient account, for our present purpose, of virtue and vice in general, and of their various forms. As to further aspects of the subject, it is not difficult to discern the facts; it is evident that things productive of virtue are noble, as tending towards virtue; and also the effects of virtue, that is, the signs of its presence and the acts to which it leads. And since the signs of virtue, and such acts as it is the mark of a virtuous man to do or have done to him, are noble, it follows that all deeds or signs of courage, and everything done courageously, must be noble things; and so with what is just and actions done justly. (Not, however, actions justly done to us; here justice is unlike the other virtues; 'justly' does not always mean 'nobly'; when a man is punished, it is more shameful that this should be justly than unjustly done to him). The same is true of the other virtues. Again, those actions are noble for which the reward is simply honour, or honour more than money. So are those in which a man aims at something desirable for some one else's sake; actions good absolutely, such as those a man does for his country without thinking of himself; actions good in their own nature; actions that are not good simply for the individual, since individual interests are selfish. Noble also are those actions whose advantage may be enjoyed after death, as opposed to those whose advantage is enjoyed during one's lifetime: for the latter are more likely to be for one's own sake only. Also, all actions done for the sake of others, since less than other actions are done for one's own sake; and all successes which benefit others and not oneself; and services done to one's benefactors, for this is just; and good deeds generally, since they are not directed to one's own profit. And the opposites of those things of which men feel ashamed, for men are ashamed of saying, doing, or intending to do shameful things. So when Alcaeus said

> *Something I fain would say to thee,*
> *Only shame restraineth me,*

Sappho wrote

> *If for things good and noble thou wert yearning,*
> *If to speak baseness were thy tongue not burning,*
> *No load of shame would on thine eyelids weigh;*
> *What thou with honour wishest thou wouldst say.*

Those things, also, are noble for which men strive anxiously, without feeling fear; for they feel thus about the good things which lead to fair fame. Again, one quality or action is nobler than another if it is that of a naturally finer being: thus a man's will be nobler than a woman's. And those qualities are noble which give more pleasure to other people than to their possessors; hence the nobleness of justice and just actions. It is noble to avenge oneself on one's enemies and not to come to terms with them; for requital is just, and the just is noble; and not to surrender is a sign of courage. Victory, too, and honour belong to the class of noble things, since they are desirable even when they yield no fruits, and they prove our superiority in good qualities. Things that deserve to be remembered are noble, and the more they deserve this, the nobler they are. So are the things that continue even after death; those which are always attended by honour; those which are exceptional; and those which are possessed by one person alone—these last are more readily remembered than others. So again are possessions that bring no profit, since they are more fitting than others for a gentleman. So are the distinctive qualities of a particular people, and the symbols of what it specially admires, like long hair in Sparta, where this is a mark of a free man, as it is not easy to perform any menial task when one's hair is long. Again, it is noble not to practise any sordid craft, since it is the mark of a free man not to live at another's beck and call. We are also to assume, when we wish either to praise a man or blame him, that qualities closely allied to those which he actually has are identical with them; for instance, that the cautious man is cold-blooded and treacherous, and that the stupid man is an honest fellow or the thick-skinned man a good-tempered one. We can always idealize any given man by drawing on the virtues akin to his actual qualities; thus we may say that the passionate and excitable man is 'outspoken'; or that the arrogant man is 'superb' or 'impressive'. Those who run to extremes will be said to possess the corresponding good qualities; rashness will be called courage, and extravagance generosity. That will be what most people think; and at the same time this method enables an advocate to draw a misleading inference from the motive, arguing that if a man runs into danger needlessly, much more will he do so in a noble cause; and if a man is open-handed to any one and every one, he will be so to his friends also, since it is the extreme form of goodness to be good to everybody.

We must also take into account the nature of our particular audience when making a speech of praise; for, as Socrates used to say, it is not difficult to praise the Athenians to an Athenian audience. If the audience esteems a given quality, we must say that our hero has that quality, no matter whether we are addressing Scythians or Spartans or philosophers. Everything, in fact, that is esteemed we are to represent as noble. After all, people regard the two things as much the same.

All actions are noble that are appropriate to the man who does them: if, for instance, they are worthy of his ancestors or of his own past career. For it makes for happiness, and is a noble thing, that he should add to the honour he already has. Even inappropriate actions are noble if they are better and nobler than the appropriate ones would be; for instance, if one who was just an average person when all went well becomes a hero in adversity, or if he becomes better and easier to get on with the higher he rises. Compare the saying of Iphicrates, 'Think what I was and what I am'; and the epigram on the victor at the Olympic games,

In time past, bearing a yoke on my shoulders, of wood un-shaven, [16]

and the encomium of Simonides,

A woman whose father, whose husband, whose brethren were princes all.

Since we praise a man for what he has actually done, and fine actions are distinguished from others by being intentionally good, we must try to prove that our hero's noble acts are intentional. This is all the easier if we can make out that he has often acted so before, and therefore we must assert coincidences and accidents to have been intended. Produce a number of good actions, all of the same kind, and people will think that they must have been intended, and that they prove the good qualities of the man who did them.

Praise is the expression in words of the eminence of a man's good qualities, and therefore we must display his actions as the product of such qualities. Encomium refers to what he has actually done; the mention of accessories, such as good birth and education, merely helps to make our story credible—good fathers are likely to have good sons, and good training is likely to produce good character. Hence it is only when a man has already done something that we bestow *encomiums* upon him. Yet the actual deeds are evidence of the doer's character: even if a man has not actually done a given good thing, we shall bestow *praise* on him, if we are sure that he is the sort of man who *would* do it. To call any one blest is, it may be added, the same thing as to call him happy; but these are not the same thing as to bestow praise and encomiums upon him; the two latter are a part of 'calling happy', just as goodness is a part of happiness.

To praise a man is in one respect akin to urging a course of action. The suggestions which would be made in the latter case become encomiums when differently expressed. When we know what action or character is required, then, in order to express these facts as suggestions for action, we have to change and re-

[16] Cf. I. 7, for this and the previous quotation.

verse our form of words. Thus the statement 'A man should be proud not of what he owes to fortune but of what he owes to himself', if put like this, amounts to a suggestion; to make it into praise we must put it thus, 'Since he is proud not of what he owes to fortune but of what he owes to himself.' Consequently, whenever you want to praise any one, think what you would urge people to do; and when you want to urge the doing of anything, think what you would praise a man for having done. Since suggestion may or may not forbid an action, the praise into which we convert it must have one or other of two opposite forms of expression accordingly.

There are, also, many useful ways of heightening the effect of praise. We must, for instance, point out that a man is the only one, or the first, or almost the only one who has done something, or that he has done it better than any one else; all these distinctions are honourable. And we must, further, make much of the particular season and occasion of an action, arguing that we could hardly have looked for it just then. If a man has often achieved the same success, we must mention this; that is a strong point; he himself, and not luck, will then be given the credit. So, too, if it is on his account that observances have been devised and instituted to encourage or honour such achievements as his own: thus we may praise Hippolochus because the first encomium ever made was for him, or Harmodius and Aristogeiton because their statues were the first to be put up in the market-place. And we may censure bad men for the opposite reason.

Again, if you cannot find enough to say of a man himself, you may pit him against others, which is what Isocrates used to do owing to his want of familiarity with forensic pleading. The comparison should be with famous men; that will strengthen your case; it is a noble thing to surpass men who are themselves great. It is only natural that methods of 'heightening the effect' should be attached particularly to speeches of praise; they aim at proving su-

---

If virtue is a faculty of beneficence, the highest kinds of it must be those which are most useful to others, and for this reason men honour most the just and the courageous, since courage is useful to others in war, justice both in war and in peace. (Page 41)

I. Wachsmuth Sc.

periority over others, and any such superiority is a form of nobleness. Hence if you cannot compare your hero with famous men, you should at least compare him with other people generally, since any superiority is held to reveal excellence. And, in general, of the lines of argument which are common to all speeches, this 'heightening of effect' is most suitable for declamations, where we take our hero's actions as admitted facts, and our business is simply to invest these with dignity and nobility. 'Examples' are most suitable to deliberative speeches; for we judge of future events by divination from past events. Enthymemes are most suitable to forensic speeches; it is our doubts about past events that most admit of arguments showing why a thing must have happened or proving that it did happen.

The above are the general lines on which all, or nearly all, speeches of praise or blame are constructed. We have seen the sort of thing we must bear in mind in making such speeches, and the materials out of which encomiums and censures are made. No special treatment of censure and vituperation is needed. Knowing the above facts, we know their contraries; and it is out of these that speeches of censure are made.

10 · The concern of the forensic speaker—wrong-doing, its motives, its perpetrators, and its victims; enumeration and elucidation of the seven causes of human action, viz. three involuntary actions are good or apparently good, pleasant or apparently pleasant

We have next to treat of Accusation and Defence, and to enumerate and describe the ingredients of the syllogisms used therein. There are three things we must ascertain—first, the nature and number of the incentives to wrong-doing; second, the state of mind of wrong-doers; third, the kind of persons who are wronged, and their condition. We will deal with these questions in order. But before that let us define the act of 'wrong-doing'.

We may describe 'wrong-doing' as injury voluntarily inflicted contrary to law. 'Law' is either special or general. By special law I mean that written law which regulates the life of a particular community; by general law, all those unwritten principles which are supposed to be acknowledged everywhere. We do things 'voluntarily' when we do them consciously and without constraint. (Not all voluntary acts are deliberate, but all deliberate acts are conscious—no one is ignorant of what he deliberately intends.) The causes of our deliberately intending harmful and wicked acts contrary to law are (1) vice, (2) lack of self-control. For the wrongs a man does to others will correspond to the bad quality or qualities that he himself possesses. Thus it is the mean man who will wrong others about money, the profligate in matters of physical pleasure, the effeminate in matters of comfort, and the coward where danger is concerned—his terror makes him abandon those who are involved in the same danger. The ambitious man does wrong for the sake of honour, the quick-tempered from anger, the lover of victory for the sake of victory, the embittered man for the sake of revenge, the stupid man because he has misguided notions of right and wrong, the shameless man because he does not mind what people think of him; and so with the rest—any wrong that any one does to others corresponds to his particular faults of character.

However, this subject has already been cleared up in part in our discussion of the virtues[17] and will be further explained later when we treat of the emotions.[18] We have now to consider the motives and states of mind of wrong-doers, and to whom they do wrong.

Let us first decide what sort of things people are trying to get or avoid when they set about doing wrong to others. For it is plain that the prosecutor must consider, out of all the aims that can ever induce us to do wrong to our neighbours, how many, and which, affect his adversary; while the defendant must consider how many, and which, do *not* affect him. Now every action of every person either is or is not due to that person himself. Of those not due to himself some are due to chance, the others to necessity; of these latter, again, some are due to compulsion, the others to na-

[17] I. 9.
[18] II. 1–11.

ture. Consequently all actions that are not due to a man himself are due either to chance or to nature or to compulsion. All actions that *are* due to a man himself and caused by himself are due either to habit or to rational or irrational craving. Rational craving is a craving for good, i.e. a *wish*—nobody wishes for anything unless he thinks it good. Irrational craving is twofold, viz. anger and appetite.

Thus every action must be due to one or other of seven causes: chance, nature, compulsion, habit, reasoning, anger, or appetite. It is superfluous further to distinguish actions according to the doers' ages, moral states, or the like; it is of course true that, for instance, young men do have hot tempers and strong appetites; still, it is not through youth that they act accordingly, but through anger or appetite. Nor, again, is action due to wealth or poverty; it is of course true that poor men, being short of money, do have an appetite for it, and that rich men, being able to command needless pleasures, do have an appetite for such pleasures: but here, again, their actions will be *due* not to wealth or poverty but to appetite. Similarly, with just men, and unjust men, and all others who are said to act in accordance with their moral qualities, their actions will really be due to one of the causes mentioned —either reasoning or emotion: due, indeed, sometimes to good dispositions and good emotions, and sometimes to bad; but that good qualities should be followed by good emotions, and bad by bad, is merely an accessory fact—it is no doubt true that the temperate man, for instance, because he is temperate, *is* always and at once attended by healthy opinions and appetites in regard to pleasant things, and the intemperate man by unhealthy ones. So we must ignore such distinctions. Still we must consider what kinds of actions and of people usually go together; for while there are no definite kinds of action associated with the fact that a man is fair or dark, tall or short, it does make a difference if he is young or old, just or unjust. And, generally speaking, all those accessory qualities that cause distinctions of human character are important: e.g. the sense of wealth or poverty, of being lucky or unlucky. This shall be dealt with later[19]—let us now deal first with the rest of the subject before us.

[19] II. 12–17.

The things that happen by chance are all those whose cause cannot be determined, that have no purpose, and that happen neither always nor usually nor in any fixed way. The definition of chance shows just what they are. Those things happen by nature which have a fixed and internal cause; they take place uniformly, either always or usually. There is no need to discuss in exact detail the things that happen contrary to nature, nor to ask whether they happen in some sense naturally or from some other cause; it would seem that chance is at least partly the cause of such events. Those things happen through compulsion which take place contrary to the desire or reason of the doer, yet through his own agency. Acts are done from habit which men do because they have often done them before. Actions are due to reasoning when, in view of any of the goods already mentioned,[20] they appear useful either as ends or as means to an end, and are performed for that reason: 'for that reason,' since even licentious persons perform a certain number of useful actions, but because they are pleasant and not because they are useful. To passion and anger are due all acts of revenge. Revenge and punishment are different things. Punishment is inflicted for the sake of the person punished; revenge for that of the punisher, to satisfy his feelings. (What anger is will be made clear when we come to discuss the emotions.[21]) Appetite is the cause of all actions that appear pleasant. Habit, whether acquired by mere familiarity or by effort, belongs to the class of pleasant things, for there are many actions not naturally pleasant which men perform with pleasure, once they have become used to them. To sum up then, all actions due to ourselves either are or seem to be either good or pleasant. Moreover, as all actions due to ourselves are done voluntarily and actions not due to ourselves are done involuntarily, it follows that all voluntary actions must either be or seem to be either good or pleasant; for I reckon among goods escape from evils or apparent evils and the exchange of a greater evil for a less (since these things are in a sense positively desirable), and likewise I count among pleasures escape from painful or apparently painful things and the exchange of a greater pain for a less. We must ascertain, then, the number

[20] I. 6.
[21] II. 2.

and nature of the things that are useful and pleasant. The useful has been previously examined in connexion with political oratory;[22] let us now proceed to examine the pleasant. Our various definitions must be regarded as adequate, even if they are not exact, provided they are clear.

11 · Definition of pleasure, and analysis of things pleasant

We may lay it down that Pleasure is a movement, a movement by which the soul as a whole is consciously brought into its normal state of being; and that Pain is the opposite. If this is what pleasure is, it is clear that the pleasant is what tends to produce this condition, while that which tends to destroy it, or to cause the soul to be brought into the opposite state, is painful. It must therefore be pleasant as a rule to move towards a natural state of being, particularly when a natural process has achieved the complete recovery of that natural state. Habits also are pleasant; for as soon as a thing has become habitual, it is virtually natural; habit is a thing not unlike nature; what happens often is akin to what happens always, natural events happening always, habitual events often. Again, that is pleasant which is not forced on us; for force is unnatural, and that is why what is compulsory is painful, and it has been rightly said

All that is done on compulsion is bitterness unto the soul.

So all acts of concentration, strong effort, and strain are necessarily painful; they all involve compulsion and force, unless we are accustomed to them, in which case it is custom that makes them pleasant. The opposites to these are pleasant; and hence ease, freedom from toil, relaxation, amusement, rest, and sleep belong to the class of pleasant things; for these are all free from any element of compulsion. Everything, too, is pleasant for which we have the desire within us, since desire is the craving for pleasure. Of the de-

[22] I. 6.

sires some are irrational, some associated with reason. By irrational I mean those which do not arise from any opinion held by the
mind. Of this kind are those known as 'natural'; for instance,
those originating in the body, such as the desire for nourishment,
namely hunger and thirst, and a separate kind of desire answering
to each kind of nourishment; and the desires connected with taste
and sex and sensations of touch in general; and those of smell,
hearing, and vision. Rational desires are those which we are induced to have; there are many things we desire to see or get because we have been told of them and induced to believe them
good. Further, pleasure is the consciousness through the senses of
a certain kind of emotion; but imagination is a feeble sort of sensation, and there will always be in the mind of a man who remembers or expects something an image or picture of what he
remembers or expects. If this is so, it is clear that memory and expectation also, being accompanied by sensation, may be accompanied by pleasure. It follows that anything pleasant is either present
and perceived, past and remembered, or future and expected,
since we perceive present pleasures, remember past ones, and expect future ones. Now the things that are pleasant to remember
are not only those that, when actually perceived as present, *were*
pleasant, but also some things that were not, provided that their
results have subsequently proved noble and good. Hence the
words

> *Sweet 'tis when rescued to remember pain,*

and

> *Even his griefs are a joy long after to one that remembers*
> *All that he wrought and endured.*[23]

The reason of this is that it is pleasant even to be merely free from
evil. The things it is pleasant to expect are those that when present
are felt to afford us either great delight or great but not painful
benefit. And in general, all the things that delight us when they are
present also do so, as a rule, when we merely remember or expect

---

[23] Cf. *Odyssey*, xv. 451–53.

them. Hence even being angry is pleasant—Homer said of wrath
that it is

> . . . *far sweeter than slow-dripping honey*[24]

for no one grows angry with a person on whom there is no prospect of taking vengeance, and we feel comparatively little anger,
or none at all, with those who are much our superiors in power.
Some pleasant feeling is associated with most of our appetites; we
are enjoying either the memory of a past pleasure or the expectation of a future one, just as persons down with fever, during their
attacks of thirst, enjoy remembering the drinks they have had and
looking forward to having more. So also a lover enjoys talking or
writing about his loved one, or doing any little thing connected
with him; all these things recall him to memory and make him actually present to the eye of imagination. Indeed, it is always the
first sign of love, that besides enjoying some one's presence, we
remember him when he is gone, and feel pain as well as pleasure,
because he is there no longer. Similarly there is an element of pleasure even in mourning and lamentation for the departed. There is
grief, indeed, at his loss, but pleasure in remembering him and as
it were seeing him before us in his deeds and in his life. We can
well believe the poet when he says

> *A twinging ache of grief rose up in everyone.*[25]

Revenge, too, is pleasant; it is pleasant to get anything that it is
painful to fail to get, and angry people suffer extreme pain when
they fail to get their revenge; but they enjoy the prospect of getting
it. Victory also is pleasant, and not merely to 'bad losers', but to
every one; the winner sees himself in the light of a champion, and
everybody has a more or less keen appetite for being that. The
pleasantness of victory implies of course that combative sports
and intellectual contests are pleasant (since in these it often happens that some one wins) and also games like knuckle-bones, ball,
dice, and draughts. And similarly with the serious sports; some of
these become pleasant when one is accustomed to them; while

[24] *Iliad*, XVIII. 125.
[25] *Odyssey*, IV. 191.

54

others are pleasant from the first, like hunting with hounds, or indeed any kind of hunting. For where there is competition, there is victory. That is why forensic pleading and debating contests are pleasant to those who are accustomed to them and have the capacity for them. Honour and good repute are among the most pleasant things of all; they make a man see himself in the character of a fine fellow, especially when he is credited with it by people whom he thinks good judges. His neighbours are better judges than people at a distance; his associates and fellow-countrymen better than strangers; his contemporaries better than posterity; sensible persons better than foolish ones; a large number of people better than a small number: those of the former class, in each case, are the more likely to be good judges of him. Honour and credit bestowed by those whom you think much inferior to yourself— e.g. children or animals—you do not value: not for its own sake, anyhow: if you do value it, it is for some other reason. Friends belong to the class of pleasant things; it is pleasant to love—if you love wine, you certainly find it delightful: and it is pleasant to be loved, for this too makes a man see himself as the possessor of goodness, a thing that every being that has a feeling for it desires to possess: to be loved means to be valued for one's own personal qualities. To be admired is also pleasant, simply because of the honour implied. Flattery and flatterers are pleasant: the flatterer is a man who, you believe, admires and likes you. To do the same thing often is pleasant, since, as we saw, anything habitual is pleasant. And to change is also pleasant: change means an approach to nature, whereas invariable repetition of anything causes the excessive prolongation of a settled condition: therefore, says the poet,

Change is in all things sweet.

That is why what comes to us only at long intervals is pleasant, whether it be a person or a thing; for it is change from what we had before, and, besides, what comes only at long intervals has the value of rarity. Learning things and wondering at things are also pleasant as a rule; wondering implies the desire of learning, so that the object of wonder is an object of desire; while in learning one is brought into one's natural condition. Conferring and receiving benefits belong to the class of pleasant things; to receive a benefit is to get what one desires; to confer a benefit implies both possession and superiority, both of which are things we try to attain. It is because beneficent acts are pleasant that people find it pleasant to put their neighbours straight again and to supply what they lack. Again, since learning and wondering are pleasant, it follows that such things as acts of imitation must be pleasant—for instance, painting, sculpture, poetry—and every product of skilful imitation; this latter, even if the object imitated is not itself pleasant; for it is not the object itself which here gives delight; the spectator draws inferences ('That is a so-and-so') and thus learns something fresh. Dramatic turns of fortune and hairbreadth escapes from perils are pleasant, because we feel all such things are wonderful.

And since what is natural is pleasant, and things akin to each other seem natural to each other, therefore all kindred and similar things are usually pleasant to each other; for instance, one man, horse, or young person is pleasant to another man, horse, or young person. Hence the proverbs 'mate delights mate', 'like to like', 'beast knows beast', 'jackdaw to jackdaw', and the rest of them. But since everything like and akin to oneself is pleasant, and since every man is himself more like and akin to himself than any one else is, it follows that all of us must be more or less fond of ourselves. For all this resemblance and kinship is present particularly in the relation of an individual to himself. And because we are all fond of ourselves, it follows that what is our own is pleasant to all of us, as for instance our own deeds and words. That is why we are usually fond of our flatterers, [our lovers,] and honour; also of our children, for our children are our own work. It is also pleasant to complete what is defective, for the whole thing thereupon becomes our own work. And since power over others is very pleasant, it is pleasant to be thought wise, for practical wisdom secures us power over others. (Scientific wisdom is also pleasant, because it is the knowledge of many wonderful things.) Again, since most of us are ambitious, it must be pleasant to disparage our neighbours as well as to have power over them. It is pleasant for a man to spend his time over what he feels he can do best; just as the poet says,

To that he bends himself,
To that each day allots most time, wherein
He is indeed the best part of himself.

Similarly, since amusement and every kind of relaxation and laughter too belong to the class of pleasant things, it follows that ludicrous things are pleasant, whether men, words, or deeds. We have discussed the ludicrous separately in the treatise on the *Art of Poetry*.

So much for the subject of pleasant things: by considering their opposites we can easily see what things are unpleasant.

12 · The characters and circumstances which lead men to commit wrong or make them victims of wrong

The above are the motives that make men do wrong to others; we are next to consider the states of mind in which they do it, and the persons to whom they do it.

They must themselves suppose that the thing can be done, and done by them: either that they can do it without being found out, or that if they are found out they can escape being punished, or that if they are punished the disadvantage will be less than the gain for themselves or those they care for. The general subject of apparent possibility and impossibility will be handled later on, since it is relevant not only to forensic but to all kinds of speaking. But it may here be said that people think that they can themselves most easily do wrong to others without being punished for it if they possess eloquence, or practical ability, or much legal experience, or a large body of friends, or a great deal of money. Their confidence is greatest if they personally possess the advantages mentioned: but even without them they are satisfied if they have friends or supporters or partners who do possess them: they can thus both commit their crimes and escape being found out and punished for committing them. They are also safe, they think, if they are on good terms with their victims or with the judges who try them. Their victims will in that case not be on their guard against being wronged, and will make some arrangement with them instead of prosecuting; while their judges will favour them because they like them, either letting them off altogether or imposing light sentences. They are not likely to be found out if their appearance contradicts the charges that might be brought against them: for instance, a weakling is unlikely to be charged with violent assault, or a poor and ugly man with adultery. Public and open injuries are the easiest to do, because nobody could at all suppose them possible, and therefore no precautions are taken. The same is true of crimes so great and terrible that no man living could be suspected of them: here too no precautions are taken. For all men guard against ordinary offences, just as they guard against ordinary diseases; but no one takes precautions against a disease that nobody has ever had. You feel safe, too, if you have either no enemies or a great many; if you have none, you expect not to be watched and therefore not to be detected; if you have a great many, you will be watched, and therefore people will think you can never risk an attempt on them, and you can defend your innocence by pointing out that you could never have taken such a risk. You may also trust to hide your crime by the way you do it or the place you do it in, or by some convenient means of disposal.

You may feel that even if you are found out you can stave off a trial, or have it postponed, or corrupt your judges: or that even if you are sentenced you can avoid paying damages, or can at least postpone doing so for a long time: or that you are so badly off that you will have nothing to lose. You may feel that the gain to be got by wrong-doing is great or certain or immediate, and that the penalty is small or uncertain or distant. It may be that the advantage to be gained is greater than any possible retribution: as in the case of despotic power, according to the popular view. You may consider your crimes as bringing you solid profit, while their punishment is nothing more than being called bad names. Or the opposite argument may appeal to you: your crimes may bring you some credit (thus you may, incidentally, be avenging your father or mother, like Zeno), whereas the punishment may amount to a fine, or banishment, or something of that sort. People may be led on to wrong others by either of these motives or feelings; but no man by both—they will affect people of quite opposite characters. You may be encouraged by having often escaped detection or punishment already; or by having often tried and failed; for in crime, as in war, there are men who will always refuse to give up the struggle. You may get your pleasure on the spot and the pain later, or the gain on the spot and the loss later. That is what appeals to weak-willed persons—and weakness of will may be shown with regard to all the objects of desire. It may on the contrary appeal to you—as it does appeal to self-controlled and sensible people—that the pain and loss are immediate, while the pleasure and profit come later and last longer. You may feel able to make it appear that your crime was due to chance, or to necessity, or to natural causes, or to habit: in fact, to put it generally, as if you had failed to do right rather than actually done wrong. You may be able to trust other people to judge you equitably. You may be stimulated by being in want: which may mean that you want necessaries, as poor people do, or that you want luxuries, as rich people do. You may be encouraged by having a particularly good reputation, because that will save you from being suspected: or by having a particularly bad one, because nothing you are likely to do will make it worse.

The above, then, are the various states of mind in which a man sets about doing wrong to others. The kind of people to whom he does wrong, and the ways in which he does it, must be considered next. The people to whom he does it are those who have what he wants himself, whether this means necessities or luxuries and materials for enjoyment. His victims may be far off or near at hand. If they are near, he gets his profit quickly; if they are far off, vengeance is slow, as those think who plunder the Carthaginians. They may be those who are trustful instead of being cautious and watchful, since all such people are easy to elude. Or those who are too easygoing to have enough energy to prosecute an offender. Or sensitive people, who are not apt to show fight over questions of money. Or those who have been wronged already by many people, and yet have not prosecuted; such men must surely be the proverbial 'Mysian prey'. Or those who have either never or often been wronged before; in neither case will they take precautions; if they have never been wronged they think they never will, and if they have often been wronged they feel that surely it cannot happen again. Or those whose character has been attacked in the past, or is exposed to attack in the future: they will be too much frightened of the judges to make up their minds to prosecute, nor can they win their case if they do: this is true of those who are hated or unpopular. Another likely class of victim is those who their injurer can pretend have, themselves or through their ancestors or friends, treated badly, or intended to treat badly, the man himself, or his ancestors, or those he cares for; as the proverb says, 'wickedness needs but a pretext'. A man may wrong his enemies, because that is pleasant: he may equally wrong his friends, because that is easy. Then there are those who have no friends, and those who lack eloquence and practical capacity; these will either not attempt to prosecute, or they will come to terms, or failing that they will lose their case. There are those whom it does not pay to waste time in waiting for trial or damages, such as foreigners and small farmers; they will settle for a trifle, and always be ready to leave off. Also those who have themselves wronged others, either often, or in the same way as they are now being wronged themselves—for it is felt that next to no wrong is done to people when it is the same wrong as they have often themselves done to others: if, for instance, you assault a man who has been accustomed to behave with violence to others. So too with those who have done wrong to others, or have meant to, or mean to, or are likely to do so; there is something fine and pleasant in wronging such persons, it seems as though almost no wrong were done. Also those by doing wrong to whom we shall be gratifying our friends, or those we admire or love, or our masters, or in general the people by reference to whom we mould our lives. Also those whom we may wrong and yet be sure of equitable treatment. Also those against whom we have had any grievance, or any previous differences with them, as Callippus had when he behaved as he did to Dion: here too it seems as if almost no wrong were being done. Also those who are on the point of being wronged by others if we fail to wrong them ourselves, since here we feel we have no time left for thinking the matter over. So Aenesidemus is said to have sent the 'cottabus' prize to Gelon, who had just reduced a town to slavery, because Gelon had got there first and forestalled his own attempt. Also those by wronging whom we shall be able to do many righteous acts; for we feel that we can then easily cure the harm done. Thus Jason the Thessalian said that it is a duty to do some unjust acts in order to be able to do many just ones.

Among the kinds of wrong done to others are those that are done universally, or at least commonly: one expects to be forgiven for doing these. Also those that can easily be kept dark, as where things that can rapidly be consumed like eatables are concerned, or things that can easily be changed in shape, colour, or combination, or things that can easily be stowed away almost anywhere— portable objects that you can stow away in small corners, or things so like others of which you have plenty already that nobody can tell the difference. There are also wrongs of a kind that shame prevents the victim speaking about, such as outrages done to the women in his household or to himself or to his sons. Also those for which you would be thought very litigious to prosecute any one—trifling wrongs, or wrongs for which people are usually excused.

The above is a fairly complete account of the circumstances under which men do wrong to others, of the sort of wrongs they do, of the sort of persons to whom they do them, and of their reasons for doing them.

13 · Actions, just and unjust, may be classified in relation to the law and the persons affected

It will now be well to make a complete classification of just and unjust actions. We may begin by observing that they have been defined relatively to two kinds of law, and also relatively to two classes of persons. By the two kinds of law I mean particular law and universal law. Particular law is that which each community lays down and applies to its own members: this is partly written and partly unwritten. Universal law is the law of Nature. For there really is, as every one to some extent divines, a natural justice and injustice that is binding on all men, even on those who have no association or covenant with each other. It is this that Sophocles'

Antigone clearly means when she says that burial of Polyneices was a just act in spite of the prohibition: she means that it was just by nature.

> Not of to-day or yesterday it is,
> But lives eternal: none can date its birth.

And so Empedocles, when he bids us kill no living creature, says that doing this is not just for some people while unjust for others,

> Nay, but, an all-embracing law, through the realms of the sky
> Unbroken it stretcheth, and over the earth's immensity.

And as Alcidamas says in his Messeniac Oration. . . .

The actions that we ought to do or not to do have also been divided into two classes as affecting either the whole community or some one of its members. From this point of view we can perform just or unjust acts in either of two ways—towards one definite person, or towards the community. The man who is guilty of adultery or assault is doing wrong to some definite person; the man who avoids service in the army is doing wrong to the community.

Thus the whole class of unjust actions may be divided into two classes, those affecting the community, and those affecting one or more other persons. We will next, before going further, remind ourselves of what 'being wronged' means. Since it has already been settled that 'doing a wrong' must be intentional, 'being wronged' must consist in having an injury done to you by some one who *intends* to do it. In order to be wronged, a man must (1) suffer actual harm, (2) suffer it against his will. The various possible forms of harm are clearly explained by our previous separate discussion of goods and evils. We have also seen that a voluntary action is one where the doer knows what he is doing. We now see that every accusation must be of an action affecting either the community or some individual. The doer of the action must either understand and intend the action, or not understand and intend it. In the former case, he must be acting either from deliberate choice or from passion. (Anger will be discussed when we speak of the passions, the motives for crime and the state of mind of the criminal have already been discussed.) Now it often happens that a man will admit an act, but will not admit the prosecutor's label for the act nor the facts which that label implies. He will admit that he took a thing but not that he 'stole' it; that he struck some one first, but not that he committed 'outrage'; that he had intercourse with a woman, but not that he committed 'adultery'; that he is guilty of theft, but not that he is guilty of 'sacrilege', the object stolen not being consecrated; that he has encroached, but not that he has 'encroached on State lands'; that he has been in communication with the enemy, but not that he has been guilty of 'treason'. Here therefore we must be able to distinguish what is theft, outrage, or adultery, from what is not, if we are to be able to make the justice of our case clear, no matter whether our aim is to establish a man's guilt or to establish his innocence. Wherever such charges are brought against a man, the question is whether he is or is not guilty of a criminal offence. It is deliberate purpose that constitutes wickedness and criminal guilt, and such names as 'outrage' or 'theft' imply deliberate purpose as well as the mere action. A blow does not always amount to 'outrage', but only if it is struck with some such purpose as to insult the man struck or gratify the striker himself. Nor does taking a thing without the owner's knowledge always amount to 'theft', but only if it is taken with the intention of keeping it and injuring the owner. And as with these charges, so with all the others.

We saw that there are two kinds of right and wrong conduct towards others, one provided for by written ordinances, the other by unwritten. We have now discussed the kind about which the laws have something to say. The other kind has itself two varieties. First, there is the conduct that springs from exceptional goodness or badness, and is visited accordingly with censure and loss of honour, or with praise and increase of honour and decorations: for instance, gratitude to, or requital of, our benefactors, readiness to help our friends, and the like. The second kind makes up for the defects of a community's written code of law. This is what we call equity; people regard it as just; it is, in fact, the sort of justice which goes beyond the written law. Its existence partly is and partly is not intended by legislators; not intended, where they have noticed no defect in the law; intended, where they find themselves unable to define things exactly, and are obliged to legislate as if that held good always which in fact only holds good usually; or where it is not easy to be complete owing to the endless possible cases presented, such as the kinds and sizes of weapons that may be used to inflict wounds—a lifetime would be too short to make out a complete list of these. If, then, a precise statement is impossible and yet legislation is necessary, the law must be expressed in wide terms; and so, if a man has no more than a finger-ring on his hand when he lifts it to strike or actually strikes another man, he is guilty of a criminal act according to the unwritten words of the law; but he is innocent really, and it is equity that declares him to be so. From this definition of equity it is plain what sort of actions, and what sort of persons, are equitable or the reverse. Equity must be applied to forgivable actions; and it must make us distinguish between criminal acts on the one hand, and errors of judgement, or misfortunes, on the other. (A 'misfortune' is an act, not due to moral badness, that has unexpected results: an 'error of judgement' is an act, also not due to moral badness, that has results that might have been expected: a 'criminal act' has results that might have been expected, but *is* due to moral badness, for that is the source of all actions inspired by our appetites.) Equity bids us be merciful to the weakness of human nature; to think less about the laws than about the man who framed them, and less about what he said than about what he meant; not to consider the actions of the accused so much as his intentions, nor this or that detail so much as the whole story; to ask not what a man is now but what he has always or usually been. It bids us remember benefits rather than injuries, and benefits received rather than benefits conferred; to be patient when we are wronged; to settle a dispute by negotiation and not by force; to prefer arbitration to litigation—for an arbitrator goes by the equity of a case, a judge by the strict law, and arbitration was invented with the express purpose of securing full power for equity.

The above may be taken as a sufficient account of the nature of equity.

Victory also is pleasant, and not merely to 'bad losers', but to every one; the winner sees himself in the light of a champion, and everybody has an appetite for being that. (Page 54)

J. Wachsmuth Sc.

14 · The worse of two wrong acts done to others is that which is prompted by the worse disposition

The worse of two acts of wrong done to others is that which is prompted by the worse disposition. Hence the most trifling acts may be the worst ones; as when Callistratus charged Melanopus with having cheated the temple-builders of three consecrated half-obols. The converse is true of just acts. This is because the greater is here potentially contained in the less: there is no crime that a man who has stolen three consecrated half-obols would shrink from committing. Sometimes, however, the worse act is reckoned not in this way but by the greater harm that it does. Or it may be because no punishment for it is severe enough to be adequate; or the harm done may be incurable—a difficult and even hopeless crime to defend; or the sufferer may not be able to get his injurer legally punished, a fact that makes the harm incurable, since legal punishment and chastisement are the proper cure. Or again, the man who has suffered wrong may have inflicted some fearful punishment on himself; then the doer of the wrong ought in justice to receive a still more fearful punishment. Thus Sophocles, when pleading for retribution to Euctemon, who had cut his own throat because of the outrage done to him, said he would not fix a penalty less than the victim had fixed for himself. Again, a man's crime is worse if he has been the first man, or the only man, or almost the only man, to commit it: or if it is by no means the first time he has gone seriously wrong in the same way: or if his crime has led to the thinking-out and invention of measures to prevent and punish similar crimes—thus in Argos a penalty is inflicted on a man on whose account a law is passed, and also on those on whose account the prison was built: or if a crime is specially brutal, or specially deliberate: or if the report of it awakes more terror than pity. There are also such rhetorically effective ways of putting it as the following: That the accused has disregarded and broken not one but many solemn obligations like oaths, promises, pledges, or rights of intermarriage between states—here the crime is worse because it consists of many crimes; and that the crime was committed in the very place where criminals are punished, as for example perjurers do—it is argued that a man who will commit a crime in a law-court would commit it anywhere. Further, the worse deed is that which involves the doer in special shame; that whereby a man wrongs his benefactors—for he does more than one wrong, by not merely doing them harm but failing to do them good; that which breaks the unwritten laws of justice —the better sort of man will be just without being forced to be so, and the written laws depend on force while the unwritten ones do not. It may however be argued otherwise, that the crime is worse which breaks the written laws: for the man who commits crimes for which terrible penalties are provided will not hesitate over crimes for which no penalty is provided at all.—So much, then, for the comparative badness of criminal actions.

15 · The non-technical or extrinsic modes of persuasion: laws, witnesses, contracts, tortures, and oaths

There are also the so-called 'non-technical' means of persuasion; and we must now take a cursory view of these, since they are specially characteristic of forensic oratory. They are five in number: laws, witnesses, contracts, tortures, oaths.

First, then, let us take laws and see how they are to be used in persuasion and dissuasion, in accusation and defence. If the written law tells against our case, clearly we must appeal to the universal law, and insist on its greater equity and justice. We must argue that the juror's oath 'I will give my verdict according to my honest opinion' means that one will not simply follow the letter of the written law. We must urge that the principles of equity are permanent and changeless, and that the universal law does not change either, for it is the law of nature, whereas written laws often do change. This is the bearing in the lines in Sophocles' *Antigone*, where Antigone pleads that in burying her brother she had broken Creon's law, but not the unwritten law:

> *Not of to-day or yesterday they are,*
> *But live eternal: ⟨none can date their birth.⟩*
> *Not I would fear the wrath of any man*
> *⟨And brave God's vengeance⟩ for defying these.*

We shall argue that justice indeed is true and profitable, but that sham justice is not, and that consequently the written law is not, because it does not fulfil the true purpose of law. Or that justice is like silver, and must be assayed by the judges, if the genuine is to be distinguished from the counterfeit. Or that the better man is, the more he will follow and abide by the unwritten law in preference to the written. Or perhaps that the law in question contradicts some other highly-esteemed law, or even contradicts itself. Thus it may be that one law will enact that all contracts must be held binding, while another forbids us ever to make illegal contracts. Or if a law is ambiguous, we shall turn it about and consider which construction best fits the interests of justice or utility, and then follow that way of looking at it. Or if, though the law still exists, the situation to meet which it was passed exists no longer, we must do our best to prove this and to combat the law thereby. If however the written law supports our case, we must urge that the oath 'to give my verdict according to my honest opinion' is not meant to make the judges give a verdict that is contrary to the law, but to save them from the guilt of perjury if they misunderstand what the law really means. Or that no one chooses what is absolutely good, but every one what is good for himself. Or that not to use the laws is as bad as to have no laws at all. Or that, as in the other arts, it does not pay to try to be cleverer than the doctor: for less harm comes from the doctor's mistakes than from the growing habit of disobeying authority. Or that trying to be cleverer than the laws is just what is forbidden by those codes of law that are accounted best. — So far as the laws are concerned, the above discussion is probably sufficient.

As to witnesses, they are of two kinds, the ancient and the recent; and these latter, again, either do or do not share in the risks of the trial. By 'ancient' witnesses I mean the poets and all other notable persons whose judgements are known to all. Thus the Athenians appealed to Homer[26] as a witness about Salamis; and the men of Tenedos not long ago appealed to Periander of Corinth in their dispute with the people of Sigeum; and Cleophon supported his accusation of Critias by quoting the elegiac verse of

[26] *Iliad*, II. 657–58.

Solon, maintaining that discipline had long been slack in the family of Critias, or Solon would never have written,

Pray thee, bid the red-haired Critias do what his father commands him.

These witnesses are concerned with past events. As to future events we shall also appeal to soothsayers: thus Themistocles quoted the oracle about 'the wooden wall' as a reason for engaging the enemy's fleet. Further, proverbs are, as has been said, one form of evidence. Thus if you are urging somebody not to make a friend of an old man, you will appeal to the proverb,

Never show an old man kindness.

Or if you are urging that he who has made away with fathers should also make away with their sons, quote,

Fool, who slayeth the father and leaveth his sons to avenge him.

'Recent' witnesses are well-known people who have expressed their opinions about some disputed matter: such opinions will be useful support for subsequent disputants on the same points: thus Eubulus used in the law-courts against the reply Plato had made to Archibius, 'It has become the regular custom in this country to admit that one is a scoundrel'. There are also those witnesses who share the risk of punishment if their evidence is pronounced false. These are valid witnesses to the fact that an action was or was not done, that something is or is not the case; they are not valid witnesses to the quality of an action, to its being just or unjust, useful or harmful. On such questions of *quality* the opinion of detached persons is highly trustworthy. Most trustworthy of all are the 'ancient' witnesses, since they cannot be corrupted.

In dealing with the evidence of witnesses, the following are useful arguments. If you have no witnesses on your side, you will argue that the judges must decide from what is probable; that this is meant by 'giving a verdict in accordance with one's honest opinion'; that probabilities cannot be bribed to mislead the court; and that probabilities are never convicted of perjury. If you *have* witnesses, and the other man has not, you will argue that probabilities cannot be put on their trial, and that we could do without the evidence of witnesses altogether if we need do no more than balance the pleas advanced on either side.

The evidence of witnesses may refer either to ourselves or to our opponent; and either to questions of fact or to questions of personal character: so, clearly, we need never be at a loss for useful evidence. For if we have no evidence of fact supporting our own case or telling against that of our opponent, at least we can always find evidence to prove our own worth or our opponent's worthlessness. Other arguments about a witness—that he is a friend or an enemy or neutral, or has a good, bad, or indifferent reputation, and any other such distinctions—we must construct upon the same general lines as we use for the regular rhetorical proofs.

Concerning contracts argument can be so far employed as to increase or diminish their importance and their credibility; we shall try to increase both if they tell in our favour, and to diminish both if they tell in favour of our opponent. Now for confirming or upsetting the credibility of contracts, the procedure is just the same as for dealing with witnesses, for the credit to be attached to contracts depends upon the character of those who have signed them or have the custody of them. The contract being once admitted genuine, we must insist on its importance, if it supports our case. We may argue that a contract is a law, though of a special and limited kind; and that, while contracts do not of course make the law binding, the law does make any lawful contract binding, and that the law itself as a whole is a sort of contract, so that any one who disregards or repudiates any contract is repudiating the law itself. Further, most business relations—those, namely, that are voluntary—are regulated by contracts, and if these lose their binding force, human intercourse ceases to exist. We need not go very deep to discover the other appropriate arguments of this kind. If, however, the contract tells against us and for our opponents, in the first place those arguments are suitable which we can use to fight a law that tells against us. We do not regard ourselves as bound to observe a bad law which it was a mistake ever to pass: and it is ridiculous to suppose that we are bound to observe a bad and mistaken contract. Again, we may argue that the duty of the judge as umpire is to decide what is just, and therefore he must ask where justice lies, and not what this or that document means. And that it is impossible to pervert justice by fraud or by force, since it is founded on nature, but a party to a contract may be the victim of either fraud or force. Moreover, we must see if the contract contravenes either universal law or any written law of our own or another country; and also if it contradicts any other previous or subsequent contract; arguing that the subsequent is the binding contract, or else that the previous one was right and the subsequent one fraudulent—whichever way suits us. Further, we must consider the question of utility, noting whether the contract is against the interest of the judges or not; and so on—these arguments are as obvious as the others.

Examination by torture is one form of evidence, to which great weight is often attached because it is in a sense compulsory. Here again it is not hard to point out the available grounds for magnifying its value, if it happens to tell in our favour, and arguing that it is the only form of evidence that is infallible; or, on the other hand, for refuting it if it tells against us and for our opponent, when we may say what is true of torture of every kind alike, that people under its compulsion tell lies quite as often as they tell the truth, sometimes persistently refusing to tell the truth, sometimes recklessly making a false charge in order to be let off sooner. We ought to be able to quote cases, familiar to the judges, in which this sort of thing has actually happened. [We must say that evidence under torture is not trustworthy, the fact being that many men whether thick-witted, tough-skinned, or stout of heart endure their ordeal nobly, while cowards and timid men are full of boldness till they see the ordeal of these others; so that no trust can be placed in evidence under torture.]

In regard to oaths, a fourfold division can be made. A man may either both offer and accept an oath, or neither, or one without the other—that is, he may offer an oath but not accept one, or accept an oath but not offer one. There is also the situation that arises when an oath has already been sworn either by himself or by his opponent.

If you refuse to offer an oath, you may argue that men do not hesitate to perjure themselves; and that if your opponent does swear, you lose your money, whereas, if he does not, you think the judges will decide against him; and that the risk of an unfavourable verdict is preferable, since you trust the judges and do not trust him.

If you refuse to accept an oath, you may argue that an oath is always paid for; that you would of course have taken it if you had been a rascal, since if you *are* a rascal you had better make something by it, and you would in that case have to swear in order to succeed. Thus your refusal, you argue, must be due to high principle, not to fear of perjury: and you may aptly quote the saying of Xenophanes,

'Tis not fair that he who fears not God should challenge him who doth.

It is as if a strong man were to challenge a weakling to strike, or be struck by, him.

If you agree to accept an oath, you may argue that you trust yourself but not your opponent; and that (to invert the remark of Xenophanes) the fair thing is for the impious man to offer the oath and for the pious man to accept it; and that it would be monstrous if you yourself were unwilling to accept an oath in a case where you demand that the judges should do so before giving their verdict. If you wish to offer an oath, you may argue that piety disposes you to commit the issue to the gods; and that your opponent ought not to want other judges than himself, since you leave the decision with him; and that it is outrageous for your opponents to refuse to swear about this question, when they insist that others should do so.

Now that we see how we are to argue in each case separately, we see also how we are to argue when they occur in pairs, namely, when you are willing to accept the oath but not to offer it; to offer it but not to accept it; both to accept and to offer it; or to do neither. These are of course combinations of the cases already mentioned, and so your arguments also must be combinations of the arguments already mentioned.

If you have already sworn an oath that contradicts your present one, you must argue that it is not perjury, since perjury is a crime, and a crime must be a voluntary action, whereas actions due to the force or fraud of others are involuntary. You must further reason from this that perjury depends on the intention and not on the spoken words. But if it is your opponent who has already sworn an oath that contradicts his present one, you must say that if he does not abide by his oaths he is the enemy of society, and that this is the reason why men take an oath before administering the laws. 'My opponents insist that you, the judges, must abide by the oath you have sworn, and yet they are not abiding by their own oaths.' And there are other arguments which may be used to magnify the importance of the oath.—[So much, then, for the 'non-technical' modes of persuasion.]

BOOK II

1 · The orator must not only try to make the argument of his speech demonstrative and worthy of belief, he must also make his own character look right and be able to influence the emotions, or moral affections, of the jury who try the case

We have now considered the materials to be used in supporting or opposing a political measure, in pronouncing eulogies or censures, and for prosecution and defence in the law-courts. We have considered the received opinions on which we may best base our arguments so as to convince our hearers—those opinions with which our enthymemes deal, and out of which they are built, in each of the three kinds of oratory, according to what may be called the special needs of each.

But since rhetoric exists to affect the giving of decisions—the hearers decide between one political speaker and another, and a legal verdict *is* a decision—the orator must not only try to make the argument of his speech demonstrative and worthy of belief; he must also make his own character look right and put his hearers, who are to decide, into the right frame of mind. Particularly in political oratory, but also in lawsuits, it adds much to an orator's influence that his own character should look right and that he should be thought to entertain the right feelings towards his hearers; and also that his hearers themselves should be in just the right frame of mind. That the orator's own character should look right is particularly important in political speaking: that the audience should be in the right frame of mind, in lawsuits. When people are feeling friendly and placable, they think one sort of thing; when they are feeling angry or hostile, they think either something totally different or the same thing with a different intensity: when they feel friendly to the man who comes before them for judgement, they regard him as having done little wrong, if any; when they feel hostile, they take the opposite view. Again, if they are eager for, and have good hopes of, a thing that will be pleasant if it happens, they think that it certainly will happen and be good for them: whereas if they are indifferent or annoyed, they do not think so.

There are three things which inspire confidence in the orator's own character—the three, namely, that induce us to believe a thing apart from any proof of it: good sense, good moral character, and goodwill. False statements and bad advice are due to one or more of the following three causes. Men either form a false opinion through want of good sense; or they form a true opinion, but because of their moral badness do not say what they really think; or finally, they are both sensible and upright, but not well disposed to their hearers, and may fail in consequence to recommend what they know to be the best course. These are the only possible cases. It follows that any one who is thought to have all three of these good qualities will inspire trust in his audience. The way to make ourselves thought to be sensible and morally good must be gathered from the analysis of goodness already given: the way to establish your own goodness is the same as the way to establish that of others. Goodwill and friendliness of disposition will form part of our discussion of the Emotions, to which we must now turn.

The Emotions are all those feelings that so change men as to affect their judgements, and that are also attended by pain or pleasure. Such are anger, pity, fear and the like, with their opposites. We must arrange what we have to say about each of them under three heads. Take, for instance, the emotion of anger: here we must discover (1) what the state of mind of angry people is, (2) who the people are with whom they usually get angry, and (3) on what grounds they get angry with them. It is not enough to know one or even two of these points; unless we know all three, we shall be unable to arouse anger in any one. The same is true of the other emotions. So just as earlier in this work we drew up a list of useful propositions for the orator, let us now proceed in the same way to analyse the subject before us.

2 · The emotion of anger

Anger may be defined as an impulse, accompanied by pain, to a conspicuous revenge for a conspicuous slight directed without justification towards what concerns oneself or towards what concerns one's friends. If this is a proper definition of anger, it must always be felt towards some particular individual, e.g. Cleon, and not 'man' in general. It must be felt because the other has done or intended to do something to him or one of his friends. It must always be attended by a certain pleasure—that which arises from the expectation of revenge. For since nobody aims at what he thinks he cannot attain, the angry man is aiming at what he can attain, and the belief that you will attain your aim is pleasant. Hence it has been well said about wrath that it

> . . . *it is far sweeter than slow-dripping honey,*
> *clouding the hearts of men like smoke.*[27]

It is also attended by a certain pleasure because the thoughts dwell upon the act of vengeance, and the images then called up cause pleasure, like the images called up in dreams.

Now slighting is the actively entertained opinion of something as obviously of no importance. We think bad things, as well as good ones, have serious importance; and we think the same of anything that tends to produce such things, while those which have little or no such tendency we consider unimportant. There are three kinds of slighting—contempt, spite, and insolence. (1) Contempt is one kind of slighting: you feel contempt for what you consider unimportant, and it is just such things that you slight. (2) Spite is another kind; it is a thwarting another man's wishes, not

[27] *Iliad*, XVIII. 125–26.

to get something yourself but to prevent his getting it. The slight arises just from the fact that you do not aim at something for yourself: clearly you do not think that he can do you harm, for then you would be afraid of him instead of slighting him, nor yet that he can do you any good worth mentioning, for then you would be anxious to make friends with him. (3) Insolence is also a form of slighting, since it consists in doing and saying things that cause shame to the victim, not in order that anything may happen to yourself, or because anything has happened to yourself, but simply for the pleasure involved. (Retaliation is not 'insolence', but vengeance.) The cause of the pleasure thus enjoyed by the insolent man is that he thinks himself greatly superior to others when ill-treating them. That is why youths and rich men are insolent; they think themselves superior when they show insolence. One sort of insolence is to rob people of the honour due to them; you certainly slight them thus; for it is the unimportant, for good or evil, that has no honour paid to it. So Achilles says in anger:

> . . . *Agamemnon*
> *humiliated me! He has my prize,*
> *by his own whim, for himself,*[28]

and

> . . . *As though I were*
> *some riffraff or camp follower,*[29]

meaning that this is why he is angry. A man expects to be specially respected by his inferiors in birth, in capacity, in goodness, and generally in anything in which he is much their superior: as where money is concerned a wealthy man looks for respect from a poor man; where speaking is concerned, the man with a turn for oratory looks for respect from one who cannot speak; the ruler demands the respect of the ruled, and the man who thinks he ought

[28] *Iliad*, I. 412–14.
[29] *Iliad*, IX. 787–88.

to be a ruler demands the respect of the man whom he thinks he ought to be ruling. Hence it has been said

> . . . *There's passion in kings;*
> *they hold power from Zeus,*[30]

and

> *A great man in his rage is formidable*
> *for underlings; though he may keep it down*
> *he cherishes the burning in his belly*
> *until a reckoning day,*[31]

their great resentment being due to their great superiority. Then again a man looks for respect from those who he thinks owe him good treatment, and these are the people whom he has treated or is treating well, or means or has meant to treat well, either himself, or through his friends, or through others at his request.

It will be plain by now, from what has been said, (1) in what frame of mind, (2) with what persons, and (3) on what grounds people grow angry. (1) The frame of mind is that in which any pain is being felt. In that condition, a man is always aiming at something. Whether, then, another man opposes him either directly in any way, as by preventing him from drinking when he is thirsty, or indirectly, the act appears to him just the same; whether some one works against him, or fails to work with him, or otherwise vexes him while he is in this mood, he is equally angry in all these cases. Hence people who are afflicted by sickness or poverty or love or thirst or any other unsatisfied desires are prone to anger and easily roused: especially against those who slight their present distress. Thus a sick man is angered by disregard of his illness, a poor man by disregard of his poverty, a man waging war by disregard of the war he is waging, a lover by disregard of his love, and so throughout, any other sort of slight being enough if special slights are wanting. Each man is predisposed, by the emotion now controlling him, to his own particular anger.

[30] *Iliad,* II. 224–25.
[31] *Iliad,* I. 93–96.

Further, we are angered if we happen to be expecting a contrary result: for a quite unexpected evil is specially painful, just as the quite unexpected fulfilment of our wishes is specially pleasant. Hence it is plain what seasons, times, conditions, and periods of life tend to stir men easily to anger, and where and when this will happen; and it is plain that the more we are under these conditions, the more easily we are stirred.

These, then, are the frames of mind in which men are easily stirred to anger. The persons with whom we get angry are those who laugh, mock, or jeer at us, for such conduct is insolent. Also those who inflict injuries upon us that are marks of insolence. These injuries must be such as are neither retaliatory nor profitable to the doers: for only then will they be felt to be due to insolence. Also those who speak ill of us, and show contempt for us, in connexion with the things we ourselves most care about: thus those who are eager to win fame as philosophers get angry with those who show contempt for their philosophy; those who pride themselves upon their appearance get angry with those who show contempt for their appearance and so on in other cases. We feel particularly angry on this account if we suspect that we are in fact, or that people think we are, lacking completely or to any effective extent in the qualities in question. For when we are convinced that we excel in the qualities for which we are jeered at, we can ignore the jeering. Again, we are angrier with our friends than with other people, since we feel that our friends ought to treat us well and not badly. We are angry with those who have usually treated us with honour or regard, if a change comes and they behave to us otherwise: for we think that they feel contempt for us, or they would still be behaving as they did before. And with those who do not return our kindnesses or fail to return them adequately, and with those who oppose us though they are our inferiors: for all such persons seem to feel contempt for us; those who oppose us seem to think us inferior to themselves, and those who do not return our kindnesses seem to think that those kindnesses were conferred

---

Equity bids us be merciful to the weakness of human nature; to think less about the laws than about the man who framed them, and less about what he said than about what he meant. (Page 64)

by inferiors. And we feel particularly angry with men of no account at all, if they slight us. For, by our hypothesis, the anger caused by the slight is felt towards people who are not justified in slighting us, and our inferiors are not thus justified. Again, we feel angry with friends if they do not speak well of us or treat us well; and still more, if they do the contrary; or if they do not perceive our needs, which is why Plexippus is angry with Meleager in Antiphon's play; for this want of perception shows that they are slighting us—we do not fail to perceive the needs of those for whom we care. Again we are angry with those who rejoice at our misfortunes or simply keep cheerful in the midst of our misfortunes, since this shows that they either hate us or are slighting us. Also with those who are indifferent to the pain they give us: this is why we get angry with bringers of bad news. And with those who listen to stories about us or keep on looking at our weaknesses; this seems like either slighting us or hating us; for those who love us share in all our distresses and it must distress any one to keep on looking at his own weaknesses. Further, with those who slight us before five classes of people: namely, (1) our rivals, (2) those whom we admire, (3) those whom we wish to admire us, (4) those for whom we feel reverence, (5) those who feel reverence for us: if any one slights us before such persons, we feel particularly angry. Again, we feel angry with those who slight us in connexion with what we are as honourable men bound to champion—our parents, children, wives, or subjects. And with those who do not return a favour, since such a slight is unjustifiable. Also with those who reply with humorous levity when we are speaking seriously, for such behavior indicates contempt. And with those who treat us less well than they treat everybody else; it is another mark of contempt that they should think we do not deserve what every one else deserves. Forgetfulness, too, causes anger, as when our own names are forgotten, trifling as this may be; since forgetfulness is felt to be another sign that we are being slighted; it is due to negligence, and to neglect us is to slight us.

The persons with whom we feel anger, the frame of mind in which we feel it, and the reasons why we feel it, have now all been set forth. Clearly the orator will have to speak so as to bring his hearers into a frame of mind that will dispose them to anger, and to represent his adversaries as open to such charges and possessed of such qualities as do make people angry.

3 · Calmness, as opposed to anger

Since growing calm is the opposite of growing angry, and calmness the opposite of anger, we must ascertain in what frames of mind men are calm, towards whom they feel calm, and by what means they are made so. Growing calm may be defined as a settling down or quieting of anger. Now we get angry with those who slight us; and since slighting is a voluntary act, it is plain that we feel calm towards those who do nothing of the kind, or who do or seem to do it involuntarily. Also towards those who intended to do the opposite of what they did do. Also towards those who treat themselves as they have treated us: since no one can be supposed to slight himself. Also towards those who admit their fault and are sorry: since we accept their grief at what they have done as satisfaction, and cease to be angry. The punishment of servants shows this: those who contradict us and deny their offence we punish all the more, but we cease to be incensed against those who agree that they deserved their punishment. The reason is that it is shameless to deny what is obvious, and those who are shameless towards us slight us and show contempt for us: anyhow, we do not feel shame before those of whom we are thoroughly contemptuous. Also we feel calm towards those who humble themselves before us and do not gainsay us; we feel that they thus admit themselves our inferiors, and inferiors feel fear, and nobody can slight any one so long as he feels afraid of him. That our anger ceases towards those who humble themselves before us is shown even by dogs, who do not bite people when they sit down. We also feel calm towards those who are serious when we are serious, because then we feel that we are treated seriously and not contemptuously. Also towards those who have done us more kindnesses than we have done them. Also towards those who pray to us and beg for mercy, since they humble themselves by doing so. Also towards those who do not insult or mock at or slight any one at all, or not any worthy person or any one like ourselves. In general, the things that make us calm may be inferred by seeing what the opposites are of those that make us angry. We are not angry with people we fear or respect, as long as we fear or respect them; you cannot be afraid of a person and also at the same time angry with him. Again, we feel no anger, or comparatively little, with those who have done what they did through anger: we do not feel that they have done it from a wish to slight us, for no one slights people when angry with them, since slighting is painless, and anger is painful. Nor do we grow angry with those who reverence us.

As to the frame of mind that makes people calm, it is plainly the opposite to that which makes them angry, as when they are amusing themselves or laughing or feasting; when they are feeling prosperous or successful or satisfied; when, in fine, they are enjoying freedom from pain, or inoffensive pleasure, or justifiable hope. Also when time has passed and their anger is no longer fresh, for time puts an end to anger. And vengeance previously taken on one person puts an end to even greater anger felt against another person. Hence Philocrates, being asked by some one, at a time when the public was angry with him, 'Why don't you defend yourself?' did right to reply, 'The time is not yet.' 'Why, when *is* the time?' 'When I see some one else calumniated.' For men become calm when they have spent their anger on somebody else. This happened in the case of Ergophilus: though the people were more irritated against him than against Callisthenes, they acquitted him because they had condemned Callisthenes to death the day before. Again, men become calm if they have convicted the offender; or if he has already suffered worse things than they in their anger would have themselves inflicted upon him; for they feel as if they were already avenged. Or if they feel that they themselves are in the wrong and are suffering justly (for anger is not excited by what is just), since men no longer think then that they are suffering without justification; and anger, as we have seen, means this. Hence we ought always to inflict a preliminary punishment in words: if that is done, even slaves are less aggrieved by the actual punishment. We also feel calm if we think that the offender will not see that he is punished on our account and because of the way he has treated us. For anger has to do with individuals. This is plain from the definition. Hence the poet has well written:

> . . . Tell *him*
> Odysseus, raider of cities, took your eye,[32]

implying that Odysseus would not have considered himself avenged unless the Cyclops perceived both by whom and for what he had been blinded. Consequently we do not get angry with any one who cannot be aware of our anger, and in particular we cease to be angry with people once they are dead, for we feel that the worst has been done to them, and that they will neither feel pain nor anything else that we in our anger aim at making them feel. And therefore the poet has well made Apollo say, in order to put a stop to the anger of Achilles against the dead Hector,

> . . . *we gods will turn against him,*
> *seeing him outrage the insensate earth!*[33]

It is now plain that when you wish to calm others, you must draw upon these lines of argument; you must put your hearers into the corresponding frame of mind, and represent those with whom they are angry as formidable, or as worthy of reverence, or as benefactors, or as involuntary agents, or as much distressed at what they have done.

4 · Friendship and Enmity

Let us now turn to Friendship and Enmity, and ask towards whom these feelings are entertained, and why. We will begin by defining friendship and friendly feeling. We may describe friendly feeling towards any one as wishing for him what you believe to be good things, not for your own sake but for his, and being inclined, so far as you can, to bring these things about. A friend is one who

[32] *Odyssey,* IX. 526–27.
[33] *Iliad,* XXIV. 63–64.

feels thus and excites these feelings in return: those who think they feel thus towards each other think themselves friends. This being assumed, it follows that your friend is the sort of man who shares your pleasure in what is good and your pain in what is unpleasant, for your sake and for no other reason. This pleasure and pain of his will be the token of his good wishes for you, since we all feel glad at getting what we wish for, and pained at getting what we do not. Those, then, are friends to whom the same things are good and evil; and those who are, moreover, friendly or unfriendly to the same people; for in that case they must have the same wishes, and thus by wishing for each other what they wish for themselves, they show themselves each other's friends. Again, we feel friendly to those who have treated us well, either ourselves or those we care for, whether on a large scale, or readily, or at some particular crisis; provided it was for our own sake. And also to those who we think *wish* to treat us well. And also to our friends' friends, and to those who like, or are liked by, those whom we like ourselves. And also to those who are enemies to those whose enemies we are, and dislike, or are disliked by, those whom we dislike. For all such persons think the things good which we think good, so that they wish what is good for us; and this, as we saw, is what friends must do. And also to those who are willing to treat us well where money or our personal safety is concerned: and therefore we value those who are liberal, brave, or just. The just we consider to be those who do not live on others; which means those who work for their living, especially farmers and others who work with their own hands. We also like temperate men, because they are not unjust to others; and, for the same reason, those who mind their own business. And also those whose friends we wish to be, if it is plain that they wish to be our friends: such are the morally good, and those well thought of by every one, by the best men, or by those whom we admire or who admire us. And also those with whom it is pleasant to live and spend our days: such are the good-tempered, and those who are not too ready to show us our mistakes, and those who are not cantankerous or quarrelsome—such people are always wanting to fight us, and those who fight us we feel wish for the opposite of what we wish for ourselves—and those who have the tact to make and take a joke; here both parties have the same object in view, when they can stand being made fun of as well as do it prettily themselves. And we also feel friendly towards those who praise such good qualities as we possess, and especially if they praise the good qualities that we are not too sure we *do* possess. And towards those who are cleanly in their person, their dress, and all their way of life. And towards those who do not reproach us with what we have done amiss to them or they have done to help us, for both actions show a tendency to criticize us. And towards those who do not nurse grudges or store up grievances, but are always ready to make friends again; for we take it that they will behave to us just as we find them behaving to every one else. And towards those who are not evil speakers and who are aware of neither their neighbours' bad points nor our own, but of our good ones only, as a good man always will be. And towards those who do not try to thwart us when we are angry or in earnest, which would mean being ready to fight us. And towards those who have some serious feeling towards us, such as admiration for us, or belief in our goodness, or pleasure in our company; especially if they feel like this about qualities in us for which we especially wish to be admired, esteemed, or liked. And towards those who are like ourselves in character and occupation, provided they do not get in our way or gain their living from the same source as we do—for then it will be a case of 'potter against potter':

Potter to potter and builder to builder begrudge their reward.

And those who desire the same things as we desire, if it is possible for us both to share them together; otherwise the same trouble arises here too. And towards those with whom we are on such terms that, while we respect their opinions, we need not blush before them for doing what is conventionally wrong: as well as towards those before whom we should be ashamed to do anything really wrong. Again, our rivals, and those whom we should like to envy us—though without ill-feeling—either we like these people or at least we wish them to like us. And we feel friendly towards those whom we help to secure good for themselves, provided we are not likely to suffer heavily by it ourselves. And those who feel as friendly to us when we are not with them as when we are—

which is why all men feel friendly towards those who are faithful to their dead friends. And, speaking generally, towards those who are really fond of their friends and do not desert them in trouble; of all good men, we feel most friendly to those who show their goodness as friends. Also towards those who are honest with us, including those who will tell us of their own weak points: it has just been said that with our friends we are not ashamed of what is conventionally wrong, and if we do have this feeling, we do not love them; if therefore we do not have it, it looks as if we *did* love them. We also like those with whom we do not feel frightened or uncomfortable—nobody can like a man of whom he feels frightened. Friendship has various forms—comradeship, intimacy, kinship, and so on.

Things that cause friendship are: doing kindnesses; doing them unasked; and not proclaiming the fact when they are done, which shows that they were done for our own sake and not for some other reason. Enmity and Hatred should clearly be studied by reference to their opposites. Enmity may be produced by anger or spite or calumny. Now whereas anger arises from offences against oneself, enmity may arise even without that; we may hate people merely because of what we take to be their character. Anger is always concerned with individuals—a Callias or a Socrates—whereas hatred is directed also against classes: we all hate any thief and any informer. Moreover, anger can by cured by time; but hatred cannot. The one aims at giving pain to its object, the other at doing him harm; the angry man wants his victims to feel; the hater does not mind whether they feel or not. All painful things are felt; but the greatest evils, injustice and folly, are the least felt, since their presence causes no pain. And anger is accompanied by pain, hatred is not; the angry man feels pain, but the hater does not. Much may happen to make the angry man pity those who offend him, but the hater under no circumstances wishes to pity a man whom he has once hated: for the one would have the offenders suffer for what they have done; the other would have them cease to exist.

It is plain from all this that we can prove people to be friends or enemies; if they are not, we can make them out to be so; if they claim to be so, we can refute their claim; and if it is disputed whether an action was due to anger or to hatred, we can attribute it to whichever of these we prefer.

5 · Fear and Confidence

To turn next to Fear, what follows will show the things and persons of which, and the states of mind in which, we feel afraid. Fear may be defined as a pain or disturbance due to a mental picture of some destructive or painful evil in the future. Of destructive or painful evils only; for there are some evils, e.g. wickedness or stupidity, the prospect of which does not frighten us: I mean only such as amount to great pains or losses. And even these only if they appear not remote but so near as to be imminent: we do not fear things that are a very long way off: for instance, we all know we shall die, but we are not troubled thereby, because death is not close at hand. From this definition it will follow that fear is caused by whatever we feel has great power of destroying us, or of harming us in ways that tend to cause us great pain. Hence the very indications of such things are terrible, making us feel that the terrible thing itself is close at hand; the approach of what is terrible is just what we mean by 'danger'. Such indications are the enmity and anger of people who have power to do something to us; for it is plain that they have the will to do it, and so they are on the point of doing it. Also injustice in possession of power; for it is the unjust man's will to do evil that makes him unjust. Also outraged virtue in possession of power; for it is plain that, when outraged, it always has the will to retaliate, and now it has the power to do so. Also fear felt by those who have the power to do something to us, since such persons are sure to be ready to do it. And since most men tend to be bad—slaves to greed, and cowards in danger—it is, as a rule, a terrible thing to be at another man's mercy; and therefore, if we have done anything horrible, those in the secret terrify us with the thought that they may betray or desert us. And those who can do us wrong are terrible to us when we are liable to be wronged; for as a rule men do wrong to others whenever they have the power to do it. And those who have been wronged, or believe themselves to be wronged, are terrible; for they are always looking out for their opportunity. Also those who have done people wrong, if they possess power, since they stand in fear of retaliation: we have already said that wickedness possessing power is terrible. Again, our rivals for a thing cause us fear when we cannot both have it at once; for we are always at war with such men. We also fear those who are to be feared by stronger people than ourselves: if they can hurt those stronger people, still more can they hurt us; and, for the same reason, we fear those whom those stronger people are actually afraid of. Also those who have destroyed people stronger than we are. Also those who are attacking people weaker than we are: either they are already formidable, or they will be so when they have thus grown stronger. Of those we have wronged, and of our enemies or rivals, it is not the passionate and outspoken whom we have to fear, but the quiet, dissembling, unscrupulous; since we never know when they are upon us, we can never be sure they are at a safe distance. All terrible things are more terrible if they give us no chance of retrieving a blunder—either no chance at all, or only one that depends on our enemies and not ourselves. Those things are also worse which we cannot, or cannot easily, help. Speaking generally, anything causes us to feel fear that when it happens to, or threatens, others causes us to feel pity.

The above are, roughly, the chief things that are terrible and are feared. Let us now describe the conditions under which we ourselves feel fear. If fear is associated with the expectation that something destructive will happen to us, plainly nobody will be afraid who believes nothing can happen to him; we shall not fear things that we believe cannot happen to us, nor people who we believe cannot inflict them upon us; nor shall we be afraid at times when we think ourselves safe from them. It follows therefore that fear is felt by those who believe something to be likely to happen to them, at the hands of particular persons, in a particular form, and at a particular time. People do not believe this when they are, or think they are, in the midst of great prosperity, and are in consequence insolent, contemptuous, and reckless—the kind of character produced by wealth, physical strength, abundance of friends, power: nor yet when they feel they have experienced every kind of horror already and have grown callous about the future, like men who are being flogged and are already nearly dead—if they are to feel the anguish of uncertainty, there must be some faint expectation of escape. This appears from the fact that fear sets us thinking what can be done, which of course nobody does when things are hopeless. Consequently, when it is advisable that the audience should be frightened, the orator must make them feel that they really are in danger of something, pointing out that it has happened to others who were stronger than they are, and is happening, or has happened, to people like themselves, at the hands of unexpected people, in an unexpected form, and at an unexpected time.

Having now seen the nature of fear, and of the things that cause it, and the various states of mind in which it is felt, we can also see what Confidence is, about what things we feel it, and under what conditions. It is the opposite of fear, and what causes it is the opposite of what causes fear; it is, therefore, the expectation associated with a mental picture of the nearness of what keeps us safe and the absence or remoteness of what is terrible: it may be due either to the near presence of what inspires confidence or to the absence of what causes alarm. We feel it if we can take steps—many, or important, or both—to cure or prevent trouble; if we have neither wronged others nor been wronged by them; if we have either no rivals at all or no strong ones; if our rivals who are strong are our friends or have treated us well or been treated well by us; or if those whose interest is the same as ours are the more numerous party, or the stronger, or both.

As for our own state of mind, we feel confidence if we believe we have often succeeded and never suffered reverses, or have often met danger and escaped it safely. For there are two reasons why human beings face danger calmly: they may have no experience of it, or they may have means to deal with it: thus when in danger at sea people may feel confident about what will happen either because they have no experience of bad weather, or because their experience gives them the means of dealing with it. We also feel confident whenever there is nothing to terrify other people like ourselves, or people weaker than ourselves, or people than whom we believe ourselves to be stronger—and we believe this if we have conquered them, or conquered others who are as strong as they are, or stronger. Also if we believe ourselves superior to our rivals in the number and importance of the advantages that make men formidable—wealth, physical strength, strong bodies of supporters, extensive territory, and the possession of all, or the most important, appliances of war. Also if we have wronged no one, or not many, or not those of whom we are afraid; and generally, if our relations with the gods are satisfactory, as will be shown especially by signs and oracles. The fact is that anger makes us confident—that anger is excited by our knowledge that we are not the wrongers but the wronged, and that the divine power is always supposed to be on the side of the wronged. Also when, at the outset of an enterprise, we believe that we cannot and shall not fail, or that we shall succeed completely.—So much for the causes of fear and confidence.

6 · Shame and Shamelessness

We now turn to Shame and Shamelessness; what follows will explain the things that cause these feelings, and the persons before whom, and the states of mind under which, they are felt. Shame may be defined as pain or disturbance in regard to bad things, whether present, past, or future, which seem likely to involve us in discredit; and shamelessness as contempt or indifference in regard to these same bad things. If this definition be granted, it follows that we feel shame at such bad things as we think are disgraceful to ourselves or to those we care for. These evils are, in the first place, those due to moral badness. Such are throwing away one's shield or taking to flight; for these bad things are due to cowardice. Also, withholding a deposit or otherwise wronging people about money; for these acts are due to injustice. Also, having carnal intercourse with forbidden persons, at wrong times, or in wrong places; for these things are due to licentiousness. Also, making profit in petty or disgraceful ways, or out of helpless persons, e.g. the poor, or the dead—whence the proverb 'He would pick a corpse's pocket'; for all this is due to low greed and meanness. Also, in money matters, giving less help than you might, or none at all, or accepting help from those worse off than yourself; so also borrowing when it will seem like begging; begging when it will seem like asking the return of a favour; asking such a return when it will seem like begging; praising a man *in order that* it may seem like begging; and going on begging in spite of failure: all such actions are tokens of meanness. Also, praising people to their face, and praising extravagantly a man's good points and glozing over his weaknesses, and showing extravagant sympathy with his grief when you are in his presence, and all that sort of thing; all this shows the disposition of a flatterer. Also, refusing to endure hardships that are endured by people who are older, more delicately brought up, of higher rank, or generally less capable of endurance than ourselves: for all this shows effeminacy. Also, accepting benefits, especially accepting them often, from another man, and then abusing him for conferring them: all this shows a mean, ignoble disposition. Also, talking incessantly about yourself, making loud professions, and appropriating the merits of others; for this is due to boastfulness. The same is true of the actions due to any of the other forms of badness of moral character, of the tokens of such badness, &c.: they are all disgraceful and shameless. Another sort of bad thing at which we feel shame is, lacking a share in the honourable things shared by every one else, or by all or nearly all who are like ourselves. By 'those like ourselves' I mean those of our own race or country or age or family, and generally those who are on our own level. Once we are on a level with others, it is a disgrace to be, say, less well educated than they are; and so with other advantages: all the more so, in each case, if it is seen to be our own fault: wherever we are ourselves to blame for our present, past, or future circumstances, it follows at once that this is to a greater extent due to our moral badness. We are moreover ashamed of having done to us, having had done, or being about to have done to us acts that involve us in dishonour and reproach; as when we surrender our persons, or lend ourselves to vile deeds, e.g. when we submit to outrage. And acts of yielding to the lust of others are shameful whether willing or unwilling (yielding to force being an instance of unwillingness), since unresisting submission to them is due to unmanliness or cowardice.

These things, and others like them, are what cause the feeling of shame. Now since shame is a mental picture of disgrace, in which we shrink from the disgrace itself and not from its consequences, and we only care what opinion is held of us because of the people who form that opinion, it follows that the people before whom we feel shame are those whose opinion of us matters to us. Such persons are: those who admire us, those whom we admire, those by whom we wish to be admired, those with whom we are competing, and those whose opinion of us we respect. We admire those, and wish those to admire us, who possess any good thing that is highly esteemed; or from whom we are very anxious to get something that they are able to give us—as a lover feels. We compete with our equals. We respect, as true, the views of sensible people, such as our elders and those who have been well educated. And we feel more shame about a thing if it is done openly, before all men's eyes. Hence the proverb, 'shame dwells in the eyes'. For this reason we feel most shame before those who will always be with us and those who notice what we do, since in both cases eyes are upon us. We also feel it before those not open to the same imputation as ourselves: for it is plain that their opinions about it are the opposite of ours. Also before those who are hard on any one whose conduct they think wrong; for what a man does himself, he is said not to resent when his neighbours do it: so that of course he does resent their doing what he does not do himself. And before those who are likely to tell everybody about you; not telling others is as good as not believing you wrong. People are likely to tell others about you if you have wronged them, since they are on the lookout to harm you; or if they speak evil of everybody, for those who attack the innocent will be still more ready to attack the guilty. And before those whose main occupation is with their neighbours' failings—people like satirists and writers of comedy; these are really a kind of evil-speakers and tell-tales. And before those who have never yet known us come to grief, since their attitude to us has amounted to admiration so far: that is why we feel ashamed to refuse those a favour who ask one for the first time—

we have not as yet lost credit with them. Such are those who are just beginning to wish to be our friends; for they have seen our best side only (hence the appropriateness of Euripides' reply to the Syracusans): and such also are those among our old acquaintances who know nothing to our discredit. And we are ashamed not merely of the actual shameful conduct mentioned, but also of the evidences of it: not merely, for example, of actual sexual intercourse, but also of its evidences; and not merely of disgraceful acts but also of disgraceful talk. Similarly we feel shame not merely in the presence of persons mentioned but also of those who will tell them what we have done, such as their servants or friends. And, generally, we feel no shame before those upon whose opinions we quite look down as untrustworthy (no one feels shame before small children or animals); nor are we ashamed of the same things before intimates as before strangers, but before the former of what seem genuine faults, before the latter of what seem conventional ones.

The conditions under which we shall feel shame are these: first, having people related to us like those before whom, as has been said, we feel shame. These are, as was stated, persons whom we admire, or who admire us, or by whom we wish to be admired, or from whom we desire some service that we shall not obtain if we forfeit their good opinion. These persons may be actually looking on (as Cydias represented them in his speech on land assignments in Samos, when he told the Athenians to imagine the Greeks to be standing all around them, actually seeing the way they voted and not merely going to hear about it afterwards): or again they may be near at hand, or may be likely to find out about what we do. This is why in misfortune we do not wish to be seen by those who once wished themselves like us; for such a feeling implies admiration. And men feel shame when they have acts or exploits to their credit on which they are bringing dishonour, whether these are their own, or those of their ancestors, or those of other persons with whom they have some close connexion. Generally, we feel shame before those for whose own misconduct we should also feel it—those already mentioned; those who take us as their models; those whose teachers or advisers we have been; or other people, it may be, like ourselves, whose rivals we are. For there are many things that shame before such people makes us do or leave undone. And we feel more shame when we are likely to be continually seen by, and go about under the eyes of, those who know of our disgrace. Hence, when Antiphon the poet was to be cudgelled to death by order of Dionysius, and saw those who were to perish with him covering their faces as they went through the gates, he said, 'Why do you cover your faces? Is it lest some of these spectators should see you *to-morrow?*'

So much for Shame; to understand Shamelessness, we need only consider the converse cases, and plainly we shall have all we need.

7 · Kindness and Unkindness

To take Kindness next: the definition of it will show us towards whom it is felt, why, and in what frames of mind. Kindness—under the influence of which a man is said to 'be kind'—may be defined as helpfulness towards some one in need, not in return for anything, nor for the advantage of the helper himself, but for that of the person helped. Kindness is great if shown to one who is in great need, or who needs what is important and hard to get, or who needs it at an important and difficult crisis; or if the helper is the only, the first, or the chief person to give the help. Natural cravings constitute such needs; and in particular cravings, accompanied by pain, for what is not being attained. The appetites are cravings of this kind: sexual desire, for instance, and those which arise during bodily injuries and in dangers; for appetite is active both in danger and in pain. Hence those who stand by us in poverty or in banishment, even if they do not help us much, are yet really kind to us, because our need is great and the occasion pressing; for instance, the man who gave the mat in the Lyceum. The

---

Anger may be defined as an impulse, accompanied by pain, to a conspicuous revenge for a conspicuous slight directed without justification towards what concerns oneself or one's friends. (Page 77)

helpfulness must therefore meet, preferably, just this kind of need; and failing just this kind, some other kind as great or greater. We now see to whom, why, and under what conditions kindness is shown; and these facts must form the basis of our arguments. We must show that the persons helped are, or have been, in such pain and need as has been described, and that their helpers gave, or are giving, the kind of help described, in the kind of need described. We can also see how to eliminate the idea of kindness and make our opponents appear unkind: we may maintain that they are being or have been helpful simply to promote their own interest— this, as has been stated, is not kindness; or that their action was accidental, or was forced upon them; or that they were not doing a favour, but merely returning one, whether they know this or not —in either case the action *is* a mere return, and is therefore not a kindness even if the doer does *not* know how the case stands. In considering this subject we must look at all the 'categories': an act may be an act of kindness because (1) it is a particular thing, (2) it has a particular magnitude or (3) quality, or (4) is done at a particular time or (5) place. As evidence of the want of kindness, we may point out that a smaller service had been refused to the man in need; or that the same service, or an equal or greater one, has been given to his enemies; these facts show that the service in question was not done for the sake of the person helped. Or we may point out that the thing desired was worthless and that the helper knew it: no one will admit that he is in need of what is worthless.

8 · Pity

So much for Kindness and Unkindness. Let us now consider Pity, asking ourselves what things excite pity, and for what persons, and in what states of our mind pity is felt. Pity may be defined as a feeling of pain caused by the sight of some evil, destructive or painful, which befalls one who does not deserve it, and which we might expect to befall ourselves or some friend of ours, and more-over to befall us soon. In order to feel pity, we must obviously be capable of supposing that some evil may happen to us or some friend of ours, and moreover some such evil as is stated in our definition or is more or less of that kind. It is therefore not felt by those completely ruined, who suppose that no further evil can befall them, since the worst has befallen them already; nor by those who imagine themselves immensely fortunate—their feeling is rather presumptuous insolence, for when they think they possess all the good things of life, it is clear that the impossibility of evil befalling them will be included, this being one of the good things in question. Those who think evil *may* befall them are such as have already had it befall them and have safely escaped from it; elderly men, owing to their good sense and their experience; weak men, especially men inclined to cowardice; and also educated people, since these can take long views. Also those who have parents living, or children, or wives; for these are our own, and the evils mentioned above may easily befall them. And those who are neither moved by any courageous emotion such as anger or confidence (these emotions take no account of the future), nor by a disposition to presumptuous insolence (insolent men, too, take no account of the possibility that something evil will happen to them), nor yet by great fear (panic-stricken people do not feel pity, because they are taken up with what is happening to themselves); only those feel pity who are between these two extremes. In order to feel pity we must also believe in the goodness of at least some people; if you think nobody good, you will believe that everybody deserves evil fortune. And, generally, we feel pity whenever we are in the condition of remembering that similar misfortunes have happened to us or ours, or expecting them to happen in future.

So much for the mental conditions under which we feel pity. What we pity is stated clearly in the definition. All unpleasant and painful things excite pity if they tend to destroy and annihilate; and all such evils as are due to chance, if they are serious. The painful and destructive evils are: death in its various forms, bodily injuries and afflictions, old age, diseases, lack of food. The evils due to chance are: friendlessness, scarcity of friends (it is a pitiful thing to be torn away from friends and companions), deformity, weakness, mutilation; evil coming from a source from which good ought to have come; and the frequent repetition of such misfortunes. Also the coming of good when the worst has happened: e.g. the arrival of the Great King's gifts for Diopeithes after his death. Also that either no good should have befallen a man at all, or that he should not be able to enjoy it when it has.

The grounds, then, on which we feel pity are these or like these. The people we pity are: those whom we know, if only they are not very closely related to us—in that case we feel about them as if we were in danger ourselves. For this reason Amasis did not weep, they say, at the sight of his son being led to death, but did weep when he saw his friend begging: the latter sight was pitiful, the former terrible, and the terrible is different from the pitiful; it tends to cast out pity, and often helps to produce the opposite of pity. Again, we feel pity when the danger is near ourselves. Also we pity those who are like us in age, character, disposition, social standing, or birth; for in all these cases it appears more likely that the same misfortune may befall us also. Here too we have to remember the general principle that what we fear for ourselves excites our pity when it happens to others. Further, since it is when the sufferings of others are close to us that they excite our pity (we cannot remember what disasters happened a hundred centuries ago, nor look forward to what will happen a hundred centuries hereafter, and therefore feel little pity, if any, for such things): it follows that those who heighten the effect of their words with suitable gestures, tones, dress, and dramatic action generally, are especially successful in exciting pity: they thus put the disasters before our eyes, and make them seem close to us, just coming or just past. Anything that has just happened, or is going to happen soon, is particularly piteous: so too therefore are the tokens and the actions of sufferers—the garments and the like of those who have already suffered; the words and the like of those actually suffering—of those, for instance, who are on the point of death. Most piteous of all is it when, in such times of trial, the victims are persons of noble character: whenever they are so, our pity is especially excited, because their innocence, as well as the setting of their misfortunes before our eyes, makes their misfortunes seem close to ourselves.

9 · Indignation

Most directly opposed to pity is the feeling called Indignation. Pain at unmerited good fortune is, in one sense, opposite to pain at unmerited bad fortune, and is due to the same moral qualities. Both feelings are associated with good moral character; it is our duty both to feel sympathy and pity for unmerited distress, and to feel indignation at unmerited prosperity; for whatever is undeserved is unjust, and that is why we ascribe indignation even to the gods. It might indeed be thought that envy is similarly opposed to pity, on the ground that envy is closely akin to indignation, or even the same thing. But it is not the same. It is true that it also is a disturbing pain excited by the prosperity of others. But it is excited not by the prosperity of the undeserving but by that of people who are like us or equal to us. The two feelings have this in common, that they must be due not to some untoward thing being likely to befall ourselves, but only to what is happening to our neighbour. The feeling ceases to be envy in the one case and indignation in the other, and becomes fear, if the pain and disturbance are due to the prospect of something bad for ourselves as the result of the other man's good fortune. The feelings of pity and indignation will obviously be attended by the converse feelings of satisfaction. If you are pained by the unmerited distress of others, you will be pleased, or at least not pained, by their merited distress. Thus no good man can be pained by the punishment of parricides or murderers. These are things we are bound to rejoice at, as we must at the prosperity of the deserving; both these things are just, and both give pleasure to any honest man, since he cannot help expecting that what has happened to a man like him will happen to him too. All these feelings are associated with the same type of moral character. And their contraries are associated with the contrary type; the man who is delighted by others' misfortunes is identical with the man who envies others' prosperity. For any one who is pained by the occurrence or existence of a given thing must be pleased by that thing's non-existence or destruction. We can now see that all these feelings tend to prevent pity (though they differ among themselves, for the reasons given), so that all are equally useful for neutralizing an appeal to pity.

We will first consider Indignation—reserving the other emotions for subsequent discussion—and ask with whom, on what grounds, and in what states of mind we may be indignant. These questions are really answered by what has been said already. Indignation is pain caused by the sight of undeserved good fortune. It is, then, plain to begin with that there are some forms of good the sight of which cannot cause it. Thus a man may be just or brave, or acquire moral goodness: but we shall not be indignant with him for that reason, any more than we shall pity him for the contrary reason. Indignation is roused by the sight of wealth, power, and the like—by all those things, roughly speaking, which are deserved by good men and by those who possess the goods of nature—noble birth, beauty, and so on. Again, what is long established seems akin to what exists by nature; and therefore we feel more indignation at those possessing a given good if they have as a matter of fact only just got it and the prosperity it brings with it. The newly rich give more offence than those whose wealth is of long standing and inherited. The same is true of those who have office or power, plenty of friends, a fine family, &c. We feel the same when these advantages of theirs secure them others. For here again, the newly rich give us more offence by obtaining office through their riches than do those whose wealth is of long standing; and so in all other cases. The reason is that what the latter have is felt to be really their own, but what the others have is not; what appears to have been always what it is is regarded as real, and so the possessions of the newly rich do not seem to be really their own. Further, it is not any and every man that deserves any given kind of good; there is a certain correspondence and appropriateness in such things; thus it is appropriate for brave men, not for just men, to have fine weapons, and for men of family, not for parvenus, to make distinguished marriages. Indignation may therefore properly be felt when any one gets what is not appropriate for him, though he may be a good man enough. It may also be felt when any one sets himself up against his superior, especially against his superior in some particular respect—whence the lines

> *and shunning only Aias in the combat—*
> *Zeus took it ill when he engaged his betters,*[34]

[34] *Iliad*, XI. 622–23.

but also, even apart from that, when the inferior in any sense contends with his superior; a musician, for instance, with a just man, for justice is a finer thing than music.

Enough has been said to make clear the grounds on which, and the persons against whom, Indignation is felt—they are those mentioned, and others like him. As for the people who feel it; we feel it if we do ourselves deserve the greatest possible goods and moreover have them, for it is an injustice that those who are not our equals should have been held to deserve as much as we have. Or, secondly, we feel it if we are really good and honest people; our judgement is then sound, and we loathe any kind of injustice. Also if we are ambitious and eager to gain particular ends, especially if we are ambitious for what others are getting without deserving to get it. And, generally, if we think that we ourselves deserve a thing and that others do not, we are disposed to be indignant with those others so far as that thing is concerned. Hence servile, worthless, unambitious persons are not inclined to Indignation, since there is nothing they can believe themselves to deserve.

From all this it is plain what sort of men those are at whose misfortunes, distresses, or failures we ought to feel pleased, or at least not pained: by considering the facts described we see at once what their contraries are. If therefore our speech puts the judges in such a frame of mind as that indicated and shows that those who claim pity on certain definite grounds do not deserve to secure pity but do deserve not to secure it, it will be impossible for the judges to feel pity.

10 · Envy

To take Envy next: we can see on what grounds, against what persons, and in what states of mind we feel it. Envy is pain at the sight of such good fortune as consists of the good things already mentioned; we feel it towards our equals; not with the idea of getting something for ourselves, but because the other people have it. We shall feel it if we have, or think we have, equals; and by 'equals' I mean equals in birth, relationship, age, disposition, distinction, or wealth. We feel envy also if we fall but a little short of having everything; which is why people in high places and prosperity feel it—they think every one else is taking what belongs to themselves. Also if we are exceptionally distinguished for some particular thing, and especially if that thing is wisdom or good fortune. Ambitious men are more envious than those who are not. So also those who profess wisdom; they are ambitious—to be thought wise. Indeed, generally, those who aim at a reputation for anything are envious on this particular point. And small-minded men are envious, for everything seems great to them. The good things which excite envy have already been mentioned. The deeds or possessions which arouse the love of reputation and honour and the desire for fame, and the various gifts of fortune, are almost all subject to envy; and particularly if we desire the thing ourselves, or think we are entitled to it, or if having it puts us a little above others, or not having it a little below them. It is clear also what kind of people we envy; that was included in what has been said already: we envy those who are near us in time, place, age, or reputation. Hence the line:

Ay, kin can even be jealous of their kin.

Also our fellow-competitors, who are indeed the people just mentioned—we do not compete with men who lived a hundred centuries ago, or those not yet born, or the dead, or those who dwell near the Pillars of Hercules, or those whom, in our opinion or that of others, we take to be far below us or far above us. So too we compete with those who follow the same ends as ourselves: we compete with our rivals in sport or in love, and generally with those who are after the same things; and it is therefore these whom we are bound to envy beyond all others. Hence the saying:

Potter against potter.

We also envy those whose possession of or success in a thing is a reproach to us: these are our neighbours and equals; for it is clear that it is our own fault we have missed the good thing in question; this annoys us, and excites envy in us. We also envy those who have what we ought to have, or have got what we did have once. Hence old men envy younger men, and those who have spent much envy those who have spent little on the same thing. And men who have not got a thing, or not got it yet, envy those who have got it quickly. We can also see what things and what persons give pleasure to envious people, and in what states of mind they feel it: the states of mind in which they feel pain are those under which they will feel pleasure in the contrary things. If therefore we ourselves with whom the decision rests are put into an envious state of mind, and those for whom our pity, or the award of something desirable, is claimed are such as have been described, it is obvious that they will win no pity from us.

11 · Emulation

We will next consider Emulation, showing in what follows its causes and objects, and the state of mind in which it is felt. Emulation is pain caused by seeing the presence, in persons whose nature is like our own, of good things that are highly valued and are possible for ourselves to acquire; but it is felt not because others have these goods, but because we have not got them ourselves. It is therefore a good feeling felt by good persons, whereas envy is a bad feeling felt by bad persons. Emulation makes us take steps to secure the good things in question, envy makes us take steps to stop our neighbour having them. Emulation must therefore tend to be felt by persons who believe themselves to deserve certain good things that they have not got, it being understood that no one aspires to things which appear impossible. It is accordingly felt by the young and by persons of lofty disposition. Also by those who possess such good things as are deserved by men held in honour—these are wealth, abundance of friends, public office, and the like; on the assumption that they ought to be good men, they are emulous to gain such goods because they ought, in their belief, to belong to men whose state of mind is good. Also by those whom all others think deserving. We also feel it about anything for which our ancestors, relatives, personal friends, race, or country are specially honoured, looking upon that thing as really our own, and therefore feeling that we deserve to have it. Further, since all good things that are highly honoured are objects of emulation, moral goodness in its various forms must be such an object, and also all those good things that are useful and serviceable to others: for men honour those who are morally good, and also those who do them service. So with those good things our possession of which can give enjoyment to our neighbours—wealth and beauty rather than health. We can see, too, what persons are the objects of the feeling. They are those who have these and similar things—those already mentioned, as courage, wisdom, public office. Holders of public office—generals, orators, and all who possess such powers—can do many people a good turn. Also those whom many people wish to be like; those who have many acquaintances or friends; those whom many admire, or whom we ourselves admire; and those who have been praised and eulogized by poets or prose-writers. Persons of the contrary sort are objects of contempt: for the feeling and notion of contempt are opposite to those of emulation. Those who are such as to emulate or be emulated by others are inevitably disposed to be contemptuous of all such persons as are subject to those bad things which are contrary to the good things that are the objects of emulation: despising them for just that reason. Hence we often despise the fortunate, when luck comes to them without their having those good things which are held in honour.

This completes our discussion of the means by which the several emotions may be produced or dissipated, and upon which depend the persuasive arguments connected with the emotions.

12 · The various types of human character considered
in relation to the various emotions and moral qualities and
to the various ages and fortunes

Let us now consider the various types of human character, in relation to the emotions and moral qualities, showing how they correspond to our various ages and fortunes. By emotions I mean

Things that cause friendship are: doing kindnesses; doing them unasked; and not proclaiming the fact when they are done, which shows that they were done for our own sake and not for some other reason. (Page 88)

anger, desire, and the like; these we have discussed already. By moral qualities I mean virtues and vices; these also have been discussed already, as well as the various things that various types of men tend to will and to do. By ages I mean youth, the prime of life, and old age. By fortune I mean birth, wealth, power, and their opposites—in fact, good fortune and ill fortune.

To begin with the Youthful type of character. Young men have strong passions, and tend to gratify them indiscriminately. Of the bodily desires, it is the sexual by which they are most swayed and in which they show absence of self-control. They are changeable and fickle in their desires, which are violent while they last, but quickly over: their impulses are keen but not deep-rooted, and are like sick people's attacks of hunger and thirst. They are hot-tempered, and quick-tempered, and apt to give way to their anger; bad temper often gets the better of them, for owing to their love of honour they cannot bear being slighted, and are indignant if they imagine themselves unfairly treated. While they love honour, they love victory still more; for youth is eager for superiority over others, and victory is one form of this. They love both more than they love money, which indeed they love very little, not having yet learnt what it means to be without it—this is the point of Pittacus' remark about Amphiaraus. They look at the good side rather than the bad, not having yet witnessed many instances of wickedness. They trust others readily, because they have not yet often been cheated. They are sanguine; nature warms their blood as though with excess of wine; and besides that, they have as yet met with few disappointments. Their lives are mainly spent not in memory but in expectation; for expectation refers to the future, memory to the past, and youth has a long future before it and a short past behind it: on the first day of one's life one has nothing at all to remember, and can only look forward. They are easily cheated, owing to the sanguine disposition just mentioned. Their hot tempers and hopeful dispositions make them more courageous than older men are; the hot temper prevents fear, and the hopeful disposition creates confidence; we cannot feel fear so long as we are feeling angry, and any expectation of good makes us confident. They are shy, accepting the rules of society in which they have been trained, and not yet believing in any other standard of honour. They have exalted notions, because they have not yet been humbled by life or learnt its necessary limitations; moreover, their hopeful disposition makes them think themselves equal to great things—and that means having exalted notions. They would always rather do noble deeds than useful ones: their lives are regulated more by moral feeling than by reasoning; and whereas reasoning leads us to choose what is useful, moral goodness leads us to choose what is noble. They are fonder of their friends, intimates, and companions than older men are, because they like spending their days in the company of others, and have not yet come to value either their friends or anything else by their usefulness to themselves. All their mistakes are in the direction of doing things excessively and vehemently. They disobey Chilon's precept by overdoing everything; they love too much and hate too much, and the same thing with everything else. They think they know everything, and are always quite sure about it; this, in fact, is why they overdo everything. If they do wrong to others, it is because they mean to insult them, not to do them actual harm. They are ready to pity others, because they think every one an honest man, or anyhow better than he is: they judge their neighbour by their own harmless natures, and so cannot think he deserves to be treated in that way. They are fond of fun and therefore witty, wit being well-bred insolence.

13 · The character of Elderly Men

Such, then is the character of the Young. The character of Elderly Men—men who are past their prime—may be said to be formed for the most part of elements that are the contrary of all these. They have lived many years; they have often been taken in, and often made mistakes; and life on the whole is a bad business. The result is that they are sure about nothing and *underdo* everything. They 'think', but they never 'know'; and because of their hesitation they always add a 'possibly' or a 'perhaps', putting everything this way and nothing positively. They are cynical; that is, they tend to put the worse construction on everything. Further, their experience makes them distrustful and therefore suspicious of evil. Consequently they neither love warmly nor hate bitterly, but following the hint of Bias they love as though they will some day hate and hate as though they will some day love. They are small-minded, because they have been humbled by life: their desires are set upon nothing more exalted or unusual than what will help them to keep alive. They are not generous, because money is one of the things they must have, and at the same time their experience has taught them how hard it is to get and how easy to lose. They are cowardly, and are always anticipating danger; unlike that of the young, who are warm-blooded, their temperament is chilly; old age has paved the way for cowardice; fear is, in fact, a form of chill. They love life; and all the more when their last day has come, because the object of all desire is something we have not got, and also because we desire most strongly that which we need most urgently. They are too fond of themselves; this is one form that smallmindedness takes. Because of this, they guide their lives too much by considerations of what is useful and too little by what is noble — for the useful is what is good for oneself, and the noble what is good absolutely. They are not shy, but shameless rather; caring less for what is noble than for what is useful, they feel contempt for what people may think of them. They lack confidence in the future; partly through experience — for most things go wrong, or anyhow turn out worse than one expects; and partly because of their cowardice. They live by memory rather than by hope; for what is left to them of life is but little as compared with the long past; and hope is of the future, memory of the past. This, again, is the cause of their loquacity; they are continually talking of the past, because they enjoy remembering it. Their fits of anger are sudden but feeble. Their sensual passions have either altogether gone or have lost their vigour: consequently they do not feel their passions much, and their actions are inspired less by what they do feel than by the love of gain. Hence men at this time of life are often supposed to have a self-controlled character; the fact is that their passions have slackened, and they are slaves to the love of gain. They guide their lives by reasoning more than by moral feeling; reasoning being directed to utility and moral feeling to moral goodness. If they wrong others, they mean to injure them, not to insult them. Old men may feel pity, as well as young men, but not for the same reason. Young men feel it out of kindness; old men out of weakness, imagining that anything that befalls any one else might easily happen to them, which, as we saw, is a thought that excites pity. Hence they are querulous, and not disposed to jesting or laughter—the love of laughter being the very opposite of querulousness.

Such are the characters of Young Men and Elderly Men. People always think well of speeches adapted to, and reflecting, their own character: and we can now see how to compose our speeches so as to adapt both them and ourselves to our audiences.

14 · The character of Men in their Prime

As for Men in their Prime, clearly we shall find that they have a character between that of the young and that of the old, free from the extremes of either. They have neither that excess of confidence which amounts to rashness, nor too much timidity, but the right amount of each. They neither trust everybody nor distrust everybody, but judge people correctly. Their lives will be guided not by the sole consideration either of what is noble or of what is useful, but by both; neither by parsimony nor by prodigality, but by what is fit and proper. So, too, in regard to anger and desire; they will be brave as well as temperate, and temperate as well as brave; these virtues are divided between the young and the old; the young are brave but intemperate, the old temperate but cowardly. To put it generally, all the valuable qualities that youth and age divide between them are united in the prime of life, while all their excesses or defects are replaced by moderation and fitness. The body is in its prime from thirty to five-and-thirty; the mind about forty-nine.

15 • The Gifts of Fortune by which human character is affected—Good Birth

So much for the types of character that distinguish youth, old age, and the prime of life. We will now turn to those Gifts of Fortune by which human character is affected. First let us consider Good Birth. Its effect on character is to make those who have it more ambitious; it is the way of all men who have something to start with to add to the pile, and good birth implies ancestral distinction. The well-born man will look down even on those who are as good as his own ancestors, because any far-off distinction is greater than the same thing close to us, and better to boast about. Being well-born, which means coming of a fine stock, must be distinguished from nobility, which means being true to the family nature—a quality not usually found in the well-born, most of whom are poor creatures. In the generations of men as in the fruits of the earth, there is a varying yield; now and then, where the stock is good, exceptional men are produced for a while, and then decadence sets in. A clever stock will degenerate towards the insane type of character, like the descendants of Alcibiades or of the elder Dionysius; a steady stock towards the fatuous and torpid type, like the descendants of Cimon, Pericles, and Socrates.

16 • Wealth

The type of character produced by Wealth lies on the surface for all to see. Wealthy men are insolent and arrogant; their possession of wealth affects their understanding; they feel as if they had every good thing that exists; wealth becomes a sort of standard of value for everything else, and therefore they imagine there is nothing it cannot buy. They are luxurious and ostentatious; luxurious, because of the luxury in which they live and the prosperity which they display; ostentatious and vulgar, because, like other people's, their minds are regularly occupied with the object of their love and admiration, and also because they think that other people's idea of happiness is the same as their own. It is indeed quite natural that they should be affected thus; for if you have money, there are always plenty of people who come begging from you. Hence the saying of Simonides about wise men and rich men, in answer to Hiero's wife, who asked him whether it was better to grow rich or wise. 'Why, rich,' he said; 'for I see the wise men spending their days at the rich men's doors.' Rich men also consider themselves worthy to hold public office; for they consider they already have the things that give a claim to office. In a word, the type of character produced by wealth is that of a prosperous fool. There is indeed one difference between the type of the newly-enriched and those who have long been rich: the newly-enriched have all the bad qualities mentioned in an exaggerated and worse form—to be newly-enriched means, so to speak, *no education in riches*. The wrongs they do others are not meant to injure their victims, but spring from insolence or self-indulgence, e.g. those that end in assault or in adultery.

17 · Power

As to Power: here too it may fairly be said that the type of character it produces is mostly obvious enough. Some elements in this type it shares with the wealthy type, others are better. Those in power are more ambitious and more manly in character than the wealthy, because they aspire to do the great deeds that their power permits them to do. Responsibility makes them more serious: they have to keep paying attention to the duties their position involves. They are dignified rather than arrogant, for the respect in which they are held inspires them with dignity and therefore with moderation—dignity being a mild and becoming form of arrogance. If they wrong others, they wrong them not on a small but on a great scale.

Good fortune in certain of its branches produces the types of character belonging to the conditions just described, since these conditions are in fact more or less the kinds of good fortune that are regarded as most important. It may be added that good fortune leads us to gain all we can in the way of family happiness and bodily advantages. It does indeed make men more supercilious and more reckless; but there is one excellent quality that goes with it—piety, and respect for the divine power, in which they believe because of events which are really the result of chance.

This account of the types of character that correspond to differences of age or fortune may end here; for to arrive at the opposite types to those described, namely, those of the poor, the unfortunate, and the powerless, we have only to ask what the opposite qualities are.

18 · Retrospect on the distinct purpose of each type of oratory

The use of persuasive speech is to lead to decisions. (When we know a thing, and have decided about it, there is no further use in speaking about it.) This is so even if one is addressing a single person and urging him to do or not to do something, as when we scold a man for his conduct or try to change his views: the single person is as much your 'judge' as if he were one of many; we may say, without qualification, that any one is your judge whom you have to persuade. Nor does it matter whether we are arguing against an actual opponent or against a mere proposition; in the latter case we still have to use speech and overthrow the opposing arguments, and we attack these as we should attack an actual opponent. Our principle holds good of ceremonial speeches also; the 'onlookers' for whom such a speech is put together are treated as the judges of it. Broadly speaking, however, the only sort of person who can strictly be called a judge is the man who decides the issue in some matter of public controversy; that is, in law-suits and in political debates, in both of which there are issues to be decided. In the section on political oratory an account has already been given of the types of character that mark the different constitutions.

The manner and means of investing speeches with moral character may now be regarded as fully set forth.

Each of the main divisions of oratory has, we have seen, its own distinct purpose. With regard to each division, we have noted the accepted views and propositions upon which we may base our arguments—for political, for ceremonial, and for forensic speaking. We have further determined completely by what means speeches may be invested with the required moral character. We are now to proceed to discuss the arguments common to *all* oratory. All orators, besides their special lines of argument, are bound to use, for instance, the topic of the Possible and Impossible; and to try to show that a thing has happened, or will happen in future. Again, the topic of Size is common to all oratory; all of us have to argue that things are bigger or smaller than they seem, whether we are making political speeches, speeches of eulogy or attack, or prosecuting or defending in the law-courts. Having analysed these subjects, we will try to say what we can about the general principles of arguing by 'enthymeme' and 'example', by the addition of which we may hope to complete the project with which we set out. Of the above-mentioned general lines of argument, that concerned with Amplification is—as has been already said—most appropriate to ceremonial speeches; that concerned with the Past, to forensic speeches, where the required decision is always about the past; that concerned with Possibility and the Future, to political speeches.

19 · The four general lines of argument: the Possible and Impossible; Fact Past; Fact Future; and Degree

Let us first speak of the Possible and Impossible. It may plausibly be argued: That if it is possible for one of a pair of contraries to be or happen, then it is possible for the other: e.g. if a man can be cured, he can also fall ill; for any two contraries are equally possible, in so far as they are contraries. That if of two similar things one is possible, so is the other. That if the harder of two things is possible, so is the easier. That if a thing can come into existence in a good and beautiful form, then it can come into existence generally; thus a house can exist more easily than a beautiful house. That if the beginning of a thing can occur, so can the end; for nothing impossible occurs or begins to occur; thus the commensurability of the diagonal of a square with its side neither occurs nor can begin to occur. That if the end is possible, so is the beginning; for all things that occur have a beginning. That if that which is posterior in essence or in order of generation can come into being, so can that which is prior: thus if a man can come into being, so can a boy, since the boy comes first in order of generation; and if a boy can, so can a man, for the man also is first. That those things are possible of which the love or desire is natural; for no one, as a rule, loves or desires impossibilities. That things which are the object of any kind of science or art are possible and exist or come into existence. That anything is possible the first step in whose production depends on men or things which we can compel or persuade to produce it, by our greater strength, our control of them, or our friendship with them. That where the parts are possible, the whole is possible; and where the whole is possible, the parts are usually possible. For if the slit in front, the toe-piece, and the upper leather can be made, then shoes can be made; and if shoes, then also the front slit and toe-piece. That if a whole genus is a thing that can occur, so can the species; and if the species can occur, so can the genus: thus, if a sailing vessel can be made, so also can a trireme; and if a trireme, then a sailing vessel also. That if one of two things whose existence depends on each other is possible, so is the other; for instance, if 'double', then 'half', and if 'half', then 'double'. That if a thing can be produced without art or preparation, it can be produced still more certainly by the careful application of art to it. Hence Agathon has said:

> To some things we by art must needs attain,
> Others by destiny or luck we gain.

That if anything is possible to inferior, weaker, and stupider people, it is more so for their opposites; thus Isocrates said that it would be a strange thing if he could not discover a thing that Euthynus had found out. As for Impossibility, we can clearly get what we want by taking the contraries of the arguments stated above.

Questions of Past Fact may be looked at in the following ways: First, that if the less likely of two things has occurred, the more likely must have occurred also. That if one thing that usually follows another has happened, then that other thing has happened; that, for instance, if a man has forgotten a thing, he has also once learnt it. That if a man had the power and the wish to do a thing, he has done it; for every one does do whatever he intends to do whenever he can do it, there being nothing to stop him. That, further, he has done the thing in question either if he intended it and nothing external prevented him; or if he had the power to do it and was angry at the time; or if he had the power to do it and his heart was set upon it—for people as a rule do what they long to do, if they can; bad people through lack of self-control; good people, because their hearts are set upon good things. Again, that if a thing was 'going to happen', it has happened; if a man was 'going to do something', he has done it, for it is likely that the intention was carried out. That if one thing has happened which naturally happens before another or with a view to it, the other has happened; for instance, if it has lightened, it has also thundered; and if an action has been attempted, it has been done. That if one thing has happened which naturally happens after another, or with a view to which that other happens, then that other (that which happens first, or happens with a view to this thing) has also happened; thus, if it has thundered it has also lightened, and if an action has been done it has been attempted. Of all these sequences some are inevitable and some merely usual. The arguments for the *non*-occurrence of anything can obviously be found by considering the opposites of those that have been mentioned.

How questions of Future Fact should be argued is clear from the same considerations: That a thing will be done if there is both the power and the wish to do it; or if along with the power to do it there is a craving for the result, or anger, or calculation, prompting it. That the thing will be done, in these cases, if the man is actually setting about it, or even if he means to do it later—for usually what we mean to do happens rather than what we do not mean to do. That a thing will happen if another thing which naturally happens before it has already happened; thus, if it is clouding over, it is likely to rain. That if the means to an end have occurred, then the end is likely to occur; thus, if there is a foundation, there will be a house.

For arguments about the Greatness and Smallness of things, the greater and the lesser, and generally great things and small, what we have already said will show the line to take. In discussing deliberative oratory we have spoken about the relative greatness of various goods, and about the greater and lesser in general. Since therefore in each type of oratory the object under discussion is some kind of good—whether it is utility, nobleness, or justice—it is clear that every orator must obtain the materials of amplification through these channels. To go further than this, and try to establish abstract laws of greatness and superiority, is to argue without an object; in practical life, particular facts count more than generalizations.

Enough has now been said about these questions of possibility and the reverse, of past or future fact, and of the relative greatness or smallness of things.

20 · The two general modes of persuasion: Example and the Enthymeme, the Maxim being part of the Enthymeme

The special forms of oratorical argument having now been discussed, we have next to treat of those which are common to all kinds of oratory. These are of two main kinds, 'Example' and 'Enthymeme'; for the 'Maxim' is part of an enthymeme.

We will first treat of argument by Example, for it has the nature of induction, which is the foundation of reasoning. This form of argument has two varieties; one consisting in the mention of actual past facts, the other in the invention of facts by the speaker. Of the latter, again, there are two varieties, the illustrative parallel and the fable (e.g. the fables of Aesop, or those from Libya). As an instance of the mention of actual facts, take the following. The speaker may argue thus: 'We must prepare for war against the king of Persia and not let him subdue Egypt. For Darius of old did not cross the Aegean until he had seized Egypt; but once he had seized it, he did cross. And Xerxes, again, did not attack us until he had seized Egypt; but once he had seized it, he did cross. If therefore the present king seizes Egypt, he also will cross, and therefore we must not let him.'

The illustrative parallel is the sort of argument Socrates used: e.g. 'Public officials ought not to be selected by lot. That is like using the lot to select athletes, instead of choosing those who are fit for the contest; or using the lot to select a steersman from among a ship's crew, as if we ought to take the man on whom the lot falls, and not the man who knows most about it.'

Instances of the fable are that of Stesichorus about Phalaris, and that of Aesop in defence of the popular leader. When the people of Himera had made Phalaris military dictator, and were going to give him a bodyguard, Stesichorus wound up a long talk by telling them the fable of the horse who had a field all to himself. Presently there came a stag and began to spoil his pasturage. The horse, wishing to revenge himself on the stag, asked a man if he could help him to do so. The man said, 'Yes, if you will let me bridle you and get on to your back with javelins in my hand'. The horse agreed, and the man mounted; but instead of getting his revenge on the stag, the horse found himself the slave of the man. 'You too', said Stesichorus, 'take care lest, in your desire for revenge on your enemies, you meet the same fate as the horse. By making Phalaris military dictator, you have already let yourselves be bridled. If you let him get on to your backs by giving him a bodyguard, from that moment you will be his slaves.'

Aesop, defending before the assembly at Samos a popular leader who was being tried for his life, told this story: A fox, in crossing a river, was swept into a hole in the rocks; and, not being able to get out, suffered miseries for a long time through the swarms of fleas that fastened on her. A hedgehog, while roaming around, noticed the fox; and feeling sorry for her asked if he might remove the fleas. But the fox declined the offer; and when the hedgehog asked why, she replied, 'These fleas are by this time full of me and not sucking much blood; if you take them away, others will come with fresh appetites and drink up all the blood I have left.' 'So, men of Samos', said Aesop, 'my client will do you no further harm; he is wealthy already. But if you put him to death, others will come along who are not rich, and their peculations will empty your treasury completely.'

Fables are suitable for addresses to popular assemblies; and they have one advantage—they are comparatively easy to invent, whereas it is hard to find parallels among actual past events. You will in fact frame them just as you frame illustrative parallels: all you require is the power of thinking out your analogy, a power developed by intellectual training. But while it is easier to supply parallels by inventing fables, it is more valuable for the political speaker to supply them by quoting what has actually happened, since in most respects the future will be like what the past has been.

Where we are unable to argue by Enthymeme, we must try to demonstrate our point by this method of Example, and to convince our hearers thereby. If we *can* argue by Enthymeme, we should use our Examples as subsequent supplementary evidence. They should not precede the Enthymemes: that will give the argument an inductive air, which only rarely suits the conditions of speech-making. If they follow the Enthymemes, they have the effect of witnesses giving evidence, and this always tells. For the same reason, if you put your Examples first you must give a large number of them; if you put them last, a single one is sufficient; even a single witness will serve if he is a good one. It has now been stated how many varieties of argument by Example there are, and how and when they are to be employed.

21 · Maxims

We now turn to the use of Maxims, in order to see upon what subjects and occasions, and for what kind of speaker, they will appropriately form part of a speech. This will appear most clearly when we have defined a maxim. It is a statement; not a particular fact, such as the character of Iphicrates, but of a general kind; nor is it about any and every subject—e.g. 'straight is the contrary of curved' is not a maxim—but only about questions of practical conduct, courses of conduct to be chosen or avoided. Now an

Enthymeme is a syllogism dealing with such practical subjects. It is therefore roughly true that the premisses or conclusions of Enthymemes, considered apart from the rest of the argument, are Maxims: e.g.

> *Never should any man whose wits are sound*
> *Have his sons taught more wisdom than their fellows.*

Here we have a Maxim; add the reason or explanation, and the whole thing is an Enthymeme; thus—

> *It makes them idle; and therewith they earn*
> *Ill-will and jealousy throughout the city.*

Again,

> *There is no man in all things prosperous,*

and

> *There is no man among us all is free,*

are maxims; but the latter, taken with what follows it, is an Enthymeme—

> *For all are slaves of money or of chance.*

From this definition of a maxim it follows that there are four kinds of maxims. In the first place, the maxim may or may not have a supplement. Proof is needed where the statement is paradoxical or disputable; no supplement is wanted where the statement contains nothing paradoxical, either because the view expressed is already a known truth, e.g.

> *Chiefest of blessings is health for a man, as it seemeth to me,*

this being the general opinion: or because, as soon as the view is stated, it is clear at a glance, e.g.

> *No love is true save that which loves for ever.*

Of the Maxims that do have a supplement attached, some are part of an Enthymeme, e.g.

> *Never should any man whose wits are sound, &c.*

Others have the essential character of Enthymemes, but are not stated as parts of Enthymemes; these latter are reckoned the best; they are those in which the reason for the view expressed is simply implied, e.g.

O mortal man, nurse not immortal wrath.

To say 'it is not right to nurse immortal wrath' is a maxim; the added words 'O mortal man' give the reason. Similarly, with the words

Mortal creatures ought to cherish mortal, not immortal thoughts.

What has been said has shown us how many kinds of Maxims there are, and to what subjects the various kinds are appropriate. They must not be given without supplement if they express disputed or paradoxical views: we must, in that case, either put the supplement first and make a maxim of the conclusion, e.g. you might say, 'For my part, since both unpopularity and idleness are undesirable, I hold that it is better not to be educated'; or you may say this first, and then add the previous clause. Where a statement, without being paradoxical, is not obviously true, the reason should be added as concisely as possible. In such cases both laconic and enigmatic sayings are suitable: thus one might say what Stesichorus said to the Locrians, 'Insolence is better avoided, lest the cicalas chirp on the ground'.

The use of Maxims is appropriate only to elderly men, and in handling subjects in which the speaker is experienced. For a young man to use them is—like telling stories—unbecoming; to use them in handling things in which one has no experience is silly and ill-bred: a fact sufficiently proved by the special fondness of country fellows for striking out maxims, and their readiness to air them.

To declare a thing to be universally true when it is not is most appropriate when working up feelings of horror and indignation in our hearers; especially by way of preface, or after the facts have been proved. Even hackneyed and commonplace maxims are to be used, if they suit one's purpose: just because they are commonplace, every one seems to agree with them, and therefore they are taken for truth. Thus, any one who is calling on his men to risk an engagement without obtaining favourable omens may quote

> One and only one portent is best:
> Defend our fatherland![35]

Or, if he is calling on them to attack a stronger force—

> The battle-god's impartial.[36]

Or, if he is urging people to destroy the innocent children of their enemies—

Fool, who slayeth the father and leaveth his sons to avenge him.

Some proverbs are also maxims, e.g. the proverb 'An Attic neighbour'. You are not to avoid uttering maxims that contradict such sayings as have become public property (I mean such sayings as 'know thyself' and 'nothing in excess') if doing so will raise your hearers' opinion of your character, or convey an effect of strong emotion—e.g. an angry speaker might well say, 'It is not true that we ought to know ourselves: anyhow, if this man had known himself, he would never have thought himself fit for an army command.' It will raise people's opinion of our character to say, for instance, 'We ought not to follow the saying that bids us treat our friends as future enemies: much better to treat our enemies as future friends.' The moral purpose should be implied partly by the very wording of our maxim. Failing this, we should add our reason: e.g. having said 'We should treat our friends, not as the saying advises, but as if they were going to be our friends always', we should add 'for the other behaviour is that of a traitor': or we might put it, 'I disapprove of that saying. A true friend will treat his friend as if he were going to be his friend for ever'; and again, 'Nor do I approve of the saying "nothing in excess": we are bound to hate bad men excessively.'

One great advantage of Maxims to a speaker is due to the want of intelligence in his hearers, who love to hear him succeed

---

[35] *Iliad*, XII. 267–69.
[36] *Iliad*, XVIII. 359.

in expressing as a universal truth the opinions which they hold themselves about particular cases. I will explain what I mean by this, indicating at the same time how we are to hunt down the maxims required. The maxim, as has been already said, is a general statement and people love to hear stated in general terms what they already believe in some particular connexion: e.g. if a man happens to have bad neighbours or bad children, he will agree with any one who tells him, 'Nothing is more annoying than having neighbours', or, 'Nothing is more foolish than to be the parent of children.' The orator has therefore to guess the subjects on which his hearers really hold views already, and what those views are, and then must express, as general truths, these same views on these same subjects. This is one advantage of using maxims. There is another which is more important—it invests a speech with moral character. There is moral character in every speech in which the moral purpose is conspicuous: and maxims always produce this effect, because the utterance of them amounts to a general declaration of moral principles: so that, if the maxims are sound, they display the speaker as a man of sound moral character. So much for the Maxim—its nature, varieties, proper use, and advantages.

22 · Enthymemes

We now come to the Enthymemes, and will begin the subject with some general consideration of the proper way of looking for them, and then proceed to what is a distinct question, the lines of argument to be embodied in them. It has already been pointed out that the Enthymeme is a syllogism, and in what sense it is so. We have also noted the differences between it and the syllogism of dialectic. Thus we must not carry its reasoning too far back, or the length of

---

Young men have strong passions, and tend to gratify them indiscriminately. Nature warms their blood as though with excess of wine; and besides that, they have as yet met with few disappointments. (Page 108)

I. Wachsmuth Sculps.

our argument will cause obscurity: nor must we put in all the steps that lead to our conclusion, or we shall waste words in saying what is manifest. It is this simplicity that makes the uneducated more effective than the educated when addressing popular audiences—makes them, as the poets tell us, 'charm the crowd's ears more finely'. Educated men lay down broad general principles; uneducated men argue from common knowledge and draw obvious conclusions. We must not, therefore, start from any and every accepted opinion, but only from those we have defined—those accepted by our judges or by those whose authority they recognize: and there must, moreover, be no doubt in the minds of most, if not all, of our judges that the opinions put forward really are of this sort. We should also base our arguments upon probabilities as well as upon certainties.

The first thing we have to remember is this. Whether our argument concerns public affairs or some other subject, we must know some, if not all, of the facts about the subject on which we are to speak and argue. Otherwise we can have no materials out of which to construct arguments. I mean, for instance, how could we advise the Athenians whether they should go to war or not, if we did not know their strength, whether it was naval or military or both, and how great it is; what their revenues amount to; who their friends and enemies are; what wars, too, they have waged, and with what success; and so on? Or how could we eulogize them if we knew nothing about the sea-fight at Salamis, or the battle of Marathon, or what they did for the Heracleidae, or any other facts like that? All eulogy is based upon the noble deeds—real or imaginary—that stand to the credit of those eulogized. On the same principle, invectives are based on facts of the opposite kind: the orator looks to see what base deeds—real or imaginary—stand to the discredit of those he is attacking, such as treachery to the cause of Hellenic freedom, or the enslavement of their gallant allies against the barbarians (Aegina, Potidaea, &c.), or any other misdeeds of this kind that are recorded against them. So, too, in a court of law: whether we are prosecuting or defending, we must pay attention to the existing facts of the case. It makes no difference whether the subject is the Lacedaemonians or the Athenians, a man or a god; we must do the same thing. Suppose it to be Achilles whom we are to advise, to praise or blame, to accuse or defend; here too we must take the facts, real or imaginary; these must be our material, whether we are to praise or blame him for the noble or base deeds he has done, to accuse or defend him for his just or unjust treatment of others, or to advise him about what is or is not to his interest. The same thing applies to any subject whatever. Thus, in handling the question whether justice is or is not a good, we must start with the real facts about justice and goodness. We see, then, that this is the only way in which any one ever proves anything, whether his arguments are strictly cogent or not: not all facts can form his basis, but only those that bear on the matter in hand: nor, plainly, can proof be effected otherwise by means of the speech. Consequently, as appears in the *Topics*,[37] we must first of all have by us a selection of arguments about questions that may arise and are suitable for us to handle; and then we must try to think out arguments of the same type for special needs as they emerge; not vaguely and indefinitely, but by keeping our eyes on the actual facts of the subject we have to speak on, and gathering in as many of them as we can that bear closely upon it: for the more actual facts we have at our command, the more easily we prove our case; and the more closely they bear on the subject, the more they will seem to belong to that speech only instead of being commonplaces. By 'commonplaces' I mean, for example, eulogy of Achilles because he is a human being or a demi-god, or because he joined the expedition against Troy: these things are true of many others, so that this kind of eulogy applies no better to Achilles than to Diomede. The special facts here needed are those that are true of Achilles alone; such facts as that he slew Hector, the bravest of the Trojans, and Cycnus the invulnerable, who prevented all the Greeks from landing, and again that he was the youngest man who joined the expedition, and was not bound by oath to join it, and so on.

Here, again, we have our first principle of selection of Enthymemes—that which refers to the lines of argument selected. We will now consider the various elementary classes of enthymemes. (By an 'elementary class' of enthymeme I mean the same thing as a

[37] *Topics*, I. 14.

'line of argument'.) We will begin, as we must begin, by observing that there are two kinds of enthymemes. One kind proves some affirmative or negative proposition; the other kind disproves one. The difference between the two kinds is the same as that between syllogistic proof and disproof in dialectic. The demonstrative enthymeme is formed by the conjunction of compatible propositions; the refutative, by the conjunction of incompatible propositions.

We may now be said to have in our hands the lines of argument for the various *special* subjects that it is useful or necessary to handle, having selected the propositions suitable in various cases. We have, in fact, already ascertained the lines of argument applicable to enthymemes about good and evil, the noble and the base, justice and injustice, and also to those about types of character, emotions, and moral qualities. Let us now lay hold of certain facts about the whole subject, considered from a different and more general point of view. In the course of our discussion we will take note of the distinction between lines of proof and lines of disproof: and also of those lines of argument used in what seem to be enthymemes, but are not, since they do not represent valid syllogisms. Having made all this clear, we will proceed to classify Objections and Refutations, showing how they can be brought to bear upon enthymemes.

23 · The twenty-eight lines of argument on which
Enthymemes, demonstrative and refutative, can be based

1. One line of positive proof is based upon consideration of the opposite of the thing in question. Observe whether that opposite has the opposite quality. If it has not, you refute the original proposition; if it has, you establish it. E.g. 'Temperance is beneficial; for licentiousness is hurtful'. Or, as in the Messenian speech, 'If war is the cause of our present troubles, peace is what we need to put things right again'. Or—

For if not even evil-doers should
Anger us if they meant not what they did,
Then can we owe no gratitude to such
As were constrained to do the good they did us.

Or—

Since in this world liars may win belief,
Be sure of the opposite likewise—that this world
Hears many a true word and believes it not.

2. Another line of proof is got by considering some modification of the key-word, and arguing that what can or cannot be said of the one, can or cannot be said of the other: e.g. 'just' does not always mean 'beneficial', or 'justly' would always mean 'beneficially', whereas it is *not* desirable to be justly put to death.

3. Another line of proof is based upon correlative ideas. If it is true that one man *gave* noble or just treatment to another, you argue that the other must have *received* noble or just treatment; or that where it is right to command obedience, it must have been right to obey the command. Thus Diomedon, the tax-farmer, said of the taxes: 'If it is no disgrace for you to sell them, it is no disgrace for us to buy them'. Further, if 'well' or 'justly' is true of the person to whom a thing is done, you argue that it is true of the doer. But it is possible to draw a false conclusion here. It may be just that A should be treated in a certain way, and yet *not* just that he should be so treated by B. Hence you must ask yourself two distinct questions: (1) Is it right that A should be thus treated? (2) Is it right that B should thus treat him? and apply your results properly, according as your answers are Yes or No. Sometimes in such a case the two answers differ: you may quite easily have a position like that in the *Alcmaeon* of Theodectes:

And was there none to loathe thy mother's crime?

to which question Alcmaeon in reply says,

Why, there are two things to examine here.

And when Alphesiboea asks what he means, he rejoins:

They judged her fit to die, not me to slay her.

Again there is the lawsuit about Demosthenes and the men who killed Nicanor; as they were judged to have killed him justly, it was thought that he was killed justly. And in the case of the man who was killed at Thebes, the judges were requested to decide whether it was unjust that he should be killed, since if it was not, it was argued that it could not have been unjust to kill him.

4. Another line of proof is the *a fortiori*. Thus it may be argued that if even the gods are not omniscient, certainly human beings are not. The principle here is that, if a quality does not in fact exist where it is *more* likely to exist, it clearly does not exist where it is *less* likely. Again, the argument that a man who strikes his father also strikes his neighbours follows from the principle that, if the less likely thing is true, the more likely thing is true also; for a man is less likely to strike his father than to strike his neighbours. The argument, then, may run thus. Or it may be urged that, if a thing is not true where it is more likely, it is not true where it is less likely; or that, if it is true where it is less likely, it is true where it is more likely: according as we have to show that a thing *is* or is *not* true. This argument might also be used in a case of parity, as in the lines:

> *Thou hast pity for thy sire, who has lost his sons:*
> *Hast none for Oeneus, whose brave son is dead?*

And, again, 'if Theseus did no wrong, neither did Paris'; or 'if the sons of Tyndareus did no wrong, neither did Paris'; or 'if Hector did well to slay Patroclus, Paris did well to slay Achilles'. And 'if other followers of an art are not bad men, neither are philosophers'. And 'if generals are not bad men because it often happens that they are condemned to death, neither are sophists'. And the remark that 'if each individual among you ought to think of his own city's reputation, you ought all to think of the reputation of Greece as a whole'.

5. Another line of argument is based on considerations of time. Thus Iphicrates, in the case against Harmodius, said, 'if before doing the deed I had bargained that, if I did it, I should have a statue, you would have given me one. Will you not give me one now that I *have* done the deed? You must not make promises when you are expecting a thing to be done for you, and refuse to

fulfil them when the thing has been done'. And, again, to induce the Thebans to let Philip pass through their territory into Attica, it was argued that 'if he had insisted on this before he helped them against the Phocians, they would have promised to do it. It is monstrous, therefore, that just because he threw away his advantage then, and trusted their honour, they should not let him pass through now'.

6. Another line is to apply to the other speaker what he has said against yourself. It is an excellent turn to give to a debate, as may be seen in the *Teucer*. It was employed by Iphicrates in his reply to Aristophon. 'Would *you*', he asked, 'take a bribe to betray the fleet?' 'No', said Aristophon; and Iphicrates replied, 'Very good: if you, who are Aristophon, would not betray the fleet, would I, who am Iphicrates?' Only, it must be recognized beforehand that the other man is more likely than you are to commit the crime in question. Otherwise you will make yourself ridiculous; if it is Aristeides who is prosecuting, you cannot say that sort of thing to him. The purpose is to discredit the prosecutor, who as a rule would have it appear that his character is better than that of the defendant, a pretension which it is desirable to upset. But the use of such an argument is in all cases ridiculous if you are attacking others for what you do or would do yourself, or are urging others to do what you neither do nor would do yourself.

7. Another line of proof is secured by defining your terms. Thus, 'What is the supernatural? Surely it is either a god or the work of a god. Well, any one who believes that the work of a god exists, cannot help also believing that gods exist'. Or take the argument of Iphicrates, 'Goodness is true nobility; neither Harmodius nor Aristogeiton had any nobility before they did a noble deed'. He also argued that he himself was more akin to Harmodius and Aristogeiton than his opponent was. 'At any rate, my deeds are more akin to those of Harmodius and Aristogeiton than yours are'. Another example may be found in the *Alexander*. 'Every one will agree that by incontinent people we mean those who are not satisfied with the enjoyment of one love.' A further example is to be found in the reason given by Socrates for not going to the court of Archelaus. He said that 'one is *insulted* by being unable to requite benefits, as well as by being unable to re-

quite injuries'. All the persons mentioned define their term and get at its essential meaning, and then use the result when reasoning on the point at issue.

8. Another line of argument is founded upon the various senses of a word. Such a word is 'rightly', as has been explained in the *Topics*.

9. Another line is based upon logical division. Thus, 'All men do wrong from one of three motives, A, B, or C: in my case A and B are out of the question, and even the accusers do not allege C'.

10. Another line is based upon induction. Thus from the case of the woman of Peparethus it might be argued that women everywhere can settle correctly the facts about their children. Another example of this occurred at Athens in the case between the orator Mantias and his son, when the boy's mother revealed the true facts: and yet another at Thebes, in the case between Ismenias and Stilbon, when Dodonis proved that it was Ismenias who was the father of her son Thettaliscus, and he was in consequence always regarded as being so. A further instance of induction may be taken from the *Law* of Theodectes: 'If we do not hand over our horses to the care of men who have mishandled other people's horses, nor ships to those who have wrecked other people's ships, and if this is true of everything else alike, then men who have failed to secure other people's safety are not to be employed to secure our own.' Another instance is the argument of Alcidamas: 'Every one honours the wise. Thus the Parians have honoured Archilochus, in spite of his bitter tongue; the Chians Homer, though he was not their countryman; the Mytilenaeans Sappho, though she was a woman; the Lacedaemonians actually made Chilon a member of their senate, though they are the least literary of men; the Italian Greeks honoured Pythagoras; the inhabitants of Lampsacus gave public burial to Anaxagoras, though he was an alien, and honour him even to this day.' ⟨It may be argued that peoples for whom philosophers legislate are always prosperous⟩ on the ground that the Athenians became prosperous under Solon's laws and the Lacedaemonians under those of Lycurgus, while at Thebes no sooner did the leading men become philosophers than the country began to prosper.

11. Another line of argument is founded upon some decision

already pronounced, whether on the same subject or on one like it or contrary to it. Such a proof is most effective if every one has always decided thus; but if not every one, then at any rate most people; or if all, or most, wise or good men have thus decided, or the actual judges of the present question, or those whose authority they accept, or any one whose decision they cannot gainsay because he has complete control over them, or those whom it is not seemly to gainsay, as the gods, or one's father, or one's teachers. Thus Autocles said, when attacking Mixidemides, that it was a strange thing that the Dread Goddesses could without loss of dignity submit to the judgement of the Areopagus, and yet Mixidemides could not. Or as Sappho said, 'Death is an evil thing; the gods have so judged it, or they would die'. Or again as Aristippus said in reply to Plato when he spoke somewhat too dogmatically, as Aristippus thought: 'Well, anyhow, our *friend*', meaning Socrates, 'never spoke like that'. And Hegesippus, having previously consulted Zeus at Olympia, asked Apollo at Delphi 'whether his opinion was the same as his father's', implying that it would be shameful for him to contradict his father. Thus too Isocrates argued that Helen must have been a good woman, because Theseus decided that she was; and Paris a good man, because the goddesses chose him before all others; and Evagoras also, says Isocrates, was good, since when Conon met with his misfortune he betook himself to Evagoras without trying any one else on the way.

12. Another line of argument consists in taking separately the parts of a subject. Such is that given in the *Topics*:[38] 'What *sort* of motion is the soul? for it must be this or that.' The *Socrates* of Theodectes provides an example: 'What temple has he profaned? What gods recognized by the state has he not honoured?'

13. Since it happens that any given thing usually has both good and bad consequences, another line of argument consists in using those consequences as a reason for urging that a thing should or should not be done, for prosecuting or defending any one, for eulogy or censure. E.g. education leads both to unpopularity, which is bad, and to wisdom, which is good. Hence you ei-

[38] Cf. *Topics*, II. 4; IV. I.

ther argue, 'It is therefore not well to be educated, since it is not well to be unpopular': or you answer, 'No, it is well to be educated, since it is well to be wise'. The *Art of Rhetoric* of Callippus is made up of this line of argument, with the addition of those of Possibility and the others of that kind already described.

14. Another line of argument is used when we have to urge or discourage a course of action that may be done in either of two opposite ways, and have to apply the method just mentioned to both. The difference between this one and the last is that, whereas in the last any two things are contrasted, here the things contrasted are opposites. For instance, the priestess enjoined upon her son not to take to public speaking: 'For', she said, 'if you say what is right, men will hate you; if you say what is wrong, the gods will hate you.' The reply might be, 'On the contrary, you *ought* to take to public speaking: for if you say what is right, the gods will love you; if you say what is wrong, men will love you.' This amounts to the proverbial 'buying the marsh with the salt'. It is just this situation, viz. when each of two opposites has both a good and a bad consequence opposite respectively to each other, that has been termed *divarication*.

15. Another line of argument is this: The things people approve of openly are not those which they approve of secretly: openly, their chief praise is given to justice and nobleness; but in their hearts they prefer their own advantage. Try, in face of this, to establish the point of view which your opponent has not adopted. This is the most effective of the forms of argument that contradict common opinion.

16. Another line is that of rational correspondence. E.g. Iphicrates, when they were trying to compel his son, a youth under the prescribed age, to perform one of the state duties because he was tall, said 'If you count tall boys men, you will next be voting short men boys'. And Theodectes in his *Law* said, 'You make citizens of such mercenaries as Strabax and Charidemus, as a reward of their merits; will you not make exiles of such citizens as those who have done irreparable harm among the mercenaries?'

17. Another line is the argument that if two results are the same their antecedents are also the same. For instance, it was a saying of Xenophanes that to assert that the gods had birth is as

impious as to say that they die; the consequence of both statements is that there is a time when the gods do not exist. This line
of proof assumes generally that the result of any given thing is always the same: e.g. 'you are going to decide not about Isocrates,
but about the value of the whole profession of philosophy.' Or, 'to
give earth and water' means slavery; or, 'to share in the Common
Peace' means obeying orders. We are to make either such assumptions or their opposite, as suits us best.

18. Another line of argument is based on the fact that men
do not always make the same choice on a later as on an earlier
occasion, but reverse their previous choice. E.g. the following
enthymeme: 'When we were exiles, we fought in order to return;
now we have returned, it would be strange to choose exile in order
not to have to fight'. On one occasion, that is, they chose to be
true to their homes at the cost of fighting, and on the other to
avoid fighting at the cost of deserting their homes.

19. Another line of argument is the assertion that some *possible* motive for an event or state of things is the *real* one: e.g. that
a gift was given in order to cause pain by its withdrawal. This notion underlies the lines:

> *God gives to many great prosperity.*
> *Not of good will towards them, but to make*
> *The ruin of them more conspicuous.*

Or take the passage from the *Meleager* of Antiphon:

> *To slay no boar, but to be witnesses*
> *Of Meleager's prowess unto Greece.*

Or the argument in the *Ajax* of Theodectes, that Diomede chose
out Odysseus not to do him honour, but in order that his companion might be a lesser man than himself—such a motive for doing
so is quite possible.

20. Another line of argument is common to forensic and deliberative oratory, namely, to consider inducements and deterrents, and the motives people have for doing or avoiding the
actions in question. These are the conditions which make us
bound to act if they are for us, and to refrain from action if they
are against us: that is, we are bound to act if the action is possible,

easy, and useful to ourselves or our friends or hurtful to our enemies; this is true even if the action entails loss, provided the loss is
outweighed by the solid advantage. A speaker will urge action by
pointing to such conditions, and discourage it by pointing to the
opposite. These same arguments also form the materials for accusation or defence—the deterrents being pointed out by the defence, and the inducements by the prosecution. As for the
defence, . . . This topic forms the whole *Art of Rhetoric* both of
Pamphilus and of Callippus.

21. Another line of argument refers to things which are supposed to happen and yet seem incredible. We may argue that
people could not have believed them, if they had not been true or
nearly true: even that they are the more likely to be true because
they are incredible. For the things which men believe are either
facts or probabilities: if, therefore, a thing that *is* believed is improbable and even incredible, it must be true, since it is certainly
not believed because it is at all probable or credible. An example is
what Androcles of the deme Pitthus said in his well-known ar-
raignment of the law. The audience tried to shout him down when
he observed that the laws required a law to set them right. 'Why',
he went on, 'fish need salt, improbable and incredible as this
might seem for creatures reared in salt water; and olive-cakes need
oil, incredible as it is that what produces oil should need it.'

22. Another line of argument is to refute our opponent's case
by noting any contrasts or contradictions of dates, acts, or words
that it anywhere displays; and this in any of the three following
connexions. (1) Referring to our opponent's conduct, e.g. 'He says
he is devoted to you, yet he conspired with the Thirty.' (2) Referring to our own conduct, e.g. 'He says I am litigious, and yet he
cannot prove that I have been engaged in a single lawsuit.' (3) Referring to both of us together, e.g. '*He* has never even *lent* any one
a penny, but *I* have *ransomed* quite a number of you.'

23. Another line that is useful for men and causes that have
been really or seemingly slandered, is to show why the facts are
not as supposed; pointing out that there is a reason for the false
impression given. Thus a woman, who had palmed off her son on
another woman, was thought to be the lad's mistress because she
embraced him; but when her action was explained the charge was
shown to be groundless. Another example is from the *Ajax* of

Theodectes, where Odysseus tells Ajax the reason why, though he is really braver than Ajax, he is not thought so.

24. Another line of argument is to show that if the *cause* is present, the *effect* is present, and if absent, absent. For by proving the cause you at once prove the effect, and conversely nothing can exist without its cause. Thus Thrasybulus accused Leodamas of having had his name recorded as a criminal on the slab in the Acropolis, and of erasing the record in the time of the Thirty Tyrants: to which Leodamas replied, 'Impossible: for the Thirty would have trusted me all the more if my quarrel with the commons had been inscribed on the slab.'

25. Another line is to consider whether the accused person can take or could have taken a better course than that which he is recommending or taking, or has taken. If he has *not* taken this better course, it is clear that he is not guilty, since no one deliberately and consciously chooses what is bad. This argument is, however, fallacious, for it often becomes clear after the event how the action could have been done better, though before the event this was far from clear.

26. Another line is, when a contemplated action is inconsistent with any past action, to examine them both together. Thus, when the people of Elea asked Xenophanes if they should or should not sacrifice to Leucothea and mourn for her, he advised them not to mourn for her if they thought her a goddess, and not to sacrifice to her if they thought her a mortal woman.

27. Another line is to make previous mistakes the grounds of accusation or defence. Thus, in the *Medea* of Carcinus the accusers allege that Medea has slain her children; 'at all events', they say, 'they are not to be seen'—Medea having made the mistake of sending her children away. In defence she argues that it is not her children, but Jason, whom she would have slain; for it would have been a mistake on her part not to do this if she *had* done the other. This special line of argument for enthymeme forms the whole of the *Art of Rhetoric* in use before Theodorus.

28. Another line is to draw meanings from names. Sophocles, for instance, says,

> O steel in heart as thou art steel in name.

This line of argument is common in praises of the gods. Thus, too,

Conon called Thrasybulus *rash in counsel*. And Herodicus said of Thrasymachus, 'You are always *bold in battle*'; of Polus, 'you are always *a colt*'; and of the legislator Draco that his laws were those not of a human being but of *a dragon*, so savage were they. And, in Euripides, Hecuba says of Aphrodite,

> Her name and Folly's (ἀφροσύνης) rightly begin alike,

and Chaeremon writes

> Pentheus—a name foreshadowing grief (πένθος) to come.

The Refutative Enthymeme has a greater reputation than the Demonstrative, because within a small space it works out two opposing arguments, and arguments put side by side are clearer to the audience. But of all syllogisms, whether refutative or demonstrative, those are most applauded of which we foresee the conclusions from the beginning, so long as they are not obvious at first sight—for part of the pleasure we feel is at our own intelligent anticipation; or those which we follow well enough to see the point of them as soon as the last word has been uttered.

24 · Nine topics of apparent, or sham, Enthymemes

Besides genuine syllogisms, there may be syllogisms that look genuine but are not; and since an enthymeme is merely a syllogism of a particular kind, it follows that, besides genuine enthymemes, there may be those that look genuine but are not.

1. Among the lines of argument that form the Spurious Enthymeme the first is that which arises from the particular words employed.

(*a*) One variety of this is when—as in dialectic, without having gone through any reasoning process, we make a final statement as if it were the conclusion of such a process, 'Therefore so-and-so is not true', 'Therefore also so-and-so must be true'—so too in rhetoric a compact and antithetical utterance passes for an enthymeme, such language being the proper province of enthymeme, so that it is seemingly the form of wording here that causes the illusion mentioned. In order to produce the effect of genuine reasoning by our form of wording it is useful to summarize the results of a number of previous reasonings: as 'some he saved—others he avenged—the Greeks he freed'. Each of these statements has been previously proved from other facts; but the mere collocation of them gives the impression of establishing some fresh conclusion.

(*b*) Another variety is based on the use of similar words for different things; e.g. the argument that the mouse must be a noble creature, since it gives its name to the most august of all religious rites—for such the Mysteries are. Or one may introduce, into a eulogy of the dog, the dog-star; or Pan, because Pindar said:

> *O thou blessed one!*
> *Thou whom they of Olympus call*
> *The hound of manifold shape*
> *That follows the Mother of Heaven:*

or we may argue that, because there is much disgrace in there *not* being a dog about, there is honour in *being* a dog. Or that Hermes is readier than any other god to go shares, since we never say 'shares all round' except of him. Or that speech is a very excellent thing, since good men are not said to be worth money but to be worthy of esteem—the phrase 'worthy of esteem' also having the meaning of 'worth speech'.

2. Another line is to assert of the whole what is true of the parts, or of the parts what is true of the whole. A whole and its parts are supposed to be identical, though often they are not. You have therefore to adopt whichever of these two lines better suits your purpose. That is how Euthydemus argues: e.g. that any one knows that there is a trireme in the Peiraeus, since he knows the separate details that make up this statement. There is also the argument that one who knows the letters knows the whole word, since the word is the same thing as the letters which compose it; or that, if a double portion of a certain thing is harmful to health, then a single portion must not be called wholesome, since it is absurd that two good things should make one bad thing. Put thus, the enthymeme is refutative; put as follows, demonstrative: 'For one good thing cannot be made up of two bad things.' The whole

line of argument is fallacious. Again, there is Polycrates' saying that Thrasybulus put down thirty tyrants, where the speaker adds them up one by one. Or the argument in the *Orestes* of Theodectes, where the argument is from part to whole:

'Tis right that she who slays her lord should die.

'It is right, too, that the son should avenge his father. Very good: these two things are what Orestes has done.' Still, perhaps the two things, once they are put together, do not form a right act. The fallacy might also be said to be due to omission, since the speaker fails to say by whose hand a husband-slayer should die.

3. Another line is the use of indignant language, whether to support your own case or to overthrow your opponent's. We do this when we paint a highly-coloured picture of the situation without having proved the facts of it: if the defendant does so, he produces an impression of his innocence; and if the prosecutor goes into a passion, he produces an impression of the defendant's guilt. Here there is no genuine enthymeme: the hearer infers guilt or innocence, but no proof is given, and the inference is fallacious accordingly.

4. Another line is to use a 'Sign', or single instance, as certain evidence; which, again, yields no valid proof. Thus, it might be said that lovers are useful to their countries, since the love of Harmodius and Aristogeiton caused the downfall of the tyrant Hipparchus. Or, again, that Dionysius is a thief, since he is a vicious man—there is, of course, no valid proof here; not every vicious man is a thief, though every thief is a vicious man.

5. Another line represents the accidental as essential. An instance is what Polycrates says of the mice, that they 'came to the rescue' because they gnawed through the bowstrings. Or it might be maintained that an invitation to dinner is a great honour, for it was because he was *not* invited that Achilles was 'angered' with

---

Elderly men have often been taken in, and often made mistakes; and life on the whole is a bad business. They neither love warmly nor hate bitterly, but love as though they will some day hate and hate as though they will some day love. (Page 109)

I Wachsmuth Sc.

the Greeks at Tenedos. As a fact, what angered him was the *insult* involved; it was a mere accident that this was the particular form that the insult took.

6. Another is the argument from consequence. In the *Alexander*, for instance, it is argued that Paris must have had a lofty disposition, since he despised society and lived by himself on Mount Ida: because lofty people do this kind of thing, therefore Paris too, we are to suppose, had a lofty soul. Or, if a man dresses fashionably and roams around at night, he is a rake, since that is the way rakes behave. Another similar argument points out that beggars sing and dance in temples, and that exiles can live wherever they please, and that such privileges are at the disposal of those we account happy and therefore every one might be regarded as happy if only he has those privileges. What matters, however, is the *circumstances* under which the privileges are enjoyed. Hence this line too falls under the head of fallacies by omission.

7. Another line consists in representing as causes things which are not causes, on the ground that they happened along with or before the event in question. They assume that, because B happens *after* A, it happens *because* of A. Politicians are especially fond of taking this line. Thus Demades said that the policy of Demosthenes was the cause of all the mischief, 'for after it the war occurred'.

8. Another line consists in leaving out any mention of time and circumstances. E.g. the argument that Paris was justified in taking Helen, since her father left her free to choose: here the freedom was presumably not perpetual; it could only refer to her first choice, beyond which her father's authority could not go. Or again, one might say that to strike a free man is an act of wanton outrage; but it is not so in every case—only when it is unprovoked.

9. Again, a spurious syllogism may, as in 'eristical' discussions, be based on the confusion of the absolute with that which is not absolute but particular. As, in dialectic, for instance, it may be argued that what-is-not *is*, on the ground that what-is-not *is* what-is-not; or that the unknown can be known, on the ground that it can be known to *be* unknown: so also in rhetoric a spurious

enthymeme may be based on the confusion of some particular probability with absolute probability. Now no particular probability is universally probable: as Agathon says,

> One might perchance say that was probable —
> That things improbable oft will hap to men.

For what is improbable does happen, and therefore it is probable that improbable things *will* happen. Granted this, one might argue that 'what is improbable is probable'. But this is not true absolutely. As, in eristic, the imposture comes from not adding any clause specifying relationship or reference or manner; so here it arises because the probability in question is not general but specific. It is of this line of argument that Corax's *Art of Rhetoric* is composed. If the accused is not open to the charge—for instance if a weakling be tried for violent assault—the defence is that he was not likely to do such a thing. But if he *is* open to the charge— i.e. if he is a *strong* man—the defence is still that he was not likely to do such a thing, since he could be sure that people would think he *was* likely to do it. And so with any other charge: the accused must be either open or not open to it: there is in either case an appearance of probable innocence, but whereas in the latter case the probability is genuine, in the former it can only be asserted in the special sense mentioned. This sort of argument illustrates what is meant by making the worse argument seem the better. Hence people were right in objecting to the training Protagoras undertook to give them. It was a fraud; the probability it handled was not genuine but spurious, and has a place in no art except Rhetoric and Eristic.

25 · Refutation

Enthymemes, genuine and apparent, have now been described; the next subject is their Refutation.

An argument may be refuted either by a counter-syllogism or by bringing an objection. It is clear that counter-syllogisms can be built up from the same lines of arguments as the original syllogisms: for the materials of syllogisms are the ordinary opinions of men, and such opinions often contradict each other. Objections, as appears in the *Topics*,[39] may be raised in four ways—either by directly attacking your opponent's own statement, or by putting forward another statement like it, or by putting forward a statement contrary to it, or by quoting previous decisions.

1. By 'attacking your opponent's own statement' I mean, for instance, this: if his enthymeme should assert that love is always good, the objection can be brought in two ways, either by making the general statement that 'all want is an evil', or by making the particular one that there would be no talk of 'Caunian love' if there were not evil loves as well as good ones.

2. An objection 'from a contrary statement' is raised when, for instance, the opponent's enthymeme having concluded that a good man does good to all his friends, you object, 'That proves nothing, for a bad man does not do evil to all his friends'.

3. An example of an objection 'from a like statement' is, the enthymeme having shown that ill-used men always hate their ill-users, to reply, 'That proves nothing, for well-used men do not always love those who used them well'.

4. The 'decisions' mentioned are those proceeding from well-known men; for instance, if the enthymeme employed has concluded that 'Some allowance ought to be made for drunken offenders, since they did not know what they were doing', the objection will be, 'Pittacus, then, deserves no approval, or he would not have prescribed specially severe penalties for offences due to drunkenness'.

Enthymemes are based upon one or other of four kinds of alleged fact: (1) Probabilities, (2) Examples, (3) Infallible Signs, (4) Ordinary Signs. (1) Enthymemes based upon Probabilities are those which argue from what is, or is supposed to be, usually true. (2) Enthymemes based upon Example are those which proceed by induction from one or more similar cases, arrive at a general proposition, and then argue deductively to a particular inference. (3) Enthymemes based upon Infallible Signs are those which argue from the inevitable and invariable. (4) Enthymemes based upon

[39] Cf. *Topics*, VIII. 10.

ordinary Signs are those which argue from some universal or particular proposition, true or false.

Now (1) as a Probability is that which happens usually but
not always, Enthymemes founded upon Probabilities can, it is
clear, always be refuted by raising some objection. The refutation
is not always genuine: it may be spurious: for it consists in showing not that your opponent's premiss is not probable, but only in
showing that it is not inevitably true. Hence it is always in defence
rather than in accusation that it is possible to gain an advantage
by using this fallacy. For the accuser uses probabilities to prove his
case: and to refute a conclusion as improbable is not the same
thing as to refute it as not inevitable. Any argument based upon
what usually happens is always open to objection: otherwise it
would not be a probability but an invariable and necessary truth.
But the judges think, if the refutation takes this form, either that
the accuser's case is not probable or that they must not decide it;
which, as we said, is a false piece of reasoning. For they ought to
decide by considering not merely what *must* be true but also what
is *likely* to be true: this is, indeed, the meaning of 'giving a verdict
in accordance with one's honest opinion'. Therefore it is not
enough for the defendant to refute the accusation by proving that
the charge is not *bound* to be true: he must do so by showing that
it is not *likely* to be true. For this purpose his objection must state
what is more usually true than the statement attacked. It may do
so in either of two ways: either in respect of frequency or in respect of exactness. It will be most convincing if it does so in both
respects; for if the thing in question *both* happens *oftener* as we
represent it *and* happens more *as* we represent it, the probability is
particularly great.

(2) Fallible Signs, and Enthymemes based upon them, can be
refuted even if the facts are correct, as was said at the outset. For
we have shown in the *Analytics*[40] that no Fallible Sign can form
part of a valid logical proof.

(3) Enthymemes depending on examples may be refuted in
the same way as probabilities. If we have a negative instance, the
argument is refuted, in so far as it is proved not inevitable, even

---

[40] *Prior Analytics*, II. 27.

though the positive examples are more similar and more frequent. And if the positive examples *are* more numerous and more frequent, we must contend that the present case is dissimilar, or that its conditions are dissimilar, or that it is different in some way or other.

(4) It will be impossible to refute Infallible Signs, and Enthymemes resting on them, by showing in any way that they do not form a valid logical proof: this, too, we see from the *Analytics*. All we can do is to show that the fact alleged does not exist. If there is no doubt that it does, and that it is an Infallible Sign, refutation now becomes impossible: for this is equivalent to a demonstration which is clear in every respect.

26 · Correction of two errors, possible or actual:
Amplification and Depreciation do not constitute an
element of enthymeme, in the sense of 'a line of
enthymematic argument'; refutative enthymemes are not
a different species from constructive

Amplification and Depreciation are not an element of enthymeme. By 'an element of enthymeme' I mean the same thing as 'a line of enthymematic argument'—a general class embracing a large number of particular kinds of enthymeme. Amplification and Depreciation are one kind of enthymeme, viz. the kind used to show that a thing is great or small; just as there are other kinds used to show that a thing is good or bad, just or unjust, and anything else of the sort. All these things are the *subject-matter* of syllogisms and enthymemes; none of these is the line of argument of an enthymeme; no more, therefore, are Amplification and Depreciation. Nor are Refutative Enthymemes a different species from Constructive. For it is clear that refutation consists either in offering positive proof or in raising an objection. In the first case we prove the opposite of our adversary's statements. Thus, if he shows that a thing has happened, we show that it has not; if he shows that it has not happened, we show that it has. This, then, could not be the distinction if there were one, since the same means are employed by both parties, enthymemes being adduced to show that the fact is or is not so-and-so. An objection, on the other hand, is not an enthymeme at all, as was said in the *Topics,* it consists in stating some accepted opinion from which it will be clear that our opponent has not reasoned correctly or has made a false assumption.

Three points must be studied in making a speech; and we have now completed the account of (1) Examples, Maxims, Enthymemes, and in general the *thought*-element—the way to invent and refute arguments. We have next to discuss (2) Style, and (3) Arrangement.

BOOK III

1 · Style: delivery and the art of language

In making a speech one must study three points: first, the means of producing persuasion; second, the style, or language, to be used; third, the proper arrangement of the various parts of the speech. We have already specified the sources of persuasion. We have shown that these are three in number; what they are; and why there are only these three: for we have shown that persuasion must in every case be effected either (1) by working on the emotions of the judges themselves, (2) by giving them the right impression of the speakers' character, or (3) by proving the truth of the statements made.

Enthymemes also have been described, and the sources from which they should be derived; there being both special and general lines of argument for enthymemes.

Our next subject will be the style of expression. For it is not enough to know *what* we ought to say; we must also say it *as* we ought; much help is thus afforded towards producing the right impression of a speech. The first question to receive attention was naturally the one that comes first naturally—how persuasion can be produced from the facts themselves. The second is how to set these facts out in language. A third would be the proper method of delivery; this is a thing that affects the success of a speech greatly; but hitherto the subject has been neglected. Indeed, it was long before it found a way into the arts of tragic drama and epic recitation: at first poets acted their tragedies themselves. It is plain that delivery has just as much to do with oratory as with poetry. (In connexion with poetry, it has been studied by Glaucon of Teos among others.) It is, essentially, a matter of the right management of the voice to express the various emotions—of speaking loudly, softly, or between the two; of high, low, or intermediate pitch; of the various rhythms that suit various subjects. These are the three things—volume of sound, modulation of pitch, and rhythm—that a speaker bears in mind. It is those who *do* bear them in mind who usually win prizes in the dramatic contests; and just as in drama the actors now count for more than the poets, so it is in the contests of public life, owing to the defects of our political institutions. No systematic treatise upon the rules of delivery has yet been composed; indeed, even the study of language made no progress till late in the day. Besides, delivery is—very properly—not regarded as an elevated subject of inquiry. Still, the whole business of rhetoric being concerned with appearances, we must pay attention to the subject of delivery, unworthy though it is, because we cannot do without it. The right thing in speaking really is that we should be satisfied not to annoy our hearers, without trying to delight them: we ought in fairness to fight our case with no help beyond the bare facts: nothing, therefore, should matter except the proof of those facts. Still, as has been already said, other things affect the result considerably, owing to the defects of our hearers. The arts of language cannot help having a small but real importance, whatever it is we have to expound to others: the way in which a thing is said does affect its intelligibility. Not, however, so much importance as people think. All such arts are fanciful and meant to charm the hearer. Nobody uses fine language when teaching geometry.

When the principles of delivery have been worked out, they will produce the same effect as on the stage. But only very slight attempts to deal with them have been made and by a few people, as by Thrasymachus in his 'Appeals to Pity'. Dramatic ability is a natural gift, and can hardly be systematically taught. The principles of good diction can be so taught, and therefore we have men of ability in this direction too, who win prizes in their turn, as well as those speakers who excel in delivery—speeches of the written or literary kind owe more of their effect to their direction than to their thought.

It was naturally the poets who first set the movement going;

for words represent things, and they had also the human voice at their disposal, which of all our organs can best represent other things. Thus the arts of recitation and acting were formed, and others as well. Now it was because poets seemed to win fame through their fine language when their thoughts were simple enough, that the language of oratorical prose at first took a poetical colour, e.g. that of Gorgias. Even now most uneducated people think that poetical language makes the finest discourses. That is not true: the language of prose is distinct from that of poetry. This is shown by the state of things to-day, when even the language of tragedy has altered its character. Just as iambics were adopted, instead of tetrameters, because they are the most prose-like of all metres, so tragedy has given up all those words, not used in ordinary talk, which decorated the early drama and are still used by the writers of hexameter poems. It is therefore ridiculous to imitate a poetical manner which the poets themselves have dropped; and it is now plain that we have not to treat in detail the whole question of style, but may confine ourselves to that part of it which concerns our present subject, rhetoric. The other—the poetical—part of it has been discussed in the treatise on the *Art of Poetry*.[41]

2 · Style: clarity and appropriateness

We may, then, start from the observations there made, including the definition of style. Style to be good must be clear, as is proved by the fact that speech which fails to convey a plain meaning will fail to do just what speech has to do. It must also be appropriate, avoiding both meanness and undue elevation; poetical language is certainly free from meanness, but it is not appropriate to prose. Clearness is secured by using the words (nouns and verbs alike) that are current and ordinary. Freedom from meanness, and positive adornment too, are secured by using the other words men-

[41] *Poetics, 20–22.*

tioned in the *Art of Poetry*.[42] Such variation from what is usual makes the language appear more stately. People do not feel towards strangers as they do towards their own countrymen, and the same thing is true of their feeling for language. It is therefore well to give to everyday speech an unfamiliar air: people like what strikes them, and are struck by what is out of the way. In verse such effects are common, and there they are fitting: the persons and things there spoken of are comparatively remote from ordinary life. In prose passages they are far less often fitting because the subject-matter is less exalted. Even in poetry, it is not quite appropriate that fine language should be used by a slave or a very young man, or about very trivial subjects: even in poetry the style, to be appropriate, must sometimes be toned down, though at other times heightened. We can now see that a writer must disguise his art and give the impression of speaking naturally and not artificially. Naturalness is persuasive, artificiality is the contrary; for our hearers are prejudiced and think we have some design against them, as if we were mixing their wines for them. It is like the difference between the quality of Theodorus' voice and the voices of all other actors: his really seems to be that of the character who is speaking, theirs do not. We can hide our purpose successfully by taking the single words of our composition from the speech of ordinary life. This is done in poetry by Euripides, who was the first to show the way to his successors.

Language is composed of nouns and verbs. Nouns are of the various kinds considered in the treatise on Poetry. Strange words, compound words, and invented words must be used sparingly and on few occasions: on *what* occasions we shall state later. The reason for this restriction has been already indicated: they depart from what is suitable, in the direction of excess. In the language of prose, besides the regular and proper terms for things, metaphorical terms only can be used with advantage. This we gather from the fact that these two classes of terms, the proper or regular and the metaphorical—these and no others—are used by everybody in conversation. We can now see that a good writer can produce a style that is distinguished without being obtrusive, and is at the

---

[42] *Poetics*, 21–22.

same time clear, thus satisfying our definition of good oratorical prose. Words of ambiguous meaning are chiefly useful to enable the sophist to mislead his hearers. Synonyms are useful to the poet, by which I mean words whose ordinary meaning is the same, e.g. πορεύεσθαι (*advancing*) and βαδίζειν (*proceeding*); these two are ordinary words and have the same meaning.

In the *Art of Poetry,* as we have already said, will be found definitions of these kinds of words; a classification of Metaphors; and mention of the fact that metaphor is of great value both in poetry and in prose. Prose-writers must, however, pay specially careful attention to metaphor, because their other resources are scantier than those of poets. Metaphor, moreover, gives style clearness, charm, and distinction as nothing else can: and it is not a thing whose use can be taught by one man to another. Metaphors, like epithets, must be fitting, which means that they must fairly correspond to the thing signified: failing this, their inappropriateness will be conspicuous: the want of harmony between two things is emphasized by their being placed side by side. It is like having to ask ourselves what dress will suit an old man; certainly not the crimson cloak that suits a young man. And if you wish to pay a compliment, you must take your metaphor from something better in the same line; if to disparage, from something worse. To illustrate my meaning: since opposites are in the same class, you do what I have suggested if you say that a man who begs 'prays', and a man who prays 'begs'; for praying and begging are both varieties of asking. So Iphicrates called Callias a 'mendicant priest' instead of a 'torch-bearer', and Callias replied that Iphicrates must be uninitiated or he would have called him not a 'mendicant priest' but a 'torch-bearer'. Both are religious titles, but one is honourable and the other is not. Again, somebody calls actors 'hangers-on of Dionysus', but they call themselves 'artists': each of these terms is a metaphor, the one intended to throw dirt at the actor, the other to dignify him. And pirates now call themselves 'purveyors'. We can thus call a crime a mistake, or a mistake a crime. We can say that a thief 'took' a thing, or that he 'plundered' his victim. An expression like that of Euripides' Telephus,

King of the oar, on Mysia's coast he landed,

is inappropriate; the word 'king' goes beyond the dignity of the subject, and so the art is *not* concealed. A metaphor may be amiss because the very syllables of the words conveying it fail to indicate sweetness of vocal utterance. Thus Dionysius the Brazen in his elegies calls poetry 'Calliope's screech'. Poetry and screeching are both, to be sure, vocal utterances. But the metaphor is bad, because the sounds of 'screeching', unlike those of poetry, are discordant and unmeaning. Further, in using metaphors to give names to nameless things, we must draw them not from remote but from kindred and similar things, so that the kinship is clearly perceived as soon as the words are said. Thus in the celebrated riddle

I marked how a man glued bronze with fire
to another man's body,

the process is nameless; but both it and gluing are a kind of application, and that is why the application of the cupping-glass is here called a 'gluing'. Good riddles do, in general, provide us with satisfactory metaphors: for metaphors imply riddles, and therefore a good riddle can furnish a good metaphor. Further, the materials of metaphors must be beautiful; and the beauty, like the ugliness, of all words may, as Licymnius says, lie in their sound or in their meaning. Further, there is a third consideration—one that upsets the fallacious argument of the sophist Bryson, that there is no such thing as foul language, because in whatever words you put a given thing your meaning is the same. This is untrue. One term may describe a thing more truly than another, may be more like it, and set it more intimately before our eyes. Besides, two different words will represent a thing in two different lights; so on this ground also one term must be held fairer or fouler than another. For both of two terms will indicate what *is* fair, or what *is* foul, but not simply their fairness or their foulness, or if so, at any rate not in an equal degree. The materials of metaphor must be beautiful to the ear, to the understanding, to the eye or some other physical sense.

All the valuable qualities that youth and age divide between them are united in the prime of life, while all their excesses and defects are replaced by moderation and fitness. (Page 111)

T. Wanner Sculp.

It is better, for instance, to say 'rosy-fingered morn', than 'crimson-fingered' or, worse still, 'red-fingered morn'. The epithets that we apply, too, may have a bad and ugly aspect, as when Orestes is called a 'mother-slayer'; or a better one, as when he is called his 'father's avenger'. Simonides, when the victor in the mule-race offered him a small fee, refused to write him an ode, because, he said, it was so unpleasant to write odes to half-asses: but on receiving an adequate fee, he wrote

Hail to you, daughters of storm-footed steeds,

though of course they were daughters of asses too. The same effect is attained by the use of diminutives, which make a bad thing less bad and a good thing less good. Take, for instance, the banter of Aristophanes in the *Babylonians* where he uses 'goldlet' for 'gold', 'cloaklet' for 'cloak', 'scofflet' for 'scoff', and 'plaguelet'. But alike in using epithets and in using diminutives we must be wary and must observe the mean.

3 · Common faults in prose style

Bad taste in language may take any of four forms:—

(1) The misuse of compound words. Lycophron, for instance, talks of the '*many-visaged* heaven' above the '*giant-crested* earth', and again the '*strait-pathed* shore'; and Gorgias of the '*pauper-poet* flatterer' and 'oath-breaking and *over-oath-keeping*'. Alcidamas uses such expressions as 'the soul filling with rage and face becoming *flame-flushed*', and 'he thought their enthusiasm would be *issue-fraught*' and '*issue-fraught* he made the persuasion of his words', and '*sombre-hued* is the floor of the sea'. The way all these words are compounded makes them, we feel, fit for verse only. This, then, is one form in which bad taste is shown.

(2) Another is the employment of strange words. For instance, Lycophron talks of 'the *prodigious* Xerxes' and '*spoliative* Sciron'; Alcidamas of 'a *toy* for poetry' and 'the *witlessness* of nature', and says '*whetted* with the *unmitigated* temper of his spirit'.

(3) A third form is the use of long, unseasonable, or frequent

epithets. It is appropriate enough for a poet to talk of 'white milk', but in prose such epithets are sometimes lacking in appropriateness or, when spread too thickly, plainly reveal the author turning his prose into poetry. Of course we must use some epithets, since they lift our style above the usual level and give it an air of distinction. But we must aim at the due mean, or the result will be worse than if we took no trouble at all; we shall get something actually bad instead of something merely not good. That is why the epithets of Alcidamas seem so tasteless; he does not use them as the seasoning of the meat, but as the meat itself, so numerous and swollen and aggressive are they. For instance, he does not say 'sweat', but 'the *moist* sweat'; not 'to the Isthmian games', but 'to the *world-concourse* of the Isthmian games'; not 'laws', but 'the laws *that are monarchs of states*'; not 'at a run', but '*his heart impelling him to speed of foot*'; not 'a school of the Muses', but '*Nature's* school of the Muses had he inherited'; and so '*frowning* care of heart', and 'achiever' not of 'popularity' but of '*universal* popularity', and '*dispenser* of pleasure to his audience', and 'he concealed it' not 'with boughs' but 'with boughs *of the forest trees*', and 'he clothed' not 'his body' but '*his body's nakedness*', and 'his soul's desire was *counter-imitative*' (this is at one and the same time a compound and an epithet, so that it seems a poet's effort), and 'so *extravagant* the excess of his wickedness'. We thus see how the inappropriateness of such poetical language imports absurdity and tastelessness into speeches, as well as the obscurity that comes from all this verbosity—for when the sense is plain, you only obscure and spoil its clearness by piling up words.

The ordinary use of compound words is where there is no term for a thing and some compound can be easily formed, like 'pastime' (χρονοτριβεῖν); but if this is much done, the prose character disappears entirely. We now see why the language of compounds is just the thing for writers of dithyrambs, who love sonorous noises; strange words for writers of epic poetry, which is a proud and stately affair; and metaphor for iambic verse, the metre which (as has been already said) is widely used to-day.

(4) There remains the fourth region in which bad taste may be shown, metaphor. Metaphors like other things may be inappropriate. Some are so because they are ridiculous; they are in-

deed used by comic as well as tragic poets. Others are too grand
and theatrical; and these, if they are far-fetched, may also be obscure. For instance, Gorgias talks of 'events that are green and full
of sap', and says 'foul was the deed you sowed and evil the harvest
you reaped'. That is too much like poetry. Alcidamas, again,
called philosophy 'a fortress that threatens the power of law', and
the *Odyssey* 'a goodly looking-glass of human life', and talked
about 'offering no such toy to poetry': all these expressions fail,
for the reasons given, to carry the hearer with them. The address
of Gorgias to the swallow, when she had let her droppings fall on
him as she flew overhead, is in the best tragic manner. He said,
'Nay, shame, O Philomela'. Considering her as a bird, you could
not call her act shameful; considering her as a girl, you could; and
so it was a good gibe to address her as what she was once and not
as what she is.

4 · Similes and metaphors

The Simile also is a metaphor; the difference is but slight. When
the poet says of Achilles that he

> . . . *came up like a fierce lion*
> *that a whole countryside is out to kill.*[43]

this is a simile; when he says of him 'the lion leapt', it is a metaphor—here, since both are courageous, he has transferred to
Achilles the name of 'lion'. Similes are useful in prose as well as in
verse; but not often, since they are of the nature of poetry. They
are to be employed just as metaphors are employed, since they are
really the same thing except for the difference mentioned.

The following are examples of similes. Androtion said of
Idrieus that he was like a terrier let off the chain, that flies at you
and bites you—Idrieus too was savage now that he was let out of
his chains. Theodamas compared Archidamus to an Euxenus who

[43] *Iliad*, xx. 192–93.

could not do geometry—a proportional simile, implying that Euxenus is an Archidamus who *can* do geometry. In Plato's *Republic* those who strip the dead are compared to curs which bite the stones thrown at them but do not touch the thrower, and there is the simile about the Athenian people, who are compared to a ship's captain who is strong but a little deaf; and the one about poets' verses, which are likened to persons who lack beauty but possess youthful freshness—when the freshness has faded the charm perishes, and so with verses when broken up into prose. Pericles compared the Samians to children who take their pap but go on crying; and the Boeotians to holm-oaks, because they were ruining one another by civil wars just as one oak causes another oak's fall. Demosthenes said that the Athenian people were like sea-sick men on board ship. Again, Demosthenes compared the political orators to nurses who swallow the bit of food themselves and then smear the children's lips with the spittle. Antisthenes compared the lean Cephisodotus to frankincense, because it was his consumption that gave one pleasure. All these ideas may be expressed either as similes or as metaphors; those which succeed as metaphors will obviously do well also as similes, and similes, with the explanation omitted, will appear as metaphors. But the proportional metaphor must always apply reciprocally to either of its co-ordinate terms. For instance, if a drinking-bowl is the shield of Dionysus, a shield may fittingly be called the drinking-bowl of Ares.

5 · The foundation of good style: correctness of language

Such, then, are the ingredients of which speech is composed. The foundation of good style is correctness of language, which falls under five heads. (1) First, the proper use of connecting words, and the arrangement of them in the natural sequence which some of them require. For instance, the connective μέν (e.g. ἐγὼ μέν) requires the correlative δέ (e.g. ὁ δέ). The answering word must be brought in before the first has been forgotten, and not be widely separated from it; nor, except in the few cases where this is appropriate, is another connective to be introduced before the one required. Consider the sentence, 'But I, as soon as he told me (for Cleon had come begging and praying), took them along and set out.' In this sentence many connecting words are inserted in front of the one required to complete the sense; and if there is a long interval before 'set out', the result is obscurity. One merit, then, of good style lies in the right use of connecting words. (2) The second lies in calling things by their own special names and not by vague general ones. (3) The third is to avoid ambiguities; unless, indeed, you definitely desire to be ambiguous, as those do who have nothing to say but are pretending to mean something. Such people are apt to put that sort of thing into verse. Empedocles, for instance, by his long circumlocutions imposes on his hearers; these are affected in the same way as most people are when they listen to diviners, whose ambiguous utterances are received with nods of acquiescence—

Croesus by crossing the Halys will ruin a mighty realm.[44]

Diviners use these vague generalities about the matter in hand because their predictions are thus, as a rule, less likely to be falsified. We are more likely to be right, in the game of 'odd and even', if we simply guess 'even' or 'odd' than if we guess at the actual number; and the oracle-monger is more likely to be right if he simply says that a thing will happen than if he says *when* it will happen, and therefore he refuses to add a definite date. All these ambiguities have the same sort of effect, and are to be avoided unless we have some such object as that mentioned. (4) A fourth rule is to observe Protagoras' classification of nouns into male, female, and inanimate; for these distinctions also must be correctly given. 'Upon her arrival she said her say and departed ($\dot{\eta}$ δ' $\dot{\epsilon}\lambda\theta o\hat{v}\sigma a$ $\kappa a\grave{\iota}$ $\delta\iota a\lambda\epsilon\chi\theta\epsilon\hat{\iota}\sigma a$ $\check{\omega}\chi\epsilon\tau o$).' (5) A fifth rule is to express plurality, fewness, and unity by the correct wording, e.g. 'Having come, they struck me (οἱ δ' $\dot{\epsilon}\lambda\theta\acute{o}\nu\tau\epsilon\varsigma$ $\check{\epsilon}\tau\upsilon\pi\tau\acute{o}\nu$ $\mu\epsilon$).'

It is a general rule that a written composition should be easy to read and therefore easy to deliver. This cannot be so where

---

[44] Cf. Herodotus, I. 53. 91.

there are many connecting words or clauses, or where punctuation is hard, as in the writings of Heracleitus. To punctuate Heracleitus is no easy task, because we often cannot tell whether a particular word belongs to what precedes or what follows it. Thus, at the outset of his treatise he says, 'Though this truth is always men understand it not', where it is not clear with which of the two clauses the word 'always' should be joined by the punctuation. Further, the following fact leads to solecism, viz. that the sentence does not work out properly if you annex to two terms a third which does not suit them both. Thus either 'sound' or 'colour' will fail to work out properly with some verbs: 'perceive' will apply to both, 'see' will not. Obscurity is also caused if, when you intend to insert a number of details, you do not first make your meaning clear; for instance, if you say, 'I meant, after telling him this, that and the other thing, to set out', rather than something of this kind 'I meant to set out after telling him; then this, that, and the other thing occurred.'

6 · Impressiveness of style

The following suggestions will help to give your language impressiveness. (1) Describe a thing instead of naming it: do not say 'circle', but 'that surface which extends equally from the middle every way'. To achieve conciseness, do the opposite—put the name instead of the description. When mentioning anything ugly or unseemly, use its name if it is the description that is ugly, and describe it if it is the name that is ugly. (2) Represent things with the help of metaphors and epithets, being careful to avoid poetical effects. (3) Use plural for singular, as in poetry, where one finds

Unto havens Achaean,

though only one haven is meant, and

Here are my letter's many-leavèd folds.

(4) Do not bracket two words under one article, but put one arti-

cle with each; e.g. τῆς γυναικὸς τῆς ἡμετέρας.[45] The reverse to secure conciseness; e.g. τῆς ἡμετέρας γυναικός.[46] (5) Use plenty of connecting words; conversely, to secure conciseness, dispense with connectives, while still preserving connexion; e.g. 'having gone and spoken', and 'having gone, I spoke', respectively. (6) And the practice of Antimachus, too, is useful—to describe a thing by mentioning attributes it does not possess; as he does in talking of Teumessus—

There is a little wind-swept knoll . . .

A subject can be developed indefinitely along these lines. You may apply this method of treatment by negation either to good or to bad qualities, according to which your subject requires. It is from this source that the poets draw expressions such as the 'stringless' or 'lyreless' melody, thus forming epithets out of negations. This device is popular in proportional metaphors, as when the trumpet's note is called 'a lyreless melody'.

7 · Appropriateness of style

Your language will be *appropriate* if it expresses emotion and character, and if it corresponds to its subject. 'Correspondence to subject' means that we must neither speak casually about weighty matters, nor solemnly about trivial ones; nor must we add ornamental epithets to commonplace nouns, or the effect will be comic, as in the works of Cleophon, who can use phrases as absurd as 'O queenly fig-tree'. To express emotion, you will employ the language of anger in speaking of outrage; the language of disgust and discreet reluctance to utter a word when speaking of impiety or foulness; the language of exultation for a tale of glory, and that of humiliation for a tale of pity; and so in all other cases.

This aptness of language is one thing that makes people believe in the truth of your story: their minds draw the false conclu-

[45] 'that wife of ours.'
[46] 'our wife.'

sion that you are to be trusted from the fact that others behave as you do when things are as you describe them; and therefore they take your story to be true, whether it is so or not. Besides, an emotional speaker always makes his audience feel with him, even when there is nothing in his arguments; which is why many speakers try to overwhelm their audience by mere noise.

Furthermore, this way of proving your story by displaying these signs of its genuineness expresses your personal character. Each class of men, each type of disposition, will have its own appropriate way of letting the truth appear. Under 'class' I include differences of age, as boy, man, or old man; of sex, as man or woman; of nationality, as Spartan or Thessalian. By 'dispositions' I here mean those dispositions only which determine the character of a man's life, for it is not every disposition that does this. If, then, a speaker uses the very words which are in keeping with a particular disposition, he will reproduce the corresponding character; for a rustic and an educated man will not say the same things nor speak in the same way. Again, some impression is made upon an audience by a device which speech-writers employ to nauseous excess, when they say 'Who does not know this?' or 'It is known to everybody.' The hearer is ashamed of his ignorance, and agrees with the speaker, so as to have a share of the knowledge that everybody else possesses.

All the variations of oratorical style are capable of being used in season or out of season. The best way to counteract any exaggeration is the well-worn device by which the speaker puts in some criticism of himself; for then people feel it must be all right for him to talk thus, since he certainly knows what he is doing. Further, it is better not to have everything always just corresponding to everything else—your hearers will see through you less easily thus. I mean for instance, if your words are harsh, you should not extend this harshness to your voice and your countenance and have everything else in keeping. If you do, the artificial character of each detail becomes apparent; whereas if you adopt one device and not another, you are using art all the same and yet nobody notices it. (To be sure, if mild sentiments are expressed in harsh tones and harsh sentiments in mild tones, you become comparatively unconvincing.) Compound words, fairly plentiful epithets, and strange words best suit an emotional speech. We forgive an angry man for talking about a wrong as 'heaven-high' or 'colossal'; and we excuse such language when the speaker has his hearers already in his hands and has stirred them deeply either by praise or blame or anger or affection, as Isocrates, for instance, does at the end of his *Panegyric,* with his 'name and fame' and 'in that they brooked'. Men do speak in this strain when they are deeply stirred, and so, once the audience is in a like state of feeling, approval of course follows. This is why such language is fitting in poetry, which is an inspired thing. This language, then, should be used either under stress of emotion, or ironically, after the manner of Gorgias and of the passages in the *Phaedrus.*

8 · Prose rhythm

The form of a prose composition should be neither metrical nor destitute of rhythm. The metrical form destroys the hearer's trust by its artificial appearance, and at the same time it diverts his attention, making him watch for metrical recurrences, just as children catch up the herald's question, 'Whom does the freedman choose as his advocate?', with the answer 'Cleon!' On the other hand, unrhythmical language is too unlimited; we do not want the limitations of metre, but some limitation we must have, or the effect will be vague and unsatisfactory. Now it is number that limits all things; and it is the numerical limitation of the forms of a composition that constitutes rhythm, of which metres are definite sections. Prose, then, is to be rhythmical, but not metrical, or it will become not prose but verse. It should not even have too precise a prose rhythm, and therefore should only be rhythmical to a certain extent.

Of the various rhythms, the heroic has dignity, but lacks the tones of the spoken language. The iambic is the very language of ordinary people, so that in common talk iambic lines occur oftener than any others: but in a speech we need dignity and the power of taking the hearer out of his ordinary self. The trochee is too much akin to wild dancing: we can see this in tetrameter verse, which is one of the trochaic rhythms.

There remains the paean, which speakers began to use in the time of Thrasymachus, though they had then no name to give it. The paean is a third class of rhythm, closely akin to both the two already mentioned; it has in it the ratio of three to two, whereas the other two kinds have the ratio of one to one, and two to one respectively. Between the two last ratios comes the ratio of one-and-a-half to one, which is that of the paean.

Now the other two kinds of rhythm must be rejected in writing prose, partly for the reasons given, and partly because they are too metrical; and the paean must be adopted, since from this alone of the rhythms mentioned no definite metre arises, and therefore it is the least obtrusive of them. At present the same form of paean is employed at the beginning as at the end of sentences, whereas the end should differ from the beginning. There are two opposite kinds of paean, one of which is suitable to the beginning of a sentence, where it is indeed actually used; this is the kind that begins with a long syllable and ends with three short ones, as

$$\Delta\bar{\alpha}\lambda\check{o}\gamma\check{e}\nu\bar{e}s \mid \bar{e}\acute{\iota}\tau\bar{e}\ \Lambda\check{v}\kappa\hat{\iota} \mid \alpha\nu,^{47}$$

and

$$\mathrm{X}\rho\bar{v}\sigma\check{e}\check{o}\kappa\check{o}\mu\big|\bar{\alpha}\ \text{''}\check{E}\kappa\check{\alpha}\tau\check{e} \mid \pi\alpha\hat{\iota}\ \Delta\iota\acute{o}s.^{48}$$

The other paean begins, conversely, with three short syllables and ends with a long one, as

$$\check{\mu}\epsilon\tau\check{\alpha}\ \delta\bar{e}\ \gamma\bar{\alpha}\nu \mid \check{v}\delta\check{\alpha}\tau\check{\alpha}\ \tau'\ \check{\omega}\kappa\big|\epsilon\check{\alpha}\nu\grave{o}\nu\ \bar{\eta}\big|\phi\check{\alpha}\nu\check{\iota}\sigma\check{e}\ \nu\check{v}\xi.^{49}$$

This kind of paean makes a real close: a short syllable can give no effect of finality, and therefore makes the rhythm appear truncated. A sentence should break off with the long syllable: the fact

---

[47] 'O Delos-born, or if perchance Lycia (thou callest thy birthplace).'
[48] 'Golden-haired Archer, son of Zeus.'
[49] 'After earth and its waters, night shrouded the Ocean from sight.'

that it is over should be indicated not by the scribe, or by his period-mark in the margin, but by the rhythm itself.

We have now seen that our language must be rhythmical and not destitute of rhythm, and what rhythms, in what particular shape, make it so.

9 · Periodic style

The language of prose must be either free-running, with its parts united by nothing except the connecting words, like the preludes in dithyrambs; or compact and antithetical, like the strophes of the old poets. The free-running style is the ancient one, e.g. 'Herein is set forth the inquiry of Herodotus the Thurian.'[50] Every one used this method formerly; not many do so now. By 'free-running' style I mean the kind that has no natural stopping-places, and comes to a stop only because there is no more to say of that subject. This style is unsatisfying just because it goes on indefinitely—one always likes to sight a stopping-place in front of one: it is only at the goal that men in a race faint and collapse; while they see the end of the course before them, they can keep on going. Such, then, is the free-running kind of style; the compact is that which is in periods. By a period I mean a portion of speech that has in itself a beginning and an end, being at the same time not too big to be taken in at a glance. Language of this kind is satisfying and easy to follow. It is satisfying, because it is just the reverse of indefinite; and moreover, the hearer always feels that he is grasping something and has reached some definite conclusion; whereas it is unsatisfactory to see nothing in front of you and get nowhere. It is easy to follow, because it can easily be remembered; and this because language when in periodic form can be numbered, and number is the easiest of all things to remember. That is why verse, which is measured, is always more easily remembered than prose, which is not: the measures of verse can be numbered. The period

[50] Herodotus, I. 1, opening.

must, further, not be completed until the sense is complete: it must not be capable of breaking off abruptly, as may happen with the following iambic lines of Sophocles—

> *Calydon's soil is this; of Pelops' land*
> *⟨The smiling plains face us across the strait.⟩*

By a wrong division of the words the hearer may take the meaning to be the reverse of what it is: for instance, in the passage quoted, one might imagine that Calydon is in the Peloponnesus.

A Period may be either divided into several members or simple. The period of several members is a portion of speech (1) complete in itself, (2) divided into parts, and (3) easily delivered at a single breath—as a whole, that is; not by fresh breath being taken at the division. A member is one of the two parts of such a period. By a 'simple' period, I mean that which has only one member. The members, and the whole periods, should be neither curt nor long. A member which is too short often makes the listener stumble; he is still expecting the rhythm to go on to the limit his mind has fixed for it; and if meanwhile he is pulled back by the speaker's stopping, the shock is bound to make him, so to speak, stumble. If, on the other hand, you go on too long, you make him feel left behind, just as people who when walking pass beyond the boundary before turning back leave their companions behind. So too if a period is too long you turn it into a speech, or something like a dithyrambic prelude. The result is much like the preludes that Democritus of Chios jeered at Melanippides for writing instead of antistrophic stanzas—

> *He that sets traps for another man's feet*
> *Is like to fall into them first;*
> *And long-winded preludes do harm to us all,*
> *But the preluder catches it worst.*

Which applies likewise to long-membered orators. Periods whose members are altogether too short are not periods at all; and the result is to bring the hearer down with a crash.

The periodic style which is divided into members is of two kinds. It is either simply divided, as in 'I have often wondered at the conveners of national gatherings and the founders of athletic contests'; or it is antithetical, where, in each of the two members, one of one pair of opposites is put along with one of another pair, or the same word is used to bracket two opposites, as 'They aided both parties—not only those who stayed behind but those who accompanied them: for the latter they acquired new territory larger than that at home, and to the former they left territory at home that was large enough'. Here the contrasted words are 'staying behind' and 'accompanying', 'enough' and 'larger'. So in the example, 'Both to those who want to get property and to those who desire to enjoy it', where 'enjoyment' is contrasted with 'getting'. Again, 'it often happens in such enterprises that the wise men fail and the fools succeed'; 'they were awarded the prize of valour immediately, and won the command of the sea not long afterwards'; 'to sail through the mainland and march through the sea, by bridging the Hellespont and cutting through Athos'; 'nature gave them their country and law took it away again'; 'some of them perished in misery, others were saved in disgrace'; 'Athenian citizens keep foreigners in their houses as servants, while the city of Athens allows her allies by thousands to live as the foreigner's slaves'; and 'to possess in life or to bequeath at death'. There is also what some one said about Peitholaus and Lycophron in a law-court, 'These men used to sell you when they were at home, and now they have come to you here and bought you'. All these passages have the structure described above. Such a form of speech is satisfying, because the significance of contrasted ideas is easily felt, especially when they are thus put side by side, and also because it has the effect of a logical argument; it is by putting two opposing conclusions side by side that you prove one of them false.

Such, then, is the nature of *antithesis*. *Parisosis* is making the two members of a period equal in length. *Paromoeosis* is making the extreme words of both members like each other. This must happen either at the beginning or at the end of each member. If at the beginning, the resemblance must always be between whole words; at the end, between final syllables or inflexions of the same word or the same word repeated. Thus, at the beginning and

ἀγρὸν γὰρ ἔλαβεν ἀργὸν παρ' αὐτου⁵¹

At the end

δωρητοί τ' ἐπέλοντο παράρρητοί τ' ἐπέεσσιν.⁵²

and

οὐκ ᾠήθησαν αὐτὸν παιδίον τετοκέναι,
ἀλλ' αὐτοῦ αἴτιον γεγονέναι,⁵³

and

ἐν πλείσταις δὲ φροντίσι καὶ ἐν ἐλαχίσταις ἐλπίσιν.⁵⁴

An example of inflexions of the same word is

ἄξιος δὲ σταθῆναι χαλκοῦς, οὐκ ἄξιος ὢν χαλκοῦ,⁵⁵

Of the same word repeated,

σὺ δ' αὐτὸν καὶ ζῶντα ἔλεγες κακῶς καὶ νῦν γράφεις κακῶς.⁵⁶

Of one syllable,

τί δ' ἂν ἔπαθες δεινόν, εἰ ἄνδρ' εἶδες ἀργόν;⁵⁷

It is possible for the same sentence to have all these features to-gether—*antithesis, parison,* and *homoeoteleuton.* (The possible beginnings of periods have been pretty fully enumerated in the

⁵¹ 'A field he took from him, a fallow field.' Aristophanes.
⁵² 'They were still amenable to gifts and to persuasion.' *Iliad,* ix. 639–40.
⁵³ 'They did not imagine that he *had borne* the child, but that he was the cause of its *having been borne.*' Anonymous.
⁵⁴ 'In the midst of plenteous cares and exiguous hopes.' Anonymous.
⁵⁵ 'Is he worthy to have a copper statue, when he is not worth a copper?' Anonymous.
⁵⁶ 'When he was alive you spoke evil of him, and now you write evil of him.' Anonymous.
⁵⁷ 'Would it have been very shocking to you if you had seen a man idling?' Anonymous.

Theodectea.) There are also spurious antitheses, like that of Epicharmus—

> *There one time I as their guest did stay,*
> *And they were my hosts on another day.*

10 · Smart and popular sayings

We may now consider the above points settled, and pass on to say something about the way to devise lively and taking sayings. Their actual invention can only come through natural talent or long practice; but this treatise may indicate the way it is done. We may deal with them by enumerating the different kinds of them. We will begin by remarking that we all naturally find it agreeable to get hold of new ideas easily: words express ideas, and therefore those words are the most agreeable that enable us to get hold of new ideas. Now strange words simply puzzle us; ordinary words convey only what we know already; it is from metaphor that we can best get hold of something fresh. When the poet calls old age 'a withered stalk', he conveys a new idea, a new fact, to us by means of the general notion of 'lost bloom', which is common to both things. The similes of the poets do the same, and therefore, if they are good similes, give an effect of brilliance. The simile, as has been said before, is a metaphor, differing from it only in the way it is put; and just because it is longer it is less attractive. Besides, it does not say outright that 'this' *is* 'that', and therefore the hearer is less interested in the idea. We see, then, that both speech and reasoning are lively in proportion as they make us seize a new idea promptly. For this reason people are not much taken either by obvious arguments (using the word 'obvious' to mean what is plain to everybody and needs no investigation), nor by those which puzzle us when we hear them stated, but only by those which convey their information to us as soon as we hear them, provided we had not the information already; or which the mind only just fails to keep up with. These two kinds do convey to us a sort of information: but the obvious and the obscure kinds convey nothing, either at once or later on. It is these qualities, then, that, so far as the meaning of what is said is concerned, make an argument acceptable. So far as the style is concerned, it is the antithetical form that appeals to us, e.g. 'judging that the peace common to all the rest was a war upon their own private interests', where there is an antithesis between war and peace. It is also good to use metaphorical words; but the metaphors must not be far-fetched, or they will be difficult to grasp, nor obvious, or they will have no effect. The words, too, ought to set the scene before our eyes; for events ought to be seen in progress rather than in prospect. So we must aim at these three points: Antithesis, Metaphor, and Actuality.

Of the four kinds of Metaphor the most taking is the proportional kind. Thus Pericles, for instance, said that the vanishing from their country of the young men who had fallen in the war was 'as if the spring were taken out of the year'. Leptines, speaking of the Lacedaemonians, said that he would not have the Athenians let Greece 'lose one of her two eyes'. When Chares was pressing for leave to be examined upon his share in the Olynthiac war, Cephisodotus was indignant, saying that he wanted his examination to take place 'while he had his fingers upon the people's throat'. The same speaker once urged the Athenians to march to Euboea, 'with Miltiades' decree as their rations'. Iphicrates, indignant at the truce made by the Athenians with Epidaurus and the neighbouring sea-board, said that they had stripped themselves of their travelling-money for the journey of war. Peitholaus called the state-galley 'the people's big stick', and Sestos 'the corn-bin of the Peiraeus'. Pericles bade his countrymen remove Aegina, 'that eyesore of the Peiraeus.' And Moerocles said he was no more a rascal than was a certain respectable citizen he named, 'whose rascality was worth over thirty per cent per annum to him, instead of a mere ten like his own'. There is also the iambic line of Anaxandrides about the way his daughters put off marrying—

My daughters' marriage-bonds are overdue.

Polyeuctus said of a paralytic man named Speusippus that he could not keep quiet, 'though fortune had fastened him in the pillory of disease'. Cephisodotus called warships 'painted millstones'. Diogenes the Dog called taverns 'the mess-rooms of Attica'. Aesion said that the Athenians had 'emptied' their town into Sicily: this is a graphic metaphor. 'Till all Hellas shouted aloud' may be regarded as a metaphor, and a graphic one again. Cephisodotus bade the Athenians take care not to hold too many 'parades'. Isocrates used the same word of those who 'parade' at the national festivals. Another example occurs in the Funeral Speech: 'It is fitting that Greece should cut off her hair beside the tomb of those who fell at Salamis, since her freedom and their valour are buried in the same grave.' Even if the speaker here had only said that it was right to weep when valour was being buried in their grave, it would have been a metaphor, and a graphic one; but the coupling of 'their valour' and 'her freedom' presents a kind of antithesis as well. 'The course of my words', said Iphicrates, 'lies straight through the middle of Chares' deeds': this is a proportional metaphor, and the phrase 'straight through the middle' makes it graphic. The expression 'to call in one danger to rescue us from another' is a graphic metaphor. Lycoleon said, defending Chabrias, 'They did not respect even that bronze statue of his that intercedes for him yonder'. This was a metaphor for the moment, though it would not always apply; a vivid metaphor, however; Chabrias is in danger, and his statue intercedes for him —that lifeless yet living thing which records his services to his country. 'Practising in every way littleness of mind' is metaphorical, for practising a quality implies increasing it. So is 'God kindled our reason to be a lamp within our souls', for both reason and light reveal things. So is 'we are not putting an end to our wars, but only postponing them', for both literal postponement and the making of such a peace as this apply to future action. So is such a saying as 'This treaty is a far nobler trophy than those we set up on fields of battle; *they* celebrate small gains and single successes; *it* celebrates our triumph in the war as a whole'; for both trophy and treaty are signs of victory. So is 'A country pays a heavy reckoning in being condemned by the judgement of mankind', for a reckoning is damage deservedly incurred.

RHETORIC

11 · Actuality or vividness

It has already been mentioned that liveliness is got by using the proportional type of metaphor and by being graphic (i.e. making your hearers *see* things). We have still to explain what we mean by their 'seeing things', and what must be done to effect this. By 'making them see things' I mean using expressions that represent things as in a state of activity. Thus, to say that a good man is 'four-square' is certainly a metaphor; both the good man and the square are perfect; but the metaphor does not suggest activity. On the other hand, in the expression 'with his vigour in full bloom' there is a notion of activity; and so in 'But you must roam as free as a sacred victim'; and in

> *Thereat up sprang the Hellenes to their feet,*

where 'up sprang' gives us activity as well as metaphor, for it at once suggests swiftness. So with Homer's common practice of giving metaphorical life to lifeless things: all such passages are distinguished by the effect of activity they convey. Thus,

> *Downward anon to the valley rebounded the boulder* remorse-less;*

and

> *The ⟨bitter⟩ arrow* flew;*

and

> *Flying on eagerly;* *

and

> *Stuck in the earth, still* panting *to feed on the flesh of the heroes;* *

and

> *And the point of the spear* in its fury *drove full through his breast-bone.* *

In all these examples the things have the effect of being active because they are made into living beings; shameless behaviour and fury and so on are all forms of activity. And the poet has attached these ideas to the things by means of proportional metaphors: as

* W. R. Roberts translation.

the stone is to Sisyphus, so is the shameless man to his victim. In his famous similes, too, he treats inanimate things in the same way:

Curving and crested with white, host following host without ceasing. *

Here he represents everything as moving and living; and activity is movement.

Metaphors must be drawn, as has been said already, from things that are related to the original thing, and yet not obviously so related—just as in philosophy also an acute mind will perceive resemblances even in things far apart. Thus Archytas said that an arbitrator and an altar were the same, since the injured fly to both for refuge. Or you might say that an anchor and an overhead hook were the same, since both are in a way the same, only the one secures things from below and the other from above. And to speak of states as 'levelled' is to identify two widely different things, the equality of a physical surface and the equality of political powers.

Liveliness is specially conveyed by metaphor, and by the further power of surprising the hearer; because the hearer expected something different, his acquisition of the new idea impresses him all the more. His mind seems to say, 'Yes, to be sure; I never thought of that'. The liveliness of epigrammatic remarks is due to the meaning not being just what the words say: as in the saying of Stesichorus that 'the cicalas will chirp to themselves on the ground'. Well-constructed riddles are attractive for the same reason; a new idea is conveyed, and there is metaphorical expression. So with the 'novelties' of Theodorus. In these the thought is startling, and, as Theodorus puts it, does not fit in with the ideas you already have. They are like the burlesque words that one finds in the comic writers. The effect is produced even by jokes depending upon changes of the letters of a word; this too is a surprise. You

* W. R. Roberts translation.

The type of character produced by Wealth lies on the surface for all to see. (Page 112)

find this in verse as well as in prose. The word which comes is not what the hearer imagined: thus

Onward he came, and his feet were shod with his—chilblains,

where one imagined the word would be 'sandals'. But the point should be clear the moment the words are uttered. Jokes made by altering the letters of a word consist in meaning, not just what you say, but something that gives a twist to the word used; e.g. the remark of Theodorus about Nicon the harpist Θρᾶττ᾽εἶ σύ ('you Thracian slavery'), where he pretends to mean θράττεις σύ ('you harp-player'), and surprises us when we find he means something else. So you enjoy the point when you see it, though the remark will fall flat unless you are aware that Nicon is Thracian. Or again: βούλει αὐτὸν πέρσαι.[58] In both these cases the saying must fit the facts. This is also true of such lively remarks as the one to the effect that to the Athenians their empire (ἀρχή) of the sea was not the beginning (ἀρχή) of their troubles, since they gained by it. Or the opposite one of Isocrates, that their empire (ἀρχή) *was* the beginning (ἀρχή) of their troubles. Either way, the speaker says something unexpected, the soundness of which is thereupon recognized. There would be nothing clever in saying 'empire is empire'. Isocrates means more than that, and uses the word with a new meaning. So too with the former saying, which denies that ἀρχή in one sense was ἀρχή in another sense. In all these jokes, whether a word is used in a second sense or metaphorically, the joke is good if it fits the facts. For instance, Ἀνάσχετος (proper name) οὐκ ἀνάσχετός:[59] where you say that what is so-and-so in one sense is not so-and-so in another; well, if the man is unpleasant, the joke fits the facts. Again, take—

Thou must not be a stranger stranger than
Thou should'st.

Do not the words 'thou must not be', &c., amount to saying that the stranger must not always be strange? Here again is the use of

---

[58] 'You wish to persecute him.'
[59] 'Baring is past bearing.'

one word in different senses. Of the same kind also is the much-praised verse of Anaxandrides:

> Death is most fit before you do
> Deeds that would make death fit for you.

This amounts to saying 'it is a fit thing to die when you are not fit to die', or 'it is a fit thing to die when death is not fit for you', i.e. when death is not the fit return for what you are doing. The type of language employed is the same in all these examples; but the more briefly and antithetically such sayings can be expressed, the more taking they are, for antithesis impresses the new idea more firmly and brevity more quickly. They should always have either some personal application or some merit of expression, if they are to be true without being commonplace—two requirements not always satisfied simultaneously. Thus 'a man should die having done no wrong' is true but dull: 'the right man should marry the right woman' is also true but dull. No, there must be both good qualities together, as in 'it is fitting to die when you are not fit for death'. The more a saying has these qualities, the livelier it appears: if, for instance, its wording is metaphorical, metaphorical in the right way, antithetical, and balanced, and at the same time it gives an idea of activity.

Successful similes also, as has been said above, are in a sense metaphors, since they always involve two relations like the proportional metaphor. Thus: a shield, we say, is the 'drinking-bowl of Ares', and a bow is the 'chordless lyre'. This way of putting a metaphor is not 'simple', as it would be if we called the bow a lyre or the shield a drinking-bowl. There are 'simple' similes also: we may say that a flute-player is like a monkey, or that a short-sighted man's eyes are like a lamp-flame with water dropping on it, since both eyes and flame keep winking. A simile succeeds best when it is a converted metaphor, for it is possible to say that a shield *is like* the drinking-bowl of Ares, or that a ruin *is like* a house in rags, and to say that Niceratus *is like* a Philoctetes stung by Pratys—the simile made by Thrasymachus when he saw Niceratus, who had been beaten by Pratys in a recitation competition, still going about unkempt and unwashed. It is in these respects that poets fail worst when they fail, and succeed best when they succeed, i.e. when they give the resemblance pat, as in

Those legs of his curl just like parsley leaves;

and

Just like Philammon struggling with his punch-ball.

These are all similes; and that similes are metaphors has been stated often already.

Proverbs, again, are metaphors from one species to another. Suppose, for instance, a man to start some undertaking in hope of gain and then to lose by it later on, 'Here we have once more the man of Carpathus and his hare', says he. For both alike went through the said experience.

It has now been explained fairly completely how liveliness is secured and why it has the effect it has. Successful hyperboles are also metaphors, e.g. the one about the man with a black eye, 'you would have thought he was a basket of mulberries'; here the 'black eye' is compared to a mulberry because of its colour, the exaggeration lying in the quantity of mulberries suggested. The phrase '*like* so-and-so' may introduce a hyperbole under the form of a simile. Thus

Just like *Philammon struggling with his punch-ball*

is equivalent to '*you would have thought he was* Philammon struggling with his punch-ball'; and

Those legs of his curl just like *parsley leaves*

is equivalent to 'his legs are so curly that *you would have thought* they were not legs but parsley leaves'. Hyperboles are for young men to use; they show vehemence of character; and this is why angry people use them more than other people.

> *Not if his gifts outnumbered the sea sands*
> *or all the dust grains in the world . . .*
> *The daughter of Agamemnon, son of Atreus*

> *I will not take in marriage. Let her be*
> *as beautiful as pale-gold Aphrodite,*
> *skilled as Athena of the sea-gray eyes* . . .[60]

(The Attic orators are particularly fond of this method of speech.) Consequently it does not suit an elderly speaker.

12 · Each kind of rhetoric has its own appropriate style

It should be observed that each kind of rhetoric has its own appropriate style. The style of written prose is not that of spoken oratory, nor are those of political and forensic speaking the same. Both written and spoken have to be known. To know the latter is to know how to speak good Greek. To know the former means that you are not obliged, as otherwise you are, to hold your tongue when you wish to communicate something to the general public.

The written style is the more finished: the spoken better admits of dramatic delivery—alike the kind of oratory that reflects character and the kind that reflects emotion. Hence actors look out for plays written in the latter style, and poets for actors competent to act in such plays. Yet poets whose plays are meant to be read *are* read and circulated: Chaeremon, for instance, who is as finished as a professional speech-writer; and Licymnius among the dithyrambic poets. Compared with those of others, the speeches of professional writers sound thin in actual contests. Those of the orators, on the other hand, are good to hear spoken, but look amateurish enough when they pass into the hands of a reader. This is just because they are so well-suited for an actual tussle, and therefore contain many dramatic touches, which, being robbed of all dramatic rendering, fail to do their own proper work, and consequently look silly. Thus strings of unconnected words, and constant repetitions of words and phrases, are very

---

[60] *Iliad*, IX. 470–78.

properly condemned in written speeches: but not in spoken speeches—speakers use them freely, for they have a dramatic effect. In this repetition there must be variety of tone, paving the way, as it were, to dramatic effect; e.g. 'This is the villain among you who deceived you, who cheated you, who meant to betray you completely'. This is the sort of thing that Philemon the actor used to do in the *Old Men's Madness* of Anaxandrides, whenever he spoke the words 'Rhadamanthus and Palamedes', and also in the prologue to the *Saints* whenever he pronounced the pronoun 'I'. If one does not deliver such things cleverly, it becomes a case of 'the man who swallowed a poker'. So too with strings of unconnected words, e.g. 'I came to him; I met him; I besought him'. Such passages must be *acted*, not delivered with the same quality and pitch of voice, as though they had only one idea in them. They have the further peculiarity of suggesting that a number of separate statements have been made in the time usually occupied by one. Just as the use of conjunctions makes many statements into a single one, so the omission of conjunctions acts in the reverse way and makes a single one into many. It thus makes everything more important: e.g. 'I came to him; I talked to him; I entreated him'—what a lot of facts! the hearer thinks—'he paid no attention to anything I said'. This is the effect which Homer seeks when he writes,

> *Nireus had led three well-found ships from Syme;*
> *Nireus, Aglaia's child by Lord Kharopos;*
> *Nireus, of all Danaäns before Troy*
> *most beautifully made, after Akhilleus.*[61]

If many things are said about a man, his name must be mentioned many times; and therefore people think that, if his name is mentioned many times, many things have been said about him. So that Homer, by means of this illusion, has made a great deal of Nireus, though he has mentioned him only in this one passage, and has preserved his memory, though he nowhere says a word about him afterwards.

Now the style of oratory addressed to public assemblies is

[61] *Iliad*, II. 795–98.

really just like scene-painting. The bigger the throng, the more distant is the point of view: so that, in the one and the other, high finish in detail is superfluous and seems better away. The forensic style is more highly finished; still more so is the style of language addressed to a single judge, with whom there is very little room for rhetorical artifices, since he can take the whole thing in better, and judge of what is to the point and what is not; the struggle is less intense and so the judgement is undisturbed. This is why the same speakers do not distinguish themselves in all these branches at once; high finish is wanted least where dramatic delivery is wanted most, and here the speaker must have a good voice, and above all, a strong one. It is ceremonial oratory that is most literary, for it is meant to be read; and next to it forensic oratory.

To analyse style still further, and add that it must be agreeable or magnificent, is useless; for why should it have these traits any more than 'restraint', 'liberality', or any other moral excellence? Obviously agreeableness will be produced by the qualities already mentioned, if our definition of excellence of style has been correct. For what other reason should style be 'clear', and 'not mean' but 'appropriate'? If it is prolix, it is not clear; nor yet if it is curt. Plainly the middle way suits best. Again, style will be made agreeable by the elements mentioned, namely by a good blending of ordinary and unusual words, by the rhythm, and by the persuasiveness that springs from appropriateness.

This concludes our discussion of style, both in its general aspects and in its special applications to the various branches of rhetoric. We have now to deal with Arrangement.

13 · Arrangement of a speech

A speech has two parts. You must state your case, and you must prove it. You cannot either state your case and omit to prove it, or prove it without having first stated it; since any proof must be a proof of something, and the only use of a preliminary statement is the proof that follows it. Of these two parts the first part is called the Statement of the case, the second part the Argument, just as we distinguish between Enunciation and Demonstration. The current division is absurd. For 'narration' surely is part of a forensic speech only: how in a political speech or a speech of display can there be 'narration' in the technical sense? or a reply to a forensic opponent? or an epilogue in closely-reasoned speeches? Again, introduction, comparison of conflicting arguments, and recapitulation are only found in political speeches when there is a struggle between two policies. They *may* occur then; so may even accusation and defence, often enough; but they form no essential part of a political speech. Even forensic speeches do not always need epilogues; not, for instance, a short speech, nor one in which the facts are easy to remember, the effect of an epilogue being always a reduction in the apparent length. It follows, then, that the only necessary parts of a speech are the Statement and the Argument. These are the essential features of a speech; and it cannot in any case have more than Introduction, Statement, Argument, and Epilogue. 'Refutation of the Opponent' is part of the arguments: so is 'Comparison' of the opponent's case with your own, for that process is a magnifying of your own case and therefore a part of the arguments, since one who does this *proves* something. The Introduction does nothing like this; nor does the Epilogue—it merely reminds us of what has been said already. If we make such distinctions we shall end, like Theodorus and his followers, by distinguishing 'narration' proper from 'post-narration' and 'pre-narration', and 'refutation' from 'final refutation'. But we ought only to bring in a new name if it indicates a real species with distinct specific qualities; otherwise the practice is pointless and silly, like the way Licymnius invented names in his *Art of Rhetoric* — 'Secundation', 'Divagation', 'Ramification'.

14 · Introduction

The Introduction is the beginning of a speech, corresponding to the prologue in poetry and the prelude in flute-music; they are all beginnings, paving the way, as it were, for what is to follow. The musical prelude resembles the introduction to speeches of display;

as flute-players play first some brilliant passage they know well and then fit it on to the opening notes of the piece itself, so in speeches of display the writer should proceed in the same way; he should begin with what best takes his fancy, and then strike up his theme and lead into it; which is indeed what *is* always done. (Take as an example the introduction to the *Helen* of Isocrates—there is nothing in common between the 'eristics' and Helen.) And here, even if you travel far from your subject, it is fitting, rather than that there should be sameness in the entire speech.

The usual subject for the introductions to speeches of display is some piece of praise or censure. Thus Gorgias writes in his *Olympic Speech*, 'You deserve widespread admiration, men of Greece', praising thus those who started the festival gatherings. Isocrates, on the other hand, censures them for awarding distinctions to fine athletes but giving no prize for intellectual ability. Or one may begin with a piece of advice, thus: 'We ought to honour good men and so I myself am praising Aristeides' or 'We ought to honour those who are unpopular but not bad men, men whose good qualities have never been noticed, like Alexander son of Priam.' Here the orator gives *advice*. Or we may begin as speakers do in the law-courts; that is to say, with appeals to the audience to excuse us if our speech is about something paradoxical, difficult, or hackneyed; like Choerilus in the lines—

> But now when allotment of all has been made . . .

Introductions to speeches of display, then, may be composed of some piece of praise or censure, of advice to do or not to do something, or of appeals to the audience; and you must choose between making these preliminary passages connected or disconnected with the speech itself.

Introductions to forensic speeches, it must be observed, have the same value as the prologues of dramas and the introductions to epic poems; the dithyrambic prelude resembling the introduction to a speech of display, as

> For thee, and thy gifts, and thy battle-spoils . . .

In prologues, and in epic poetry, a foretaste of the theme is given, intended to inform the hearers of it in advance instead of keeping their minds in suspense. Anything vague puzzles them: so give them a grasp of the beginning, and they can hold fast to it and follow the argument. So we find—

> *Sing, O goddess of song, of the Wrath . . .**
> *Tell me, O Muse, of the hero . . .**
> *Lead me to tell a new tale, how there came great warfare*
> *to Europe*
> *Out of the Asian land . . .*

The tragic poets, too, let us know the pivot of their play; if not at the outset like Euripides, at least somewhere in the preface to a speech like Sophocles—

> *Polybus was my father . . .;*

and so in Comedy. This, then, is the most essential function and distinctive property of the introduction, to show what the aim of the speech is; and therefore no introduction ought to be employed where the subject is not long or intricate.

The other kinds of introduction employed are remedial in purpose, and may be used in any type of speech. They are concerned with the speaker, the hearer, the subject, or the speaker's opponent. Those concerned with the speaker himself or with his opponent are directed to removing or exciting prejudice. But whereas the defendant will begin by dealing with this sort of thing, the prosecutor will take quite another line and deal with such matters in the closing part of his speech. The reason for this is not far to seek. The defendant, when he is going to bring himself on the stage, must clear away any obstacles, and therefore must begin by removing any prejudice felt against him. But if you are to *excite* prejudice, you must do so at the close, so that the judges may more easily remember what you have said.

The appeal to the hearer aims at securing his goodwill, or at arousing his resentment, or sometimes at gaining his serious attention to the case, or even at distracting it—for gaining it is not always an advantage, and speakers will often for that reason try to make him laugh.

You may use any means you choose to make your hearer re-

* W. R. Roberts translation.

ceptive; among others giving him a good impression of your character, which always helps to secure his attention. He will be ready to attend to anything that touches himself and to anything that is important, surprising, or agreeable; and you should accordingly convey to him the impression that what you have to say is of this nature. If you wish to distract his attention, you should imply that the subject does not affect him, or is trivial or disagreeable. But observe, all this has nothing to do with the speech itself. It merely has to do with the weak-minded tendency of the hearer to listen to what is beside the point. Where this tendency is absent, no introduction is wanted beyond a summary statement of your subject, to put a sort of head on the main body of your speech. Moreover, calls for attention, when required, may come equally well in any part of a speech; in fact, the beginning of it is just where there is least slackness of interest; it is therefore ridiculous to put this kind of thing at the beginning, when every one is listening with most attention. Choose therefore any point in the speech where such an appeal is needed, and then say 'Now I beg you to note this point— it concerns you quite as much as myself'; or

I will tell you that whose like you have never yet

heard for terror, or for wonder. This is what Prodicus called 'slipping in a bit of the fifty-drachma show-lecture for the audience whenever they began to nod'. It is plain that such introductions are addressed not to ideal hearers, but to hearers as we find them. The use of introductions to excite prejudice or to dispel misgivings is universal—

My lord, I will not say that eagerly . . .

or

Why all this preface?

Introductions are popular with those whose case is weak, or looks weak; it pays them to dwell on anything rather than the actual facts of it. That is why slaves, instead of answering the questions put to them, make indirect replies with long preambles. The means of exciting in your hearers goodwill and various other feelings of the same kind have already been described. The poet finely says

> May I find love and mercy among these people,[62]

and these are the two things we should aim at. In speeches of display we must make the hearer feel that the eulogy includes either himself or his family or his way of life or something or other of the kind. For it is true, as Socrates says in the *Funeral Speech*, that 'the difficulty is not to praise the Athenians at Athens but at Sparta'.

The introductions of political oratory will be made out of the same materials as those of the forensic kind, though the nature of political oratory makes them very rare. The subject is known already, and therefore the *facts* of the case need no introduction; but you may have to say something on account of yourself or to your opponents; or those present may be inclined to treat the matter either more or less seriously than you wish them to. You may accordingly have to excite or dispel some prejudice, or to make the matter under discussion seem more or less important than before: for either of which purposes you will want an introduction. You may also want one to add elegance to your remarks, feeling that otherwise they will have a casual air, like Gorgias' eulogy of the Eleans, in which, without any preliminary sparring or fencing, he begins straight off with 'Happy city of Elis!'

15 · Prejudice

In dealing with prejudice, one class of argument is that whereby you can dispel objectionable suppositions about yourself. It makes no practical difference whether such a supposition has been put into words or not, so that this distinction may be ignored. Another way is to meet any of the issues directly: to deny the alleged fact; or to say that you have done no harm, or none to *him*, or not as much as he says; or that you have done him no injustice, or not much; or that you have done nothing disgraceful, or nothing dis-

---

[62] *Odyssey*, VI. 345.

graceful enough to matter: these are the sort of questions on which the dispute hinges. Thus Iphicrates replying to Nausicrates, admitted that he had done the deed alleged, and that he had done Nausicrates harm, but not that he had done him wrong. Or you may admit the wrong, but balance it with other facts, and say that, if the deed harmed him, at any rate it was honourable; or that, if it gave him pain, at least it did him good; or something else like that. Another way is to allege that your action was due to mistake, or bad luck, or necessity—as Sophocles said he was not trembling, as his traducer maintained, in order to make people think him an old man, but because he could not help it; he would rather *not* be eighty years old. You may balance your motive against your actual deed; saying, for instance, that you did not mean to injure him but to do so-and-so; that you did not do what you are falsely charged with doing—the damage was accidental —'I should indeed be a detestable person if I had deliberately intended this result.' Another way is open when your calumniator, or any of his connexions, is or has been subject to the same grounds for suspicion. Yet another, when others are subject to the same grounds for suspicion but are admitted to be in fact innocent of the charge: e.g. 'Must I be a profligate because I am well-groomed? Then so-and-so must be one too.' Another, if other people have been calumniated by the same man or some one else, or, without being calumniated, have been suspected, like yourself now, and yet have been proved innocent. Another way is to return calumny for calumny and say, 'It is monstrous to trust the man's statements when you cannot trust the man himself.' Another is when the question has been already decided. So with Euripides' reply to Hygiaenon, who, in the action for an exchange of properties, accused him of impiety in having written a line encouraging perjury—

> My tongue hath sworn: no oath is on my soul.

Euripides said that his opponent himself was guilty in bringing into the law-courts cases whose decision belonged to the Dionysiac contests. 'If I have not already answered for my words there, I am ready to do so if you choose to prosecute me there.' Another method is to denounce calumny, showing what an enormity it is, and in particular that it raises false issues, and that it means a lack of confidence in the merits of his case. The argument from evidential circumstances is available for both parties: thus in the *Teucer* Odysseus says that Teucer is closely bound to Priam, since his mother Hesione was Priam's sister. Teucer replies that Telamon his father was Priam's enemy, and that he himself did not betray the spies to Priam. Another method, suitable for the calumniator, is to praise some trifling merit at great length, and then attack some important failing concisely; or after mentioning a number of good qualities to attack one bad one that really bears on the question. This is the method of thoroughly skilful and unscrupulous prosecutors. By mixing up the man's merits with what is bad, they do their best to make use of them to damage him.

There is another method open to both calumniator and apologist. Since a given action can be done from many motives, the former must try to disparage it by selecting the worse motive of two, the latter to put the better construction on it. Thus one might argue that Diomedes chose Odysseus as his companion because he supposed Odysseus to be the best man for the purpose; and you might reply to this that it was, on the contrary, because he was the only hero so worthless that Diomedes need not fear his rivalry.

16 · Narration

We may now pass from the subject of calumny to that of Narration.

Narration in ceremonial oratory is not continuous but intermittent. There must, of course, be some survey of the actions that form the subject-matter of the speech. The speech is a composition containing two parts. One of these is not provided by the orator's art, viz. the actions themselves, of which the orator is in no sense author. The other part is provided by his art, namely, the proof (where proof is needed) that the actions were done, the description of their quality or of their extent, or even all these three things together. Now the reason why sometimes it is not desirable to make the whole narrative continuous is that the case thus expounded is hard to keep in mind. Show, therefore, from one set of facts that your hero is, e.g. brave, and from other sets of facts that he is able, just, &c. A speech thus arranged is comparatively simple, instead of being complicated and elaborate. You will have to recall well-known deeds among others; and because they are well-known, the hearer usually needs no narration of them; none, for instance, if your object is the praise of Achilles; we all know the facts of his life—what you have to do is to apply those facts. But if your object is the praise of Critias, you *must* narrate his deeds, which not many people know of . . .

Nowadays it is said, absurdly enough, that the narration should be rapid. Remember what the man said to the baker who asked whether he was to make the cake hard or soft: 'What, can't you make it *right?*' Just so here. We are not to make long narrations, just as we are not to make long introductions or long arguments. Here, again, rightness does not consist either in rapidity or in conciseness, but in the happy mean; that is, in saying just so much as will make the facts plain, or will lead the hearer to believe that the thing has happened, or that the man has caused injury or wrong to some one, or that the facts are really as important as you wish them to be thought: or the opposite facts to establish the opposite arguments.

You may also narrate as you go anything that does credit to yourself, e.g. 'I kept telling him to do his duty and not abandon his children'; or discredit to your adversary, e.g. 'But he answered me that, wherever he might find himself, there he would find other children', the answer Herodotus[63] records of the Egyptian mutineers. Slip in anything else that the judges will enjoy.

The defendant will make less of the narration. He has to maintain that the thing has not happened, or did no harm, or was not unjust, or not so bad as is alleged. He must therefore not waste time about what is admitted fact, unless this bears on his own contention; e.g. that the thing was done, but was not wrong. Further, we must speak of events as past and gone, except where they excite pity or indignation by being represented as present. The Story told to Alcinous is an example of a brief chronicle,

[63] Cf. Herodotus, II. 30.

when it is repeated to Penelope in sixty lines. Another instance is the Epic Cycle as treated by Phayllus, and the prologue to the *Oeneus*.

The narration should depict character; to which end you must know what makes it do so. One such thing is the indication of moral purpose; the quality of purpose indicated determines the quality of character depicted and is itself determined by the end pursued. Thus it is that mathematical discourses depict no character; they have nothing to do with moral purpose, for they represent nobody as pursuing any end. On the other hand, the Socratic dialogues do depict character, being concerned with moral questions. This end will also be gained by describing the manifestations of various types of character, e.g. 'he kept walking along as he talked', which shows the man's recklessness and rough manners. Do not let your words seem inspired so much by intelligence, in the manner now current, as by moral purpose: e.g. 'I willed this; aye, it was my moral purpose; true, I gained nothing by it, still it is better thus.' For the other way shows good sense, but this shows good character; good sense making us go after what is useful, and good character after what is noble. Where any detail may appear incredible, then add the cause of it; of this Sophocles provides an example in the *Antigone*, where Antigone says she had cared more for her brother than for husband or children, since if the latter perished they might be replaced,

> But since my father and mother in their graves
> Lie dead, no brother can be born to me.

If you have no such cause to suggest, just say that you are aware that no one will believe your words, but the fact remains that such is your nature, however hard the world may find it to believe that a man deliberately does anything except what pays him.

Again, you must make use of the emotions. Relate the famil-

We must neither speak casually about weighty matters, nor solemnly about trivial ones; nor must we add ornamental epithets to commonplace nouns, or the effect will be comic, as in the works of Cleophon, who can use phrases as absurd as 'O queenly fig-tree'. (Page 162)

iar manifestations of them, and those that distinguish yourself and your opponent; for instance, 'he went away scowling at me'. So Aeschines described Cratylus as 'hissing with fury and shaking his fists'. These details carry conviction: the audience take the truth of what they know as so much evidence for the truth of what they do not. Plenty of such details may be found in Homer:

> . . . *Hearing this,*
> *the old nurse hid her face between her hands*
> *and wept hot tears . . .*[64]

a true touch—people beginning to cry do put their hands over their eyes.

Bring yourself on the stage from the first in the right character, that people may regard you in that light; and the same with your adversary; but do not let them see what you are about. How easily such impressions may be conveyed we can see from the way in which we get some inkling of things we know nothing of by the mere look of the messenger bringing news of them. Have some narrative in many different parts of your speech; and sometimes let there be none at the beginning of it.

In political oratory there is very little opening for narration; nobody can 'narrate' what has not yet happened. If there is narration at all, it will be of past events, the recollection of which is to help the hearers to make better plans for the future. Or it may be employed to attack some one's character, or to eulogize him— only then you will not be doing what the political speaker, as such, has to do.

If any statement you make is hard to believe, you must guarantee its truth, and at once offer an explanation, and then furnish it with such particulars as will be expected. Thus Carcinus' Jocasta, in his *Oedipus*, keeps guaranteeing the truth of her answers to the inquiries of the man who is seeking her son; and so with Haemon in Sophocles.

---

[64] *Odyssey*, XIX. 390–92.

RHETORIC

17 · Arguments

The duty of the Arguments is to attempt demonstrative proofs. These proofs must bear directly upon the question in dispute, which must fall under one of four heads. (1) If you maintain that the act *was not committed,* your main task in court is to prove this. (2) If you maintain that the act *did no harm,* prove this. If you maintain that (3) the act was *less* than is alleged, or (4) *justified,* prove these facts, just as you would prove the act not to have been committed if you were maintaining that.

It should be noted that only where the question in dispute falls under the first of these heads can it be true that one of the two parties is necessarily a rogue. Here ignorance cannot be pleaded, as it might if the dispute were whether the act was justified or not. This argument must therefore be used in this case only, not in the others.

In ceremonial speeches you will develop your case mainly by arguing that what has been done is, e.g., noble and useful. The facts themselves are to be taken on trust; proof of them is only submitted on those rare occasions when they are not easily credible or when they have been set down to some one else.

In political speeches you may maintain that a proposal is impracticable; or that, though practicable, it is unjust, or will do no good, or is not so important as its proposer thinks. Note any falsehoods about irrelevant matters—they will look like proof that his other statements also are false. Argument by 'example' is highly suitable for political oratory, argument by 'enthymeme' better suits forensic. Political oratory deals with future events, of which it can do no more than quote past events as examples. Forensic oratory deals with what is or is not *now* true, which can better be demonstrated, because not contingent—there is no contingency in what has now already happened. Do not use a continuous succession of enthymemes: intersperse them with other matter, or they will spoil one another's effect. There are limits to their number—

Friend, you have spoken as much *as a sensible man would have spoken* —*

* W. Rhys Roberts translation.

'as *much*' says Homer, not 'as *well*'. Nor should you try to make enthymemes on every point; if you do, you will be acting just like some students of philosophy, whose conclusions are more familiar and believable than the premisses from which they draw them. And avoid the enthymeme form when you are trying to rouse feeling; for it will either kill the feeling or will itself fall flat: all simultaneous motions tend to cancel each other either completely or partially. Nor should you go after the enthymeme form in a passage where you are depicting character—the process of demonstration can express neither moral character nor moral purpose. Maxims should be employed in the Arguments—and in the Narration too—since these do express character: 'I have given him this, though I am quite aware that one should "Trust no man".' Or if you are appealing to the emotions: 'I do not regret it, though I have been wronged; if he has the profit on his side, I have justice on mine.'

Political oratory is a more difficult task than forensic; and naturally so, since it deals with the future, whereas the pleader deals with the past, which, as Epimenides of Crete said, even the diviners already know. (Epimenides did not practise divination about the future; only about the obscurities of the past.) Besides, in forensic oratory you have a basis in the law; and once you have a starting-point, you can prove anything with comparative ease. Then again, political oratory affords few chances for those leisurely digressions in which you may attack your adversary, talk about yourself, or work on your hearers' emotions; fewer chances indeed, than any other affords, unless your set purpose is to divert your hearers' attention. Accordingly, if you find yourself in difficulties, follow the lead of the Athenian speakers, and that of Isocrates, who makes regular attacks upon people in the course of a political speech, e.g. upon the Lacedaemonians in the *Panegyricus,* and upon Chares in the speech about the allies. In ceremonial oratory, intersperse your speech with bits of episodic eulogy, like Isocrates, who is always bringing some one forward for this purpose. And this is what Gorgias meant by saying that he always found something to talk about. For if he speaks of Achilles, he praises Peleus, then Aeacus, then Zeus; and in like manner the virtue of valour, describing its good results, and saying what it is like.

Now if you have proofs to bring forward, bring them forward, and your moral discourse as well; if you have no enthymemes, then fall back upon moral discourse: after all, it is more fitting for a good man to display himself as an honest fellow than as a subtle reasoner. Refutative enthymemes are more popular than demonstrative ones: their logical cogency is more striking: the facts about two opposites always stand out clearly when the two are put side by side.

The 'Reply to the Opponent' is not a separate division of the speech; it is part of the Arguments to break down the opponent's case, whether by objection or by counter-syllogism. Both in political speaking and when pleading in court, if you are the first speaker you should put your own arguments forward first, and then meet the arguments on the other side by refuting them and pulling them to pieces beforehand. If, however, the case for the other side contains a great variety of arguments, begin with these, like Callistratus in the Messenian assembly, when he demolished the arguments likely to be used against him before giving his own. If you speak later, you must first, by means of refutation and counter-syllogism, attempt some answer to your opponent's speech, especially if his arguments have been well received. For just as our minds refuse a favourable reception to a *person* against whom they are prejudiced, so they refuse it to a speech when they have been favourably impressed by the speech on the other side. You should, therefore, make room in the minds of the audience for your coming speech; and this will be done by getting your opponent's speech out of the way. So attack that first—either the whole of it, or the most important, successful, or vulnerable points in it, and thus inspire confidence in what you have to say yourself—

> *First, champion will I be of Goddesses . . .*
> *Never, I ween, would Hera . . . .*

where the speaker has attacked the silliest argument first. So much for the Arguments.

With regard to the element of moral character: there are assertions which, if made about yourself, may excite dislike, appear tedious, or expose you to the risk of contradiction; and other things which you cannot say about your opponent without seeming abusive or ill-bred. Put such remarks, therefore, into the mouth of some third person. This is what Isocrates does in the *Philippus* and in the *Antidosis,* and Archilochus in his satires. The latter represents the father himself as attacking his daughter in the lampoon

> *Think nought impossible at all,*
> *Nor swear that it shall not befall . . .*

and puts into the mouth of Charon the carpenter the lampoon which begins

> *Nor for the wealth of Gyes . . .*

So too Sophocles makes Haemon appeal to his father on behalf of Antigone as if it were others who were speaking.

Again, sometimes you should restate your enthymemes in the form of maxims; e.g. 'Wise men will come to terms in the hour of success; for they will gain most if they do'. Expressed as an enthymeme, this would run, '*If* we ought to come to terms when doing so will enable us to gain the greatest advantage, *then* we ought to come to terms in the hour of success.'

18 · Interrogation and jests

Next as to Interrogation. The best moment to employ this is when your opponent has so answered one question that the putting of just one more lands him in absurdity. Thus Pericles questioned Lampon about the way of celebrating the rites of the Saviour Goddess. Lampon declared that no uninitiated person could be told of them. Pericles then asked, 'Do you know them yourself?' 'Yes', answered Lampon. 'Why,' said Pericles, 'how can that be, when you are uninitiated?'

Another good moment is when one premiss of an argument is obviously true, and you can see that your opponent must say 'yes' if you ask him whether the other is true. Having first got this answer about the other, do not go on to ask him about the obviously true one, but just state the conclusion yourself. Thus, when Meletus denied that Socrates believed in the existence of gods but admitted that he talked about a supernatural power, Socrates proceeded to ask whether 'supernatural beings were not either children of the gods or in some way divine?' 'Yes', said Meletus. 'Then', replied Socrates, 'is there any one who believes in the existence of children of the gods and yet not in the existence of the gods themselves?' Another good occasion is when you expect to show that your opponent is contradicting either his own words or what every one believes. A fourth is when it is impossible for him to meet your question except by an evasive answer. If he answers 'True, and yet not true', or 'Partly true and partly not true', or 'True in one sense but not in another', the audience thinks he is in difficulties, and applauds his discomfiture. In other cases do not attempt interrogation; for if your opponent gets in an objection, you are felt to have been worsted. You cannot ask a series of questions owing to the incapacity of the audience to follow them; and for this reason you should also make your enthymemes as compact as possible.

In replying, you must meet ambiguous questions by drawing reasonable distinctions, not by a curt answer. In meeting questions that seem to involve you in a contradiction, offer the explanation at the outset of your answer, before your opponent asks the next question or draws his conclusion. For it is not difficult to see the drift of his argument in advance. This point, however, as well as the various means of refutation, may be regarded as known to us from the *Topics*.[65]

When your opponent in drawing his conclusion puts it in the form of a question, you must justify your answer. Thus when Sophocles was asked by Peisander whether he had, like the other members of the Board of Safety, voted for setting up the Four Hundred, he said 'Yes.' 'Why, did you not think it wicked?'— 'Yes.'—'So *you* committed this wickedness?'—'Yes', said Sophocles, 'for there was nothing better to do.' Again, the Lacedaemonian, when he was being examined on his conduct as ephor, was asked whether he thought that the other ephors had been justly

[65] *Topics*, VIII.

put to death. 'Yes', he said. 'Well then', asked his opponent, 'did not *you* propose the same measures as they?'—'Yes.'—'Well then, would not *you* too be justly put to death?'—'Not at all', said he; '*they* were bribed to do it, and I did it from conviction.' Hence you should not ask any further questions after drawing the conclusion, nor put the conclusion itself in the form of a further question, unless there is a large balance of truth on your side.

As to jests. These are supposed to be of some service in controversy. Gorgias said that you should kill your opponents' earnestness with jesting and their jesting with earnestness; in which he was right. Jests have been classified in the *Poetics*. Some are becoming to a gentleman, others are not; see that you choose such as become *you*. Irony better befits a gentleman than buffoonery; the ironical man jokes to amuse himself, the buffoon to amuse other people.

19 · The Epilogue or conclusion

The Epilogue has four parts. You must (1) make the audience well-disposed towards yourself and ill-disposed towards your opponent, (2) magnify or minimize the leading facts, (3) excite the required state of emotion in your hearers, and (4) refresh their memories.

(1) Having shown your own truthfulness and the untruthfulness of your opponent, the natural thing is to commend yourself, censure him, and hammer in your points. You must aim at one of two objects—you must make yourself out a good man and him a bad one either in yourselves or in relation to your hearers. How this is to be managed—by what lines of argument you are to represent people as good or bad—this has been already explained.

(2) The facts having been proved, the natural thing to do next is to magnify or minimize their importance. The facts must be admitted before you can discuss how important they are; just as the body cannot grow except from something already present. The proper lines of argument to be used for this purpose of amplification and depreciation have already been set forth.

(3) Next, when the facts and their importance are clearly understood, you must excite your hearers' emotions. These emotions are pity, indignation, anger, hatred, envy, emulation, pugnacity. The lines of argument to be used for these purposes also have been previously mentioned.

(4) Finally you have to review what you have already said. Here you may properly do what some wrongly recommend doing in the introduction—repeat your points frequently so as to make them easily understood. What you *should* do in your introduction is to state your subject, in order that the point to be judged may be quite plain; in the epilogue you should summarize the arguments by which your case has been proved. The first step in this reviewing process is to observe that you have done what you undertook to do. You must, then, state what you have said and why you have said it. Your method may be a comparison of your own case with that of your opponent; and you may compare either the ways you have both handled the same point or make your comparison less direct: 'My opponent said so-and-so on this point; I said so-and-so, and this is why I said it'. Or with modest irony, e.g. 'He certainly said so-and-so, but I said so-and-so'. Or 'How vain he would have been if he had proved all this instead of *that!*' Or put it in the form of a question. 'What has *not* been proved by me?' or 'What *has* my opponent proved?' You may proceed then, either in this way by setting point against point, or by following the natural order of the arguments as spoken, first giving your own, and then separately, if you wish, those of your opponent.

For the conclusion, the disconnected style of language is appropriate, and will mark the difference between the oration and the peroration. 'I have done. You have heard me. The facts are before you. I ask for your judgement.'

J. Wangner Sculps

ON POETICS

περι ποιητικης

THE TRANSLATION OF
INGRAM BYWATER

ON POETICS

1 · Preliminary discourse on Tragedy, Epic poetry, and Comedy, as the chief forms of imitative poetry, distinguished by the means they use

Our subject being Poetry, I propose to speak not only of the art in general but also of its species and their respective capacities; of the structure of plot required for a good poem; of the number and nature of the constituent parts of a poem; and likewise of any other matters in the same line of inquiry. Let us follow the natural order and begin with the primary facts.

Epic poetry and Tragedy, as also Comedy, Dithyrambic poetry, and most flute-playing and lyre-playing, are all, viewed as a whole, modes of imitation. But at the same time they differ from one another in three ways, either by a difference of kind in their means, or by differences in the objects, or in the manner of their imitations.

I. Just as colour and form are used as means by some, who (whether by art or constant practice) imitate and portray many things by their aid, and the voice is used by others; so also in the above-mentioned group of arts, the means with them as a whole are rhythm, language, and harmony—used, however, either singly or in certain combinations. A combination of harmony and rhythm alone is the means in flute-playing and lyre-playing, and any other arts there may be of the same description, e.g. imitative piping. Rhythm alone, without harmony, is the means in the dancer's imitations; for even he, by the rhythms of his attitudes, may represent men's characters, as well as what they do and suffer. There is further an art which imitates by language alone, without harmony, in prose or in verse, and if in verse, either in some one or in a plurality of metres. This form of imitation is to this day without a name. We have no common name for a mime of Sophron or Xenarchus and a Socratic Conversation; and we should still be without one even if the imitation in the two instances were in trimeters or elegiacs or some other kind of verse—though it is the way with people to tack on 'poet' to the name of a metre, and talk of elegiac-poets and epic-poets, thinking that they call them poets not by reason of the imitative nature of their work, but indiscriminately by reason of the metre they write in. Even if a theory of medicine or physical philosophy be put forth in a metrical form, it is usual to describe the writer in this way; Homer and Empedocles, however, have really nothing in common apart from their metre; so that, if the one is to be called a poet, the other should be termed a physicist rather than a poet. We should be in the same position also, if the imitation in these instances were in all the metres, like the *Centaur* (a rhapsody in a medley of all metres) of Chaeremon; and Chaeremon one has to recognize as a poet. So much, then, as to these arts. There are, lastly, certain other arts, which combine all the means enumerated, rhythm, melody, and verse, e.g. Dithyrambic and Nomic poetry, Tragedy and Comedy; with this difference, however, that the three kinds of means are in some of them all employed together, and in others brought in separately, one after the other. These elements of difference in the above arts I term the means of their imitation.

2 · The poetic arts distinguished by their objects

II. The objects the imitator represents are actions, with agents who are necessarily either good men or bad—the diversities of human character being nearly always derivative from this primary distinction, since the line between virtue and vice is one dividing the whole of mankind. It follows, therefore, that the agents represented must be either above our own level of goodness, or beneath it, or just such as we are; in the same way as, with the painters, the personages of Polygnotus are better than we are, those of Pauson worse, and those of Dionysius just like ourselves. It is clear that each of the above-mentioned arts will admit of these differences, and that it will become a separate art by representing objects with this point of difference. Even in dancing, flute-playing, and lyre-playing such diversities are possible; and they are also possible in the nameless art that uses language, prose or verse without harmony, as its means; Homer's personages, for instance, are better than we are; Cleophon's are on our own level; and those of Hegemon of Thasos, the first writer of parodies, and Nicochares, the author of the *Diliad,* are beneath it. The same is true of the Dithyramb and the Nome: the personages may be presented in them with the difference exemplified in the . . . of . . . and Argas, and in the Cyclopses of Timotheus and Philoxenus. This difference it is that distinguishes Tragedy and Comedy also; the one would make its personages worse, and the other better, than the men of the present day.

3 · The poetic arts distinguished by the manner of their imitations

III. A third difference in these arts is in the manner in which each kind of object is represented. Given both the same means and the same kind of object for imitation, one may either (1) speak at one moment in narrative and at another in an assumed character, as Homer does; or (2) one may remain the same throughout, without any such change; or (3) the imitators may represent the whole story dramatically, as though they were actually doing the things described.

As we said at the beginning, therefore, the differences in the imitation of these arts come under three heads, their means, their objects, and their manner.

So that as an imitator Sophocles will be on one side akin to Homer, both portraying good men; and on another to Aristophanes, since both present their personages as acting and doing. This in fact, according to some, is the reason for plays being termed dramas, because in a play the personages act the story.

Hence too both Tragedy and Comedy are claimed by the Dorians as their discoveries; Comedy by the Megarians—by those in Greece as having arisen when Megara became a democracy, and by the Sicilian Megarians on the ground that the poet Epicharmus was of their country, and a good deal earlier than Chionides and Magnes; even Tragedy also is claimed by certain of the Peloponnesian Dorians. In support of this claim they point to the words 'comedy' and 'drama'. Their word for the outlying hamlets, they say, is *comae,* whereas Athenians call them *demes*—thus assuming that comedians got the name not from their *comoe* or revels, but from their strolling from hamlet to hamlet, lack of appreciation keeping them out of the city. Their word also for 'to act', they say, is *dran,* whereas Athenians use *prattein.*

So much, then, as to the number and nature of the points of difference in the imitation of these arts.

4 · The origin and development of poetry and its kinds

It is clear that the general origin of poetry was due to two causes, each of them part of human nature. Imitation is natural to man from childhood, one of his advantages over the lower animals being this, that he is the most imitative creature in the world, and learns at first by imitation. And it is also natural for all to delight in works of imitation. The truth of this second point is shown by experience: though the objects themselves may be painful to see, we delight to view the most realistic representations of them in art, the forms for example of the lowest animals and of dead bodies. The explanation is to be found in a further fact: to be learning something is the greatest of pleasures not only to the philosopher but also to the rest of mankind, however small their capacity for it; the reason of the delight in seeing the picture is that one is at the same time learning—gathering the meaning of things, e.g. that the man there is so-and-so; for if one has not seen the thing before, one's pleasure will not be in the picture as an imitation of it, but will be due to the execution or colouring or some similar cause. Imitation, then, being natural to us—as also the sense of harmony and rhythm, the metres being obviously species of rhythms—it was through their original aptitude, and by a series of improvements for the most part gradual on their first efforts, that they created poetry out of their improvisations.

Poetry, however, soon broke up into two kinds according to the differences of character in the individual poets; for the graver among them would represent noble actions, and those of noble personages; and the meaner sort the actions of the ignoble. The latter class produced invectives at first, just as others did hymns and panegyrics. We know of no such poem by any of the pre-Homeric poets, though there were probably many such writers among them; instances, however, may be found from Homer downwards, e.g. his *Margites,* and the similar poems of others. In this poetry of invective its natural fitness brought an iambic metre into use; hence our present term 'iambic', because it was the metre of their 'iambs' or invectives against one another. The result was that the old poets became some of them writers of heroic and others of iambic verse. Homer's position, however, is peculiar: just as he was in the serious style the poet of poets, standing alone not only through the literary excellence, but also through the dramatic character of his imitations, so too he was the first to outline for us the general forms of Comedy by producing not a dramatic invective, but a dramatic picture of the Ridiculous; his *Margites* in fact stands in the same relation to our comedies as the *Iliad* and *Odyssey* to our tragedies. As soon, however, as Tragedy and Comedy appeared in the field, those naturally drawn to the one line of poetry became writers of comedies instead of iambs, and those naturally drawn to the other, writers of tragedies instead of epics, because these new modes of art were grander and of more esteem than the old.

If it be asked whether Tragedy is now all that it need be in its formative elements, to consider that, and decide it theoretically and in relation to the theatres, is a matter for another inquiry.

It certainly began in improvisations—as did also Comedy; the one originating with the authors of the Dithyramb, the other with those of the phallic songs, which still survive as institutions in many of our cities. And its advance after that was little by little, through their improving on whatever they had before them at each stage. It was in fact only after a long series of changes that the movement of Tragedy stopped on its attaining to its natural form. (1) The number of actors was first increased to two by Aeschylus, who curtailed the business of the Chorus, and made the dialogue, or spoken portion, take the leading part in the play. (2) A third actor and scenery were due to Sophocles. (3) Tragedy acquired also its magnitude. Discarding short stories and a ludicrous diction, through its passing out of its satyric stage, it assumed, though only at a late point in its progress, a tone of dignity; and its metre changed then from trochaic to iambic. The reason for their original use of the trochaic tetrameter was that their poetry was satyric and more connected with dancing than it now is. As soon, however, as a spoken part came in, nature herself found the appropriate metre. The iambic, we know, is the most speakable of metres, as is shown by the fact that we very often fall into it in conversation, whereas we rarely talk hexameters, and only when we depart from the speaking tone of voice. (4) Another change was a plurality of episodes or acts. As for the remaining matters, the superadded embellishments and the account of their introduction, these must be taken as said, as it would probably be a long piece of work to go through the details.

5 · Comedy and Epic poetry

As for Comedy, it is (as has been observed) an imitation of men worse than the average; worse, however, not as regards any and every sort of fault, but only as regards one particular kind, the Ridiculous, which is a species of the Ugly. The Ridiculous may be defined as a mistake or deformity not productive of pain or harm to others; the mask, for instance, that excites laughter, is something ugly and distorted without causing pain.

Though the successive changes in Tragedy and their authors are not unknown, we cannot say the same of Comedy; its early stages passed unnoticed, because it was not as yet taken up in a serious way. It was only at a late point in its progress that a chorus of comedians was officially granted by the Archon; they used to be mere volunteers. It had also already certain definite forms at the time when the record of those termed comic poets begins. Who it was who supplied it with masks, or prologues, or a plurality of actors and the like, has remained unknown. The invented Fable, or Plot, however, originated in Sicily, with Epicharmus and Phormis; of Athenian poets Crates was the first to drop the Comedy of invective and frame stories of a general and non-personal nature, in other words, Fables or Plots.

Epic poetry, then, has been seen to agree with Tragedy to this extent, that of being an imitation of serious subjects in a grand kind of verse. It differs from it, however, (1) in that it is one kind of verse and in narrative form; and (2) in its length—which is due to its action having no fixed limit of time, whereas Tragedy endeavours to keep as far as possible within a single circuit of the sun, or something near that. This, I say, is another point of difference between them, though at first the practice in this respect was just the same in tragedies as in epic poems. They differ also (3) in their constituents, some being common to both and others peculiar to Tragedy—hence a judge of good and bad in Tragedy is a judge of that in epic poetry also. All the parts of an epic are included in Tragedy; but those of Tragedy are not all of them to be found in the Epic.

6 • Definition of Tragedy, and an analysis of its qualitative parts

Reserving hexameter poetry and Comedy for consideration hereafter,[1] let us proceed now to the discussion of Tragedy; before doing so, however, we must gather up the definition resulting from what has been said. A tragedy, then, is the imitation of an action that is serious and also, as having magnitude, complete in itself; in language with pleasurable accessories, each kind brought in separately in the parts of the work; in a dramatic, not in a nar-

[1] For hexameter poetry compare chapter 23 ff. Comedy was treated in the lost second book.

rative form; with incidents arousing pity and fear, wherewith to accomplish its catharsis of such emotions. Here by 'language with pleasurable accessories' I mean that with rhythm and harmony or song superadded; and by 'the kinds separately' I mean that some portions are worked out with verse only, and others in turn with song.

I. As they act the stories, it follows that in the first place the Spectacle (or stage-appearance of the actors) must be some part of the whole; and in the second Melody and Diction, these two being the means of their imitation. Here by 'Diction' I mean merely this, the composition of the verses; and by 'Melody', what is too completely understood to require explanation. But further: the subject represented also is an action; and the action involves agents, who must necessarily have their distinctive qualities both of character and thought, since it is from these that we ascribe certain qualities to their actions. There are in the natural order of things, therefore, two causes, Thought and Character, of their actions, and consequently of their success or failure in their lives. Now the action (that which was done) is represented in the play by the Fable or Plot. The Fable, in our present sense of the term, is simply this, the combination of the incidents, or things done in the story; whereas Character is what makes us ascribe certain moral qualities to the agents; and Thought is shown in all they say when proving a particular point or, it may be, enunciating a general truth. There are six parts consequently of every tragedy, as a whole (that is) of such or such quality, viz. a Fable or Plot, Characters, Diction, Thought, Spectacle, and Melody; two of them arising from the means, one from the manner, and three from the objects of the dramatic imitation; and there is nothing else besides these six. Of these, its formative elements, then, not a few of the dramatists have made due use, as every play, one may say, admits of Spectacle, Character, Fable, Diction, Melody, and Thought.

II. The most important of the six is the combination of the incidents of the story. Tragedy is essentially an imitation not of persons but of action and life, of happiness and misery. All human happiness or misery takes the form of action; the end for which we live is a certain kind of activity, not a quality. Character gives us qualities, but it is in our actions—what we do—that we are happy or the reverse. In a play accordingly they do not act in order to portray the Characters; they include the Characters for the sake of the action. So that it is the action in it, i.e. its Fable or Plot, that is the end and purpose of the tragedy; and the end is everywhere the chief thing. Besides this, a tragedy is impossible without action, but there may be one without Character. The tragedies of most of the moderns are characterless—a defect common among poets of all kinds, and with its counterpart in painting in Zeuxis as compared with Polygnotus; for whereas the latter is strong in character, the work of Zeuxis is devoid of it. And again: one may string together a series of characteristic speeches of the utmost finish as regards Diction and Thought, and yet fail to produce the true tragic effect; but one will have much better success with a tragedy which, however inferior in these respects, has a Plot, a combination of incidents, in it. And again: the most powerful elements of attraction in Tragedy, the Peripeties and Discoveries, are parts of the Plot. A further proof is in the fact that beginners succeed earlier with the Diction and Characters than with the construction of a story; and the same may be said of nearly all the early dramatists. We maintain, therefore, that the first essential, the life and soul, so to speak, of Tragedy is the Plot; and that the Characters come second—compare the parallel in painting, where the most beautiful colours laid on without order will not give one the same pleasure as a simple black-and-white sketch of a portrait. We maintain that Tragedy is primarily an imitation of action, and that it is mainly for the sake of the action that it imitates the personal agents. Third, comes the element of Thought, i.e. the power of saying whatever can be said, or what is appropriate to the occasion. This is what, in the speeches in Tragedy, falls under the arts of Politics and Rhetoric; for the older poets make their personages discourse like statesmen, and the moderns like rhetoricians. One must not confuse it with Character. Character in a play is that which reveals the moral purpose of the agents, i.e. the sort of thing they seek or avoid, where that is not obvious—hence there is no room for Character in a speech on a purely indifferent subject. Thought, on the other hand, is shown in all they say when proving or disproving some particular point, or enunciating some universal proposition. Fourth among the literary elements is the

Diction of the personages, i.e., as before explained, the expression of their thoughts in words, which is practically the same thing with verse as with prose. As for the two remaining parts, the Melody is the greatest of the pleasurable accessories of Tragedy. The Spectacle, though an attraction, is the least artistic of all the parts, and has least to do with the art of poetry. The tragic effect is quite possible without a public performance and actors; and besides, the getting-up of the Spectacle is more a matter for the costumier than the poet.

7 · The arrangement and length of the play

Having thus distinguished the parts, let us now consider the proper construction of the Fable or Plot, as that is at once the first and the most important thing in Tragedy. We have laid it down that a tragedy is an imitation of an action that is complete in itself, as a whole of some magnitude; for a whole may be of no magnitude to speak of. Now a whole is that which has beginning, middle, and end. A beginning is that which is not itself necessarily after anything else, and which has naturally something else after it; an end is that which is naturally after something itself, either as its necessary or usual consequent, and with nothing else after it; and a middle, that which is by nature after one thing and has also another after it. A well-constructed Plot, therefore, cannot either begin or end at any point one likes; beginning and end in it must be of the forms just described. Again: to be beautiful, a living creature, and every whole made up of parts, must not only present a certain order in its arrangement of parts, but also be of a certain definite magnitude. Beauty is a matter of size and order, and therefore impossible either (1) in a very minute creature, since our perception becomes indistinct as it approaches instantaneity; or (2) in a creature of vast size—one, say, 1,000 miles long—as in that case, instead of the object being seen all at once, the unity and wholeness of it is lost to the beholder. Just in the same way, then, as a beautiful whole made up of parts, or a beautiful living creature, must be of some size, but a size to be taken in by the eye, so a story or Plot must be of some length, but of a length to be taken in by the memory. As for the limit of its length, so far as that is relative to public performances and spectators, it does not fall within the theory of poetry. If they had to perform a hundred tragedies, they would be timed by water-clocks, as they are said to have been at one period. The limit, however, set by the actual nature of the thing is this: the longer the story, consistently with its being comprehensible as a whole, the finer it is by reason of its magnitude. As a rough general formula, 'a length which allows of the hero passing by a series of probable or necessary stages from misfortune to happiness, or from happiness to misfortune', may suffice as a limit for the magnitude of the story.

8 · Unity of Plot

The Unity of a Plot does not consist, as some suppose, in its having one man as its subject. An infinity of things befall that one man, some of which it is impossible to reduce to unity; and in like manner there are many actions of one man which cannot be made to form one action. One sees, therefore, the mistake of all the poets who have written a *Heracleid, a Theseid,* or similar poems; they suppose that, because Heracles was one man, the story also of Heracles must be one story. Homer, however, evidently understood this point quite well, whether by art or instinct, just in the same way as he excels the rest in every other respect. In writing an *Odyssey,* he did not make the poem cover all that ever befell his hero—it befell him, for instance, to get wounded on Parnassus and also to feign madness at the time of the call to arms, but the two incidents had no necessary or probable connexion with one another—instead of doing that, he took as the subject of the *Odyssey,* as also of the *Iliad,* an action with a Unity of the kind we are describing. The truth is that, just as in the other imitative arts one imitation is always of one thing, so in poetry the story, as an imitation of action, must represent one action, a complete whole, with its several incidents so closely connected that the transposal or withdrawal of any one of them will disjoin and dislocate the whole. For that which makes no perceptible difference by its presence or absence is no real part of the whole.

9 · The poet must depict the probable and the universal

From what we have said it will be seen that the poet's function is to describe, not the thing that has happened, but a kind of thing that might happen, i.e. what is possible as being probable or necessary. The distinction between historian and poet is not in the one writing prose and the other verse—you might put the work of Herodotus into verse, and it would still be a species of history; it consists really in this, that the one describes the thing that has been, and the other a kind of thing that might be. Hence poetry is something more philosophic and of graver import than history, since its statements are of the nature rather of universals, whereas those of history are singulars. By a universal statement I mean one as to what such or such a kind of man will probably or necessarily say or do—which is the aim of poetry, though it affixes proper names to the characters; by a singular statement, one as to what, say, Alcibiades did or had done to him. In Comedy this has become clear by this time; it is only when their plot is already made up of probable incidents that they give it a basis of proper names, choosing for the purpose any names that may occur to them, instead of writing like the old iambic poets about particular persons. In Tragedy, however, they still adhere to the historic names; and for this reason: what convinces is the possible; now whereas we are not yet sure as to the possibility of that which has not happened, that which has happened is manifestly possible, else it would not have come to pass. Nevertheless even in Tragedy there are some plays with but one or two known names in them, the rest being inventions; and there are some without a single known name, e.g. Agathon's *Antheus*, in which both incidents and names are of the poet's invention; and it is no less delightful on that account. So that one must not aim at a rigid adherence to the traditional stories on which tragedies are based. It would be absurd, in fact, to do so, as even the known stories are only known to a few, though they are a delight none the less to all.

It is evident from the above that the poet must be more the poet of his stories or Plots than of his verses, inasmuch as he is a poet by virtue of the imitative element in his work, and it is actions that he imitates. And if he should come to take a subject from actual history he is none the less a poet for that; since some historic occurrences may very well be in the probable and possible order of things; and it is in that aspect of them that he is their poet.

Of simple Plots and actions the episodic are the worst. I call a Plot episodic when there is neither probability nor necessity in the sequence of its episodes. Actions of this sort bad poets construct through their own fault, and good ones on account of the players. His work being for public performance, a good poet often stretches out a Plot beyond its capabilities, and is thus obliged to twist the sequence of incident.

Tragedy, however, is an imitation not only of a complete action, but also of incidents arousing pity and fear. Such incidents have the very greatest effect on the mind when they occur unexpectedly and at the same time in consequence of one another; there is more of the marvellous in them then than if they happened of themselves or by mere chance. Even matters of chance seem most marvellous if there is an appearance of design as it were in them; as for instance the statue of Mitys at Argos killed the author of Mitys' death by falling down on him when a looker-on at a public spectacle; for incidents like that we think to be not without a meaning. A Plot, therefore, of this sort is necessarily finer than others.

10 · Simple and complex Plots

Plots are either simple or complex, since the actions they represent are naturally of this twofold description. The action, proceeding in the way defined, as one continuous whole, I call simple, when the change in the hero's fortunes takes place without Peripety or Discovery; and complex, when it involves one or the other, or both. These should each of them arise out of the structure of the Plot itself, so as to be the consequence, necessary or probable, of the antecedents. There is a great difference between a thing happening *propter hoc* and *post hoc*.

11 · Peripety, Discovery, and Suffering

A Peripety is the change of the kind described from one state of things within the play to its opposite, and that too in the way we are saying, in the probable or necessary sequence of events; as it is for instance in *Oedipus:* here the opposite state of things is produced by the Messenger, who, coming to gladden Oedipus and to remove his fears as to his mother, reveals the secret of his birth. And in *Lynceus:* just as he is being led off for execution, with Danaus at his side to put him to death, the incidents preceding this bring it about that he is saved and Danaus put to death. A Discovery is, as the very word implies, a change from ignorance to knowledge, and thus to either love or hate, in the personages marked for good or evil fortune. The finest form of Discovery is one attended by Peripeties, like that which goes with the Discovery in *Oedipus.* There are no doubt other forms of it; what we have said may happen in a way in reference to inanimate things, even things of a very casual kind; and it is also possible to discover whether some one has done or not done something. But the form most directly connected with the Plot and the action of the piece is the first-mentioned. This, with a Peripety, will arouse either pity or fear—actions of that nature being what Tragedy is assumed to represent; and it will also serve to bring about the happy or unhappy ending. The Discovery, then, being of persons, it may be that of one party only to the other, the latter being already known; or both the parties may discover themselves. Iphigenia, for instance, was discovered to Orestes by sending the letter; and another Discovery was required to reveal him to Iphigenia.

Two parts of the Plot, then, Peripety and Discovery, are on

matters of this sort. A third part is Suffering; which we may define as an action of a destructive or painful nature, such as murders on the stage, tortures, woundings, and the like. The other two have been already explained.

12 · The qualitative parts of Tragedy

The parts of Tragedy to be treated as formative elements in the whole were mentioned in a previous chapter. From the point of view, however, of its quantity, i.e. the separate sections into which it is divided, a tragedy has the following parts: Prologue, Episode, Exode, and a choral portion, distinguished into Parode and Stasimon; these two are common to all tragedies, whereas songs from the stage and *Commoe* are only found in some. The Prologue is all that precedes the Parode of the chorus; an Episode all that comes in between two whole choral songs; the Exode all that follows after the last choral song. In the choral portion the Parode is the whole first statement of the chorus; a Stasimon, a song of the chorus without anapaests or trochees; a *Commos,* a lamentation sung by chorus and actor in concert. The parts of Tragedy to be used as formative elements in the whole we have already mentioned; the above are its parts from the point of view of its quantity, or the separate sections into which it is divided.

13 · The tragic hero

The next points after what we have said above will be these: (1) What is the poet to aim at, and what is he to avoid, in constructing his Plots? and (2) What are the conditions on which the tragic effect depends?

We assume that, for the finest form of Tragedy, the Plot must be not simple but complex; and further, that it must imitate actions arousing fear and pity, since that is the distinctive function of this kind of imitation. It follows, therefore, that there are three forms of Plot to be avoided. (1) A good man must not be seen passing from happiness to misery, or (2) a bad man from misery to happiness. The first situation is not fear-inspiring or piteous, but simply odious to us. The second is the most untragic that can be; it has no one of the requisites of Tragedy; it does not appeal either to the human feeling in us, or to our pity, or to our fears. Nor, on the other hand, should (3) an extremely bad man be seen falling from happiness into misery. Such a story may arouse the human feeling in us, but it will not move us to either pity or fear; pity is occasioned by undeserved misfortune, and fear by that of one like ourselves; so that there will be nothing either piteous or fear-inspiring in the situation. There remains, then, the intermediate kind of personage, a man not preeminently virtuous and just, whose misfortune, however, is brought upon him not by vice and depravity but by some error of judgement, of the number of those in the enjoyment of great reputation and prosperity; e.g. Oedipus, Thyestes, and the men of note of similar families. The perfect Plot, accordingly, must have a single, and not (as some tell us) a double issue; the change in the hero's fortunes must be not from misery to happiness, but on the contrary from happiness to misery; and the cause of it must lie not in any depravity, but in some great error on his part; the man himself being either such as we have described, or better, not worse, than that. Fact also confirms our theory. Though the poets began by accepting any tragic story that came to hand, in these days the finest tragedies are always on the story of some few houses, on that of Alcmeon, Oedipus, Orestes, Meleager, Thyestes, Telephus, or any others that may have been involved, as either agents or sufferers, in some deed of horror. The theoretically best tragedy, then, has a Plot of this description. The critics, therefore, are wrong who blame Euripides for taking this line in his tragedies, and giving many of them an unhappy ending. It is, as we have said, the right line to take. The best proof is this: on the stage, and in the public performances, such plays, properly worked out, are seen to be the most truly tragic; and Euripides, even if his execution be faulty in every other point, is seen to be nevertheless the most tragic certainly of the dramatists. After this comes the construction of Plot which some rank first, one with a double story (like the *Odyssey*) and an opposite issue for the good and the bad personages. It is ranked as first only through the weakness of the audiences; the poets merely follow their public, writing as its wishes dictate. But the pleasure here is not that of Tragedy. It belongs rather to Comedy, where the bitterest enemies in the piece (e.g. Orestes and Aegisthus) walk off good friends at the end, with no slaying of any one by any one.

14 · The tragic deed

The tragic fear and pity may be aroused by the Spectacle; but they may also be aroused by the very structure and incidents of the play—which is the better way and shows the better poet. The Plot in fact should be so framed that, even without seeing the things take place, he who simply hears the account of them shall be filled with horror and pity at the incidents; which is just the effect that the mere recital of the story in *Oedipus* would have on one. To produce this same effect by means of the Spectacle is less artistic, and requires extraneous aid. Those, however, who make use of the Spectacle to put before us that which is merely monstrous and not productive of fear, are wholly out of touch with Tragedy; not every kind of pleasure should be required of a tragedy, but only its own proper pleasure.

The tragic pleasure is that of pity and fear, and the poet has to produce it by a work of imitation; it is clear, therefore, that the causes should be included in the incidents of his story. Let us see, then, what kinds of incident strike one as horrible, or rather as piteous. In a deed of this description the parties must necessarily be either friends, or enemies, or indifferent to one another. Now when enemy does it on enemy, there is nothing to move us to pity either in his doing or in his meditating the deed, except so far as the actual pain of the sufferer is concerned; and the same is true when the parties are indifferent to one another. Whenever the tragic deed, however, is done within the family—when murder or the like is done or meditated by brother on brother, by son on father, by mother on son, or son on mother—these are the situations the poet should seek after. The traditional stories,

accordingly, must be kept as they are, e.g. the murder of Clytaem-
nestra by Orestes and of Eriphyle by Alcmeon. At the same time
even with these there is something left to the poet himself; it is for
him to devise the right way of treating them. Let us explain more
clearly what we mean by 'the right way'. The deed of horror may
be done by the doer knowingly and consciously, as in the old
poets, and in Medea's murder of her children in Euripides. Or he
may do it, but in ignorance of his relationship, and discover that
afterwards, as does the Oedipus in Sophocles. Here the deed is
outside the play; but it may be within it, like the act of the Alcmeon in Astydamas, or that of the Telegonus in *Ulysses Wounded*.
A third possibility is for one meditating some deadly injury to another, in ignorance of his relationship, to make the discovery in
time to draw back. These exhaust the possibilities, since the deed
must necessarily be either done or not done, and either knowingly
or unknowingly.

The worst situation is when the personage is with full knowledge on the point of doing the deed, and leaves it undone. It is
odious and also (through the absence of suffering) untragic; hence
it is that no one is made to act thus except in some few instances,
e.g. Haemon and Creon in *Antigone*. Next after this comes the actual perpetration of the deed meditated. A better situation than
that, however, is for the deed to be done in ignorance, and the relationship discovered afterwards, since there is nothing odious in
it, and the Discovery will serve to astound us. But the best of all is
the last; what we have in *Cresphontes*, for example, where
Merope, on the point of slaying her son, recognizes him in time; in
Iphigenia, where sister and brother are in a like position; and in
Helle, where the son recognizes his mother, when on the point of
giving her up to her enemy.

This will explain why our tragedies are restricted (as we said
just now) to such a small number of families. It was accident
rather than art that led the poets in quest of subjects to embody

---

*Whenever the tragic deed is done within the family —when murder or the
like is done or meditated by brother on brother, by son on father, by
mother on son —these are the situations the poet should seek after.* (Page
219)

this kind of incident in their Plots. They are still obliged, accordingly, to have recourse to the families in which such horrors have occurred.

On the construction of the Plot, and the kind of Plot required for Tragedy, enough has now been said.

15 • Rules for the character of the tragic personages, and a note on the use of stage-artifice

In the Characters there are four points to aim at. First and foremost, that they shall be good. There will be an element of character in the play, if (as has been observed) what a personage says or does reveals a certain moral purpose; and a good element of character, if the purpose so revealed is good. Such goodness is possible in every type of personage, even in a woman or a slave, though the one is perhaps an inferior, and the other a wholly worthless being. The second point is to make them appropriate. The Character before us may be, say, manly; but it is not appropriate in a female Character to be manly, or clever. The third is to make them like the reality, which is not the same as their being good and appropriate, in our sense of the term. The fourth is to make them consistent and the same throughout; even if inconsistency be part of the man before one for imitation as presenting that form of character, he should still be consistently inconsistent. We have an instance of baseness of character, not required for the story, in the Menelaus in *Orestes;* of the incongruous and unbefitting in the lamentation of Ulysses in *Scylla,* and in the (clever) speech of Melanippe, and of inconsistency in *Iphigenia at Aulis,* where Iphigenia the suppliant is utterly unlike other later Iphigenia. The right thing, however, is in the Characters just as in the incidents of the play to endeavour always after the necessary or the probable; so that whenever such-and-such a personage says or does such-and-such a thing, it shall be the necessary or probable outcome of his character; and whenever this incident follows on that, it shall be either the necessary or the probable consequence of it. From this one sees (to digress for a moment) that the Dénouement also should arise out of the plot itself, and not depend on a stage-artifice, as in *Medea,* or in the story of the (arrested) departure of the Greeks in the *Iliad.* The artifice must be reserved for matters outside the play—for past events beyond human knowledge, or events yet to come, which require to be foretold or announced; since it is the privilege of the Gods to know everything. There should be nothing improbable among the actual incidents. If it be unavoidable, however, it should be outside the tragedy, like the improbability in the *Oedipus* of Sophocles. But to return to the Characters. As Tragedy is an imitation of personages better than the ordinary man, we in our way should follow the example of good portrait-painters, who reproduce the distinctive features of a man, and at the same time, without losing the likeness, make him handsomer than he is. The poet in like manner, in portraying men quick or slow to anger, or with similar infirmities of character, must know how to represent them as such, and at the same time as good men, as Agathon and Homer have represented Achilles.

All these rules one must keep in mind throughout, and, further, those also for such points of stage-effect as directly depend on the art of the poet, since in these too one may often make mistakes. Enough, however, has been said on the subject in one of our published writings.

16 · The various forms of Discovery

Discovery in general has been explained already. As for the species of Discovery, the first to be noted is (1) the least artistic form of it, of which the poets make most use through mere lack of invention, Discovery by signs or marks. Of these signs some are congenital, like the 'lance-head which the Earth-born have on them', or 'stars', such as Carcinus brings in his *Thyestes;* others acquired after birth—these latter being either marks on the body, e.g. scars, or external tokens, like necklaces, or (to take another sort of instance) the ark in the Discovery in *Tyro.* Even these, however, admit of two uses, a better and a worse; the scar of Ulysses is an instance; the Discovery of him through it is made in one way by the nurse and in another by the swineherds. A Discovery using signs as a means of assurance is less artistic, as indeed are all such as imply reflection; whereas one bringing them in all of a sudden, as in the *Bath-story,* is of a better order. Next after these are (2) Discoveries made directly by the poet; which sister reveals who she is by the letter, Orestes' Discovery of himself in *Iphigenia:* whereas his sister reveals who she is by the letter, Orestes is made to say himself what the poet rather than the story demands. This, therefore, is not far removed from the first-mentioned fault, since he might have presented certain tokens as well. Another instance is the 'shuttle's voice' in the *Tereus* of Sophocles. (3) A third species is Discovery through memory, from a man's consciousness being awakened by something seen. Thus in *The Cyprioe* of Dicaeogenes, the sight of the picture makes the man burst into tears; and in the *Tale of Alcinous,* hearing the harper Ulysses is reminded of the past and weeps; the Discovery of them being the result. (4) A fourth kind is Discovery through reasoning e.g. in *The Choephoroe,* 'One like me is here; there is no one like me but Orestes; he, therefore, must be here.' Or that which Polyidus the Sophist suggested for *Iphigenia;* since it was natural for Orestes to reflect: 'My sister was sacrificed and I am to be sacrificed like her.' Or that in the *Tydeus* of Theodectes: 'I came to find a son, and am to die myself.' Or that in *The Phinidae:* on seeing the place the women inferred their fate, that they were to die there, since they had also been exposed there. (5) There is, too, a composite Discovery arising from bad reasoning on the side of the other party. An instance of it is in *Ulysses the False Messenger:* he said he should know the bow—which he had not seen; but to suppose from that that he would know it again (as though he had once seen it) was bad reasoning. (6) The best of all Discoveries, however, is that arising from the incidents themselves, when the great surprise comes about through a probable incident, like that in the *Oedipus* of Sophocles; and also in *Iphigenia;* for it was not improbable that she should wish to have a letter taken home. These last are the only Discoveries independent of the artifice of signs and necklaces. Next after them come Discoveries through reasoning.

17 · Additional rules for the construction of a play

At the time when he is constructing his Plots, and engaged on the Diction in which they are worked out, the poet should remember (1) to put the actual scenes as far as possible before his eyes. In this way, seeing everything with the vividness of an eye-witness as it were, he will devise what is appropriate, and be least likely to overlook incongruities. This is shown by what was censured in Carcinus, the return of Amphiaraus from the sanctuary; it would have passed unnoticed, if it had not been actually seen by the audience; but on the stage his play failed, the incongruity of the incident offending the spectators. (2) As far as may be, too, the poet should even act his story with the very gestures of his personages. Given the same natural qualifications, he who feels the emotions to be described will be the most convincing; distress and anger, for instance, are portrayed most truthfully by one who is feeling them at the moment. Hence it is that poetry demands a man with a special gift for it, or else one with a touch of madness in him; the former can easily assume the required mood, and the latter may be actually beside himself with emotion. (3) His story, again, whether already made or of his own making, he should first simplify and reduce to a universal form, before proceeding to lengthen it out by the insertion of episodes. The following will show how the universal element in *Iphigenia,* for instance, may be viewed: A certain maiden having been offered in sacrifice, and spirited away from her sacrificers into another land, where the custom was to sacrifice all strangers to the Goddess, she was made there the priestess of this rite. Long after that the brother of the priestess happened to come; the fact, however, of the oracle having for a certain reason bidden him go thither, and his object in going, are outside the Plot of the play. On his coming he was arrested, and about to be sacrificed, when he revealed who he was—either as Euripides puts it, or (as suggested by Polyidus) by the not improbable exclamation, 'So I too am doomed to be sacrificed, as my sister was'; and the disclosure led to his salvation. This done, the next thing, after the proper names have been fixed as a basis for the story, is to work in episodes or accessory incidents. One must mind, however, that the episodes are appropriate, like the fit of madness in Orestes, which led to his arrest, and the purifying, which brought about his salvation. In plays, then, the episodes are short; in epic poetry they serve to lengthen out the poem. The argument of the *Odyssey* is not a long one. A certain man has been abroad many years; Poseidon is ever on the watch for him, and he is all alone. Matters at home too have come to this, that his substance is being wasted and his son's death plotted by suitors to his wife. Then he arrives there himself after his grievous sufferings; reveals himself, and falls on his enemies; and the end is his salvation and their death. This being all that is proper to the *Odyssey*, everything else in it is episode.

18 · Additional rules for the construction of a play, continued

(4) There is a further point to be borne in mind. Every tragedy is in part Complication and in part Dénouement; the incidents before the opening scene, and often certain also of those within the play, forming the Complication; and the rest the Dénouement. By Complication I mean all from the beginning of the story to the point just before the change in the hero's fortunes; by Dénouement, all from the beginning of the change to the end. In the *Lynceus* of Theodectes, for instance, the Complication includes, together with the presupposed incidents, the seizure of the child and that in turn of the parents; and the Dénouement all from the indictment for the murder to the end. Now it is right, when one speaks of a tragedy as the same or not the same as another, to do so on the ground before all else of their Plot, i.e. as having the same or not the same Complication and Dénouement. Yet there are many dramatists who, after a good Complication, fail in the Dénouement. But it is necessary for both points of construction to be always duly mastered. (5) There are four distinct species of Tragedy—that being the number of the constituents also that have been mentioned: first, the complex Tragedy, which is all Peripety and Discovery; second, the Tragedy of suffering, e.g. the *Ajaxes* and *Ixions;* third, the Tragedy of character, e.g. *The*

Phthiotides[2] and *Peleus*. The fourth constituent is that of 'Spectacle', exemplified in *The Phorcides,* in *Prometheus,* and in all plays with the scene laid in the nether world. The poet's aim, then, should be to combine every element of interest, if possible, or else the more important and the major part of them. This is now especially necessary owing to the unfair criticism to which the poet is subjected in these days. Just because there have been poets before him strong in the several species of tragedy, the critics now expect the one man to surpass that which was the strong point of each one of his predecessors. (6) One should also remember what has been said more than once, and not write a tragedy on an epic body of incident (i.e. one with a plurality of stories in it), by attempting to dramatize, for instance, the entire story of the *Iliad.* In the epic owing to its scale every part is treated at proper length; with a drama, however, on the same story the result is very disappointing. This is shown by the fact that all who have dramatized the fall of Ilium in its entirety, and not part by part, like Euripides, or the whole of the Niobe story, instead of a portion, like Aeschylus, either fail utterly or have but ill success on the stage; for that and that alone was enough to ruin even a play by Agathon. Yet in their Peripeties, as also in their simple plots, the poets I mean show wonderful skill in aiming at the kind of effect they desire — a tragic situation that arouses the human feeling in one, like the clever villain (e.g. Sisyphus) deceived, or the brave wrongdoer worsted. This is probable, however, only in Agathon's sense, when he speaks of the probability of even improbabilities coming to pass. (7) The Chorus too should be regarded as one of the actors; it should be an integral part of the whole, and take a share in the action — that which it has in Sophocles, rather than in Euripides. With the later poets, however, the songs in a play of theirs have no more to do with the Plot of that than of any other tragedy. Hence it is that they are now singing intercalary pieces, a practice first introduced by Agathon. And yet what real difference is there between singing such intercalary pieces, and attempting to fit in a speech, or even a whole act, from one play into another?

---

[2] This does not agree with anything actually said before.

ARISTOTLE

19 · The Thought of the tragic personages

The Plot and Characters having been discussed, it remains to consider the Diction and Thought. As for the Thought, we may assume what is said of it in our Art of Rhetoric,[3] as it belongs more properly to that department of inquiry. The Thought of the personages is shown in everything to be effected by their language—in every effort to prove or disprove, to arouse emotion (pity, fear, anger, and the like), or to maximize or minimize things. It is clear, also, that their mental procedure must be on the same lines in their actions likewise, whenever they wish them to arouse pity or horror, or to have a look of importance or probability. The only difference is that with the act the impression has to be made without explanation; whereas with the spoken word it has to be produced by the speaker, and result from his language. What, indeed, would be the good of the speaker, if things appeared in the required light even apart from anything he says?

As regards the Diction, one subject for inquiry under this head is the turns given to the language when spoken; e.g. the difference between command and prayer, simple statement and threat, question and answer, and so forth. The theory of such matters, however, belongs to Elocution and the professors of that art. Whether the poet knows these things or not, his art as a poet is never seriously criticized on that account. What fault can one see in Homer's 'Sing of the wrath, Goddess'?—which Protagoras has criticized as being a command where a prayer was meant, since to bid one do or not do, he tells us, is a command. Let us pass over this, then, as appertaining to another art, and not to that of poetry.

20 · The ultimate constituents of language

The Diction viewed as a whole is made up of the following parts: the Letter (or ultimate element), the Syllable, the Conjunction, the Article, the Noun, the Verb, the Case, and the Speech. (1) The

[3] Cf. especially *Rhetoric*, I. 2.

Letter is an indivisible sound of a particular kind, one that may become a factor in an intelligible sound. Indivisible sounds are uttered by the brutes also, but no one of these is a Letter in our sense of the term. These elementary sounds are either vowels, semi-vowels, or mutes. A vowel is a Letter having an audible sound without the addition of another Letter. A semi-vowel, one having an audible sound by the addition of another Letter; e.g. S and R. A mute, one having no sound at all by itself, but becoming audible by an addition, that of one of the Letters which have a sound of some sort of their own; e.g. G and D. The Letters differ in various ways: as produced by different conformations or in different regions of the mouth; as aspirated, not aspirated, or sometimes one and sometimes the other; as long, short, or of variable quantity; and further as having an acute, grave, or intermediate accent. The details of these matters we must leave to the metricians. (2) A Syllable is a non-significant composite sound, made up of a mute and a Letter having a sound (a vowel or semi-vowel); for GR, without an A, is just as much a Syllable as GRA, with an A. The various forms of the Syllable also belong to the theory of metre. (3) A Conjunction is (a) a non-significant sound which, when one significant sound is formable out of several, neither hinders nor aids the union, and which, if the Speech thus formed stands by itself (apart from other Speeches), must not be inserted at the beginning of it; e.g. μέν, δή, τοι, δέ. Or (b) a non-significant sound capable of combining two or more significant sounds into one; e.g. ἀμφί, περί, &c. (4) An Article is a non-significant sound marking the beginning, end, or dividing-point of a Speech, its natural place being either at the extremities or in the middle. (5) A Noun or name is a composite significant sound not involving the idea of time, with parts which have no significance by themselves in it. It is to be remembered that in a compound we do not think of the parts as having significance also by themselves; in the name 'Theodorus', for instance, the δωρον means nothing to us. (6) A Verb is a composite significant sound involving the idea of time, with parts which (just as in the Noun) have no significance by themselves in it. Whereas the word 'man' or 'white' does not imply when, 'walks' and 'has walked' involve in addition to the idea of walking that of time present or time past. (7) A Case of a Noun or Verb is when the word means 'of' or 'to' a thing, and so forth, or

for one or many (e.g. 'man' and 'men'); or it may consist merely in
the mode of utterance, e.g. in question, command, &c. 'Walked?'
and 'Walk!' are Cases of the verb 'to walk' of this last kind. (8) A
Speech is a composite significant sound, some of the parts of
which have a certain significance by themselves. It may be observed that a Speech is not always made up of Noun and Verb; it
may be without a Verb, like the definition of man; but it will always have some part with a certain significance by itself. In the
Speech 'Cleon walks', 'Cleon' is an instance of such a part. A
Speech is said to be one in two ways, either as signifying one thing,
or as a union of several Speeches made into one by conjunction.
Thus the *Iliad* is one Speech by conjunction of several; and the
definition of man is one through its signifying one thing.

21 · The different kinds of terms

Nouns are of two kinds, either (1) simple, i.e. made up of non-
significant parts, like the word γη, or (2) double; in the latter case
the word may be made up either of a significant and a non-
significant part (a distinction which disappears in the compound),
or of two significant parts. It is possible also to have triple, quad-
ruple, or higher compounds, like most of our amplified names;
e.g. 'Hermocaicoxanthus' and the like.

Whatever its structure, a Noun must always be either (1) the
ordinary word for the thing, or (2) a strange word, or (3) a metaphor, or (4) an ornamental word, or (5) a coined word, or (6) a
word lengthened out, or (7) curtailed, or (8) altered in form. By
the ordinary word I mean that in general use in a country; and by
a strange word, one in use elsewhere. So that the same word may
obviously be at once strange and ordinary, though not in reference
to the same people; οἴγυνον, for instance, is an ordinary word in
Cyprus, and a strange word with us. Metaphor consists in giving
the thing a name that belongs to something else; the transference
being either from genus to species, or from species to genus, or
from species to species, or on grounds of analogy. That from
genus to species is exemplified in 'Here stands my ship'; for lying

at anchor is the 'standing' of a particular kind of thing. That from species to genus in 'Truly ten thousand good deeds has Ulysses wrought', where 'ten thousand', which is a particular large number, is put in place of the generic 'a large number'. That from species to species in 'Drawing the life with the bronze', and in 'Severing with the enduring bronze'; where the poet uses 'draw' in the sense of 'sever' and 'sever' in that of 'draw', both words meaning to 'take away' something. That from analogy is possible whenever there are four terms so related that the second (B) is to the first (A), as the fourth (D) to the third (C); for one may then metaphorically put D in lieu of B, and B in lieu of D. Now and then, too, they qualify the metaphor by adding on to it that to which the word it supplants is relative. Thus a cup (B) is in relation to Dionysus (A) what a shield (D) is to Ares (C). The cup accordingly will be metaphorically described as the 'shield *of Dionysus*' (D + A), and the shield as the 'cup *of Ares*' (B + C). Or to take another instance: As old age (D) is to life (C), so is evening (B) to day (A). One will accordingly describe evening (B) as the 'old age *of the day*' (D + A)—or by the Empedoclean equivalent; and old age (D) as the 'evening' or 'sunset *of life*' (B + C). It may be that some of the terms thus related have no special name of their own, but for all that they will be metaphorically described in just the same way. Thus to cast forth seed-corn is called 'sowing'; but to cast forth its flame, as said of the sun, has no special name. This nameless act (B), however, stands in just the same relation to its object, sunlight (A), as sowing (D) to the seed-corn (C). Hence the expression in the poet, 'sowing around a god-created *flame*' (D + A). There is also another form of qualified metaphor. Having given the thing the alien name, one may by a negative addition deny of it one of the attributes naturally associated with its new name. An instance of this would be to call the shield not the 'cup *of Ares*', as in the former case, but a 'cup *that holds no wine*'. . . . A coined word is a name which, being quite unknown among a people, is given by the poet himself; e.g. (for there are some words that seem to be of this origin) ἔρνυγες for horns, and ἀρητήρ for priest. A word is said to be lengthened out, when it has a short vowel made long, or an extra syllable inserted; e.g. πόληος for πόλεως, Πηληιάδεω for Πηλείδου. It is said to be curtailed, when it has lost a part; e.g.

κρῖ, δῶ, and ὄψ in μία γίνεται ἀμφοτέρων ὄψ. It is an altered word, when part is left as it was and part is of the poet's making; e.g. δεξιτερόν for δεξιόν, in δεξιτερὸν κατὰ μαζόν.

The Nouns themselves (to whatever class they may belong) are either masculines, feminines, or intermediates (neuter). All ending in N, P, Σ, or in the two compounds of this last Ψ and Ξ, are masculines. All ending in the invariably long vowels, H and Ω, and in A among the vowels that may be long, are feminines. So that there is an equal number of masculine and feminine terminations, as Ψ and Ξ are the same as Σ, and need not be counted. There is no Noun, however, ending in a mute or in either of the two short vowels, E and O. Only three (μέλι, κόμμι, πέπερι) end in I, and five in Y. The intermediates, or neuters, end in the variable vowels or in N, P, Σ.

22 · The characteristics of the language of poetry

The perfection of Diction is for it to be at once clear and not mean. The clearest indeed is that made up of the ordinary words for things, but it is mean, as is shown by the poetry of Cleophon and Sthenelus. On the other hand the Diction becomes distinguished and non-prosaic by the use of unfamiliar terms, i.e. strange words, metaphors, lengthened forms, and everything that deviates from the ordinary modes of speech.—But a whole statement in such terms will be either a riddle or a barbarism, a riddle, if made up of metaphors, a barbarism, if made up of strange words. The very nature indeed of a riddle is this, to describe a fact in an impossible combination of words (which cannot be done with the real names for things, but can be with their metaphorical substitutes); e.g. 'I saw a man glue brass on another with fire', and the like. The corresponding use of strange words results in a barbarism.—A certain admixture, accordingly, of unfamiliar terms is necessary. These, the strange word, the metaphor, the ornamental equivalent, &c., will save the language from seeming mean and prosaic, while the ordinary words in it will secure the requisite clearness. What helps most, however, to render the Diction at once clear and non-prosaic is the use of the lengthened, curtailed, and altered forms of words. Their deviation from the ordinary words will, by making the language unlike that in general use, give it a non-prosaic appearance; and their having much in common with the words in general use will give it the quality of clearness. It is not right, then, to condemn these modes of speech, and ridicule the poet for using them, as some have done; e.g. the elder Euclid, who said it was easy to make poetry if one were to be allowed to lengthen the words in the statement itself as much as one likes—a procedure he caricatured by reading Ἐπιχάρην εἶδον Μαραθῶνάδε βαδίζοντα, and οὐκ ἄν γ᾽ ἐράμενος τὸν ἐκείνου ἐλλέβορον as verses. A too apparent use of these licences has certainly a ludicrous effect, but they are not alone in that; the rule of moderation applies to all the constituents of the poetic vocabulary; even with metaphors, strange words, and the rest, the effect will be the same, if one uses them improperly and with a view to provoking laughter. The proper use of them is a very different thing. To realize the difference one should take an epic verse and see how it reads when the normal words are introduced. The same should be done too with the strange word, the metaphor, and the rest; for one has only to put the ordinary words in their place to see the truth of what we are saying. The same iambic, for instance, is found in Aeschylus and Euripides, and as it stands in the former it is a poor line; whereas Euripides, by the change of a single word, the substitution of a strange for what is by usage the ordinary word, has made it seem a fine one. Aeschylus having said in his *Philoctetes*:

φαγέδαινα ἥ μου σάρκαος ἐσθίει ποδός,

Euripides has merely altered the ἐσθίει here into θοινᾶται. Or suppose

νῦν δέ μ᾽ ἐὼν ὀλίγος τε καὶ οὐτιδανὸς καὶ ἀεικής

to be altered, by the substitution of the ordinary words, into

νυν δέ μ᾽ ἐὼν μικρός τε καὶ ἀσθενικὸς καὶ ἀειδής.

Or the line

δίφρον ἀεικέλιον καταθεὶς ὀλίγην τε τράπεζαν

into

δίφρον μοχθηρὸν καταθεὶς μικράν τε τράπεζαν.

Or ἠιόνες βοόωσιν into ἠιόνες κράζουσιν. Add to this that Ariphrades used to ridicule the tragedians for introducing expressions unknown in the language of common life, δωμάτων ἄπο (for ἄπὸ δωμάτων), σέθεν, ἐγὼ δέ νιν, 'Αχιλλέως πέρι (for περὶ Αχιλλέως), and the like. The mere fact of their not being in ordinary speech gives the Diction a non-prosaic character; but Ariphrades was unaware of that. It is a great thing, indeed, to make a proper use of these poetical forms, as also of compounds and strange words. But the greatest thing by far is to be a master of metaphor. It is the one thing that cannot be learnt from others; and it is also a sign of genius, since a good metaphor implies an intuitive perception of the similarity in dissimilars.

Of the kinds of words we have enumerated it may be observed that compounds are most in place in the dithyramb, strange words in heroic, and metaphors in iambic poetry. Heroic poetry, indeed, may avail itself of them all. But in iambic verse, which models itself as far as possible on the spoken language, only those kinds of words are in place which are allowable also in an oration, i.e. the ordinary word, the metaphor, and the ornamental equivalent.

Let this, then, suffice as an account of Tragedy, the art imitating by means of action on the stage.

23 · An Epic must preserve unity of action

As for the poetry which merely narrates or imitates by means of versified language (without action), it is evident that it has several points in common with Tragedy.

I. The construction of its stories should clearly be like that in a drama; they should be based on a single action, one that is a complete whole in itself, with a beginning, middle, and end, so as to enable the work to produce its own proper pleasure with all the organic unity of a living creature. Nor should one suppose that there is anything like them in our usual histories. A history has to deal not with one action, but with one period and all that happened in that to one or more persons, however disconnected the several events may have been. Just as two events may take place at the same time, e.g. the sea-fight off Salamis and the battle with the Carthaginians in Sicily, without converging to the same end, so too of two consecutive events one may sometimes come after the other with no one end as their common issue. Nevertheless most of our epic poets, one may say, ignore the distinction.

Herein, then, to repeat what we have said before, we have a further proof of Homer's marvellous superiority to the rest. He did not attempt to deal even with the Trojan war in its entirety, though it was a whole with a definite beginning and end— through a feeling apparently that it was too long a story to be taken in one view, or if not that, too complicated from the variety of incident in it. As it is, he has singled out one section of the whole; many of the other incidents, however, he brings in as episodes, using the Catalogue of the Ships, for instance, and other episodes to relieve the uniformity of his narrative. As for the other epic poets, they treat of one man, or one period; or else of an action which, although one, has a multiplicity of parts in it. This last is what the authors of the *Cypria* and *Little Iliad* have done. And the result is that, whereas the *Iliad* or *Odyssey* supplies materials for only one, or at most two tragedies, the *Cypria* does that for several and the *Little Iliad* for more than eight: for an *Adjudgment of Arms*, a *Philoctetes*, a *Neoptolemus*, a *Eurypylus*, a *Ulysses as Beggar*, a *Laconian Women*, a *Fall of Ilium*, and a *Departure of the Fleet;* as also a *Sinon*, and a *Women of Troy*.

24 • Points of resemblance and of difference between
Epic poetry and Tragedy

II. Besides this, Epic poetry must divide into the same species as Tragedy; it must be either simple or complex, a story of character or one of suffering. Its parts, too, with the exception of Song and Spectacle, must be the same, as it requires Peripeties, Discoveries, and scenes of suffering just like Tragedy. Lastly, the Thought and Diction in it must be good in their way. All these elements appear in Homer first; and he has made due use of them. His two poems are each examples of construction, the *Iliad* simple and a story of suffering, the *Odyssey* complex (there is Discovery throughout it) and a story of character. And they are more than this, since in Diction and Thought too they surpass all other poems.

There is, however, a difference in the Epic as compared with Tragedy, (1) in its length, and (2) in its metre. (1) As to its length, the limit already suggested will suffice: it must be possible for the beginning and end of the work to be taken in one view — a condition which will be fulfilled if the poem be shorter than the old epics, and about as long as the series of tragedies offered for one hearing. For the extension of its length epic poetry has a special advantage, of which it makes large use. In a play one cannot represent an action with a number of parts going on simultaneously; one is limited to the part on the stage and connected with the actors. Whereas in epic poetry the narrative form makes it possible for one to describe a number of simultaneous incidents; and these, if germane to the subject, increase the body of the poem. This then is a gain to the Epic, tending to give it grandeur, and also variety of interest and room for episodes of diverse kinds. Uniformity of incident by the satiety it soon creates is apt to ruin tragedies on the stage. (2) As for its metre, the heroic has been assigned it from experience; were any one to attempt a narrative poem in some one, or in several, of the other metres, the incongruity of the thing would be apparent. The heroic in fact is the gravest and weightiest of metres — which is what makes it more tolerant than the rest of strange words and metaphors, that also being a point in which the narrative form of poetry goes beyond all others. The iambic and trochaic, on the other hand, are metres of movement, the one representing that of life and action, the other that of the dance. Still more unnatural would it appear, if one were to write

---

Epic poetry and Tragedy, as also Comedy, Dithyrambic poetry, and most flute and lyre playing, are all, viewed as a whole, modes of imitation.
(Page 203)

I. Wangner Sc.

an epic in a medley of metres, as Chaeremon did. Hence it is that no one has ever written a long story in any but heroic verse; nature herself, as we have said, teaches us to select the metre appropriate to such a story.

Homer, admirable as he is in every other respect, is especially so in this, that he alone among epic poets is not unaware of the part to be played by the poet himself in the poem. The poet should say very little *in propria persona,* as he is no imitator when doing that. Whereas the other poets are perpetually coming forward in person, and say but little, and that only here and there, as imitators, Homer after a brief preface brings in forthwith a man, a woman, or some other Character—no one of them characterless, but each with distinctive characteristics.

The marvellous is certainly required in Tragedy. The Epic, however, affords more opening for the improbable, the chief factor in the marvellous, because in it the agents are not visibly before one. The scene of the pursuit of Hector would be ridiculous on the stage—the Greeks halting instead of pursuing him, and Achilles shaking his head to stop them; but in the poem the absurdity is overlooked. The marvellous, however, is a cause of pleasure, as is shown by the fact that we all tell a story with additions, in the belief that we are doing our hearers a pleasure.

Homer more than any other has taught the rest of us the art of framing lies in the right way. I mean the use of paralogism. Whenever, if A is or happens, a consequent, B, is or happens, men's notion is that, if the B is, the A also is—but that is a false conclusion. Accordingly, if A is untrue, but there is something else, B, that on the assumption of its truth follows as its consequent, the right thing then is to add on the B. Just because we know the truth of the consequent, we are in our own minds led on to the erroneous inference of the truth of the antecedent. Here is an instance, from the *Bath-story* in the *Odyssey.*

A likely impossibility is always preferable to an unconvincing possibility. The story should never be made up of improbable incidents; there should be nothing of the sort in it. If, however, such incidents are unavoidable, they should be outside the piece, like the hero's ignorance in *Oedipus* of the circumstances of Laius' death; not within it, like the report of the Pythian games in *Elec-*

tra, or the man's having come to Mysia from Tegea without uttering a word on the way, in *The Mysians.* So that it is ridiculous to say that one's Plot would have been spoilt without them, since it is fundamentally wrong to make up such Plots. If the poet has taken such a Plot, however, and one sees that he might have put it in a more probable form, he is guilty of absurdity as well as fault of art. Even in the *Odyssey* the improbabilities in the setting-ashore of Ulysses would be clearly intolerable in the hands of an inferior poet. As it is, the poet conceals them, his other excellences veiling their absurdity. Elaborate Diction, however, is required only in places where there is no action, and no Character or Thought to be revealed. Where there is Character or Thought, on the other hand, an over-ornate Diction tends to obscure them.

25 · Possible criticisms of an Epic or Tragedy, and the answers to them

As regards Problems and their Solutions, one may see the number and nature of the assumptions on which they proceed by viewing the matter in the following way. (1) The poet being an imitator just like the painter or other maker of likenesses, he must necessarily in all instances represent things in one or other of three aspects, either as they were or are, or as they are said or thought to be or to have been, or as they ought to be. (2) All this he does in language, with an admixture, it may be, of strange words and metaphors, as also of the various modified forms of words, since the use of these is conceded in poetry. (3) It is to be remembered, too, that there is not the same kind of correctness in poetry as in politics, or indeed any other art. There is, however, within the limits of poetry itself a possibility of two kinds of error, the one directly, the other only accidentally connected with the art. If the poet meant to describe the thing correctly, and failed through lack of power of expression, his art itself is at fault. But if it was through his having meant to describe it in some incorrect way (e.g. to make the horse in movement have both right legs thrown forward) that the technical error (one in a matter of, say, medicine or some other special science), or impossibilities of whatever kind they may be, have got into his description, his error in that case is not in the essentials of the poetic art. These, therefore, must be the premisses of the Solutions in answer to the criticisms involved in the Problems.

I. As to the criticisms relating to the poet's art itself. Any impossibilities there may be in his descriptions of things are faults. But from another point of view they are justifiable, if they serve the end of poetry itself—if (to assume what we have said of that end) they make the effect of either that very portion of the work or some other portion more astounding. The Pursuit of Hector is an instance in point. If, however, the poetic end might have been as well or better attained without sacrifice of technical correctness in such matters, the impossibility is not to be justified, since the description should be, if it can, entirely free from error. One may ask, too, whether the error is in a matter directly or only accidentally connected with the poetic art; since it is a lesser error in an artist not to know, for instance, that the hind has no horns, than to produce an unrecognizable picture of one.

II. If the poet's description be criticized as not true to fact, one may urge perhaps that the object ought to be as described— an answer like that of Sophocles, who said that he drew men as they ought to be, and Euripides as they were. If the description, however, be neither true nor of the thing as it ought to be, the answer must be then, that it is in accordance with opinion. The tales about Gods, for instance, may be as wrong as Xenophanes thinks, neither true nor the better thing to say; but they are certainly in accordance with opinion. Of other statements in poetry one may perhaps say, not that they are better than the truth, but that the fact was so at the time; e.g. the description of the arms: 'their spears stood upright, butt-end upon the ground'; for that was the usual way of fixing them then, as it is still with the Illyrians. As for the question whether something said or done in a poem is morally right or not, in dealing with that one should consider not only the intrinsic quality of the actual word or deed, but also the person who says or does it, the person to whom he says or does it, the time, the means, and the motive of the agent—whether he does it to attain a greater good, or to avoid a greater evil.

ON POETICS

III. Other criticisms one must meet by considering the language of the poet: (1) by the assumption of a strange word in a passage like ουρηας μὲν πρῶτον, where by ουρηας Homer may perhaps mean not mules but sentinels. And in saying of Dolon, ὅς ρ' η τοι ειδος μὲν ἔην κακός, his meaning may perhaps be, not that Dolon's body was deformed, but that his face was ugly, as ευειδής is the Cretan word for handsome-faced. So, too, ζωρότερον δὲ κέραιε may mean not 'mix the wine stronger', as though for topers, but 'mix it quicker'. (2) Other expressions in Homer may be explained as metaphorical; e.g. in ἄλλοι μέν ρα θεοί τε καὶ ανέρες ευδον ⟨ἅπαντες⟩ παννύχιοι, as compared with what he tells us at the same time, η τοι ὅτ' ες πεδίον τὸ Τρωικόν αθρήσειεν, αυλων συρίγγων †τε ομαδόν†, the word απαντες 'all', is metaphorically put for 'many', since 'all' is a species of 'many'. So also his οἴη δ' ἄμμορος is metaphorical, the best known standing 'alone'. (3) A change, as Hippias of Thasos suggested, in the mode of reading a word will solve the difficulty in δίδομεν δέ οι, and in τὸ μὲν ου καταπύθεται ὄμβρῳ. (4) Other difficulties may be solved by another punctuation; e.g. in Empedocles, αιψα δὲ θνήτ' εφύοντο, τὰ πρὶν μάθον αθάνατα ζωρά τε πρὶν κέκρητο. Or (5) by the assumption of an equivocal term, as in παρῴχηκεν δὲ πλέω νύξ, where πλέω is equivocal. Or (6) by an appeal to the custom of language. Wine-and-water we call 'wine'; and it is on the same principle that Homer speaks of a κνημὶς νεοτεύκτου κασσιτέροιο, a 'greave of new-wrought tin'. A worker in iron we call a 'brazier'; and it is on the same principle that Ganymede is described as the 'wine-server' of Zeus, though the Gods do not drink wine. This latter, however, may be an instance of metaphor. But whenever also a word seems to imply some contradiction, it is necessary to reflect how many ways there may be of understanding it in the passage in question; e.g. in Homer's τῇ ρ' ἔσχετο χάλκεον ἔγχος one should consider the possible senses of 'was stopped there'—whether by taking it in this sense or in that one will best avoid the fault of which Glaucon speaks: 'They start with some improbable presumption; and having so decreed it themselves, proceed to draw inferences, and censure the poet as though he had actually said whatever they happen to believe, if his statement conflicts with their own notion of things.' This is how Homer's silence about Icarius has been treated. Starting with the notion of his having been a Lacedaemonian, the critics think it strange for Telemachus not to have met him when he went to Lacedaemon. Whereas the fact may have been as the Cephallenians say, that the wife of Ulysses was of a Cephallenian family, and that her father's name was Icadius, not Icarius. So that it is probably a mistake of the critics that has given rise to the Problem.

Speaking generally, one has to justify (1) the Impossible by reference to the requirements of poetry, or to the better, or to opinion. For the purposes of poetry a convincing impossibility is preferable to an unconvincing possibility; and if men such as Zeuxis depicted be impossible, the answer is that it is better they should be like that, as the artist ought to improve on his model. (2) The Improbable one has to justify either by showing it to be in accordance with opinion, or by urging that at times it is not improbable; for there is a probability of things happening also against probability. (3) The contradictions found in the poet's language one should first test as one does an opponent's confutation in a dialectical argument, so as to see whether he means the same thing, in the same relation, and in the same sense, before admitting that he has contradicted either something he has said himself or what a man of sound sense assumes as true. But there is no possible apology for improbability of Plot or depravity of character, when they are not necessary and no use is made of them, like the improbability in the appearance of Aegeus in *Medea* and the baseness of Menelaus in *Orestes*.

The objections, then, of critics start with faults of five kinds: the allegation is always that something is either (1) impossible, (2) improbable, (3) corrupting, (4) contradictory, or (5) against technical correctness. The answers to these objections must be sought under one or other of the above-mentioned heads, which are twelve in number.

26 · Tragedy artistically superior to Epic poetry

The question may be raised whether the epic or the tragic is the higher form of imitation. It may be argued that, if the less vulgar is the higher, and the less vulgar is always that which addresses the better public, an art addressing any and every one is of a very vulgar order. It is a belief that their public cannot see the meaning, unless they add something themselves, that causes the perpetual movements of the performers—bad flute-players, for instance, rolling about, if quoit-throwing is to be represented, and pulling at the conductor, if Scylla is the subject of the piece. Tragedy, then, is said to be an art of this order—to be in fact just what the later actors were in the eyes of their predecessors; for Mynniscus used to call Callippides 'the ape', because he thought he so overacted his parts; and a similar view was taken of Pindarus also. All Tragedy, however, is said to stand to the Epic as the newer to the older school of actors. The one, accordingly, is said to address a cultivated audience, which does not need the accompaniment of gesture; the other, an uncultivated one. If, therefore, Tragedy is a vulgar art, it must clearly be lower than the Epic.

The answer to this is twofold. In the first place, one may urge (1) that the censure does not touch the art of the dramatic poet, but only that of his interpreter; for it is quite possible to overdo the gesturing even in an epic recital, as did Sosistratus, and in a singing contest, as did Mnasitheus of Opus. (2) That one should not condemn all movement, unless one means to condemn even the dance, but only that of ignoble people—which is the point of the criticism passed on Callippides and in the present day on others, that their women are not like gentlewomen. (3) That Tragedy may produce its effect even without movement or action in just the same way as Epic poetry; for from the mere reading of a play its quality may be seen. So that, if it be superior in all other respects, this element of inferiority is no necessary part of it.

In the second place, one must remember (1) that Tragedy has everything that the Epic has (even the epic metre being admissible), together with a not inconsiderable addition in the shape of the music (a very real factor in the pleasure of the drama) and the Spectacle. (2) That its reality of presentation is felt in the play as read, as well as in the play as acted. (3) That the tragic imitation requires less space for the attainment of its end; which is a great advantage, since the more concentrated effect is more pleasurable than one with a large admixture of time to dilute it—consider the *Oedipus* of Sophocles, for instance, and the effect of expanding it into the number of lines of the *Iliad*. (4) That there is less unity in the imitation of the epic poets, as is proved by the fact that any one work of theirs supplies matter for several tragedies; the result being that, if they take what is really a single story, it seems curt when briefly told, and thin and waterish when on the scale of length usual with their verse. In saying that there is less unity in an epic, I mean an epic made up of a plurality of actions, in the same way as the *Iliad* and *Odyssey* have many such parts, each one of them in itself of some magnitude; yet the structure of the two Homeric poems is as perfect as can be, and the action in them is as nearly as possible one action. If, then, Tragedy is superior in these respects, and also, besides these, in its poetic effect (since the two forms of poetry should give us, not any or every pleasure, but the very special kind we have mentioned), it is clear that, as attaining the poetic effect better than the Epic, it will be the higher form of art.

So much for Tragedy and Epic poetry—for these two arts in general and their species; the number and nature of their constituent parts; the causes of success and failure in them; the Objections of the critics, and the Solutions in answer to them.